修 編 序

　　不要懷疑，「**高職英文法精要**」就是高職生的聖經。英文是大多數高職生的弱點所在，但無論參加哪一種升學考試，英文都是必考科目。如何以最有效率的方式學好英文，是高職生的首要目標。

　　其實，只要懂得方法，要在英文這一科拿高分實在不難。根據編者多年來的觀察，要拿高分，有兩件事非常重要。**第一，熟記重要單字**，本公司所推出的「**四技二專 1000 字**」，統計了歷屆考試中，最常考的一千個單字，這麼珍貴的資料，是所有高職生不可或缺的。

　　第二，熟悉基本文法。編者深感對台灣的學生而言，文法是學習英文最大的困難所在。為了因應高職生的需求，特別重新修編，並出版「**高職英文法精要**」。本書以淺顯易懂的方式，來講解最重要的文法。使用本書的方法，就是先熟讀每個章節前半段的講解，然後再做後面的歷屆試題和模擬考題，做錯的題目，務必要回頭翻閱講解，徹底突破盲點，以收事半功倍之效。

　　編者相信，只要善加利用本書，文法將成為幫助您進入高等教育之門的鑰匙。本書的修編工作，係經審慎的斟酌與校閱後才完成。但仍恐有不足或缺漏之處，誠盼各屆先進不吝指正。

編者　謹識

●||| 目　録

九十三學年度四技二專統一入學測驗
考試科目彙整表

代碼	類　別（或群組）	共同科目	專　業　科　目	
01	機　械　類	國文、英文、數學 (A)	(一)	機械原理（機械力學、機件原理）
			(二)	機械製造（含實習）、機械製圖
02	汽　車　類	國文、英文、數學 (A)	(一)	汽車學（汽車原理、柴油引擎、汽車電系）
			(二)	汽車實習（含相關知識故障排除）
03	電　機　類	國文、英文、數學 (A)	(一)	基本電學、電子學
			(二)	電工機械（含實習）、電子電路實習
04	電　子　類	國文、英文、數學 (A)	(一)	基本電學、電子學
			(二)	電子電路實習、計算機概論與微處理機實習
05	化　工　類	國文、英文、數學 (A)	(一)	化學
			(二)	化工原理
06	衛　生　類	國文、英文、數學 (A)	(一)	化學
			(二)	計算機概論、生物
07	土木建築類	國文、英文、數學 (A)	(一)	工程材料、工程力學概要
			(二)	測量實習、工程圖學
08	工業設計類	國文、英文、數學 (A)	(一)	基礎製圖、設計基礎
			(二)	物理、計算機概論
09	工程與管理類工程組	國文、英文、數學 (A)	(一)	物理、化學
			(二)	基礎製圖、計算機概論
10	工程與管理類管理組	國文、英文、數學 (A)	(一)	初級會計、統計學概論
			(二)	企業管理、計算機概論

代碼	類別 （或群組）	共同科目	專業科目	
11	護理類	國文、英文、數學 (C)	(一)	解剖學、生理學、藥物學
			(二)	基本護理學、內外科護理學
12	食品類	國文、英文、數學 (B)	(一)	食品概論（食品加工、食品化學）
			(二)	生物、化學
13	商業類	國文、英文、數學 (B)	(一)	計算機概論及商業概論
			(二)	初級會計學、經濟學
14	商業設計類	國文、英文、數學 (B)	(一)	文字造形、色彩學
			(二)	圖學、設計基礎
15	幼保類	國文、英文、數學 (B)	(一)	幼兒教保概論、嬰幼兒發展與保育
			(二)	幼兒教保活動設計、教保實務
16	美容類	國文、英文、數學 (B)	(一)	家政概論
			(二)	美容技藝（美膚與保健、美容與衛生、美顏、美髮）
17	家政類	國文、英文、數學 (B)	(一)	家政概論
			(二)	家事技藝（縫紉、手工藝、烹飪）
18	農業類	國文、英文、數學 (B)	(一)	生物
			(二)	農業概論
19	語文類英文組	國文、英文、數學 (B)	(一)	計算機概論及商業概論
			(二)	英文閱讀與寫作
20	語文類日文組	國文、英文、數學 (B)	(一)	計算機概論及商業概論
			(二)	日文閱讀與寫作
21	餐旅類	國文、英文、數學 (B)	(一)	餐旅概論（觀光概論、餐飲管理）
			(二)	餐飲實務
22	海事類	國文、英文、數學 (B)	(一)	計算機概論
			(二)	船舶概論

代碼	類別 （或群組）	共同科目	專　業　科　目	
23	水　產　類	國文、英文、 數學 (B)	(一)	水產生物
			(二)	水產概論
51	電機電子群	國文、英文、 數學 (A)	(一)	基本電學、電子學
			(二)	電子電路實習、計算機概論與微處理機實習
			(二)	電工機械（含實習）、電子電路實習
52	商業語文 群 (一)	國文、英文、 數學 (B)	(一)	計算機概論及商業概論
			(二)	初級會計學、經濟學
			(二)	英文閱讀與寫作
53	商業語文 群 (二)	國文、英文、 數學 (B)	(一)	計算機概論及商業概論
			(二)	日文閱讀與寫作
			(二)	初級會計學、經濟學
54	商業語文 群 (三)	國文、英文、 數學 (B)	(一)	計算機概論及商業概論
			(二)	日文閱讀與寫作
			(二)	英文閱讀與寫作
55	商業語文 群 (四)	國文、英文、 數學 (B)	(一)	計算機概論及商業概論
			(二)	日文閱讀與寫作
			(二)	初級會計學、經濟學
			(二)	英文閱讀與寫作
56	家政美容群	國文、英文、 數學 (B)	(一)	家政概論
			(二)	美容技藝（美膚與保健、美容與衛生、美顏、美髮）
			(二)	家事技藝（縫紉、手工藝、烹飪）

* 共同科目與專業科目每科之滿分均爲 100 分。

* 數學卷分共同題部分及非共同題部分，共同題部分所有考生皆需作答，非共同題部分，考生依報名類別選擇所屬部分作答，有 A、B、C 三類。

本書製作過程

　　本書的完成，是一個工作團隊的力量。由王淑平小姐擔任總指揮，謝靜芳老師協助編輯，並經由美籍老師 Laura E. Stewart 的細心校訂，白雪嬌小姐為本書設計活潑的封面，黃淑貞小姐負責設計專業的版面，非常感謝她們辛苦的付出。此外，還要特別感謝洪偉華小姐協助校閱，以及蘇淑玲小姐、洪淑娟小姐、洪佳穗小姐、鍾明淨小姐協助打字。

PART-1

八大詞類

命題焦點

▶1. 抽象名詞與物質名詞的特性、雙重所有格的用法是焦點所在。

▶2. 常考使役動詞、連綴動詞及dare, need當本動詞和助動詞的用法，要弄清楚助動詞＋ have ＋ p.p.表示對過去的推測或該做而未做的用法。

▶3. 對等、附屬連接詞的命題率頗高。介系詞則很少考冷僻的用法。

1. 名 詞

① 可數名詞 { 普通名詞 集合名詞 }　② 不可數名詞 { 物質名詞 專有名詞 抽象名詞 }

1. 可數與不可數名詞

1. 普通名詞、集合名詞爲可數名詞，有單、複數

⑴ 指一個事物時爲單數，指兩個以上的事物時爲複數。

【例】 *a cat*（單數）　　　*two cats*（複數）

　　　an apple　　　　　*two apples*

⑵ 集合名詞代表集合體時，有單、複數之分，但指集合體的組成分子時，形態上雖然是單數，意義卻是複數。

【例】 There is only one *family* in the village.【表集合體】

（這村子只有一戶人家。）

There're a few *families* in this village.【表集合體】

（這村子有幾戶人家。）

My *family are* all well.【表組成分子】

（我的家人都安好。）

2. 物質名詞、專有名詞、抽象名詞爲不可數名詞，無複數形

⑴ 不可數名詞視爲單數，但不可接在 a 或 an 之後，可視需要，接在 the, this, that, my, your, his 等之後。

【例】 *This* coffee is too strong for me.

（這咖啡對我而言太濃了。）

Everybody desires happiness.（每個人都想要快樂。）

(2) 不可數名詞的數量表示方法。

① 不定量的表示方法

【例】 We had *little snow* last year. (去年雪下得很少。)

I don't have *much furniture*. (我的傢俱不多。)

② 以容器表示單位

【例】 a *cup* of tea　一杯茶　　　a *glass* of water　一杯水

two *bags* of rice　兩袋米　　two *bottles* of beer　兩瓶啤酒

③ 以形狀表示單位

【例】 a *piece* of chalk　一枝粉筆

a *sheet* [*piece*] of paper　一張紙

a *loaf* [two *loaves*] of bread　一 [兩] 條麵包

two *cakes* of soap　兩塊肥皂

two *lumps* of sugar　兩塊方糖

a *slice* of meat [bread]　一片肉 [麵包]

a *piece* of furniture　一件傢俱

④ 以度、量、衡表示單位

【例】 a *pound* of sugar　一磅糖　　　a *yard* of cloth　一碼布

two *gallons* of gasoline　兩加侖汽油

(3) the + 形容詞 = 複數名詞，要用複數動詞。

【例】 *The rich are* not always happy. (有錢人未必快樂。)

2. 集合名詞的用法

集合名詞：family (家庭；家人)，people (民族；人民)，

class (班級；班上的學生)，committee (委員會；委員)，

audience (觀眾；聽眾)，crowd (群眾)，party (政黨)，

army (軍隊)，police (警察)，cattle (牛；家畜)，

furniture (傢俱)

(1) **代表集合體**：和普通名詞一樣有單、複數，可加冠詞。

【例】 The Chinese are *an* old *people*.【單數】

（中國人是古老的民族。）

There are *many peoples* in Asia.【複數】

（亞洲有許多民族。）

(2) **代表集合體之組成份子**，本身為複數名詞。

【例】 The *audience were* moved by his speech.

（聽眾都為他的演講所感動。）

Our *class are* all hard workers.

（我們班的學生都很用功。）

<比較> Our *class has* forty students.（我們班上有 40 個學生。）

☞ a. 此時字形雖為單數，意義卻為複數，字尾不可以加
"s" 表示複數形。

【例】 Whose are *these cattle*?（這些牛是誰的？）

b. 做主詞時要用複數動詞。

【例】 My *family are* all early risers.

（我的家人都早起。）

c. 此類名詞的代名詞為 they, their, them。

【例】 The *committee* are divided in *their* opinions.

（委員們的意見分歧。）

3. 名詞的轉用

不可數名詞有時可當作普通可數名詞使用。

┌─────────────────────┐
│ 1. 專有名詞 ➡ 普通名詞 │
└─────────────────────┘

(1)「叫～的人」

【例】 *A Mr. Miller* came to see you.

（一位叫米勒先生的人來看你。）

There are *three Smiths* in this class.

（這班上有三位叫史密斯的人。）

(2) 「像～那樣的人、場所」

　　【例】 I want to become *an Edison*.

　　　　　（我要成為像愛迪生那樣的科學家。）

　　　　 Keelung is *the Manchester* of Taiwan.

　　　　　（基隆是台灣的曼徹斯特。）

(3) 「～全家人」

　　【例】 We invited *the Browns* to dinner.

　　　　　（我們邀請布朗全家人來吃晚餐。）

(4) 「～的作品、製品」

　　【例】 I bought *a Millet*.（我買了一幅米列的畫。）

　　　　 She has *a* new *Ford*.（她有一輛新的福特汽車。）

---

2. 物質名詞 ➡ 普通名詞

(1) 表示種類

　　【例】 This is *a* French *wine*.（這是一種法國酒。）

　　　＜比較＞ *Wine* is made from grapes.

　　　　　　（酒是用葡萄釀的。）

(2) 表示製成品

　　【例】 We smooth clothes with *an iron*.

　　　　　（我們用熨斗燙平衣服。）

　　　＜比較＞ Steel is made from *iron*.（鋼是用鐵製成的。）

(3) 表示個體

　　【例】 He has *some* gray *hairs*.（他有些白頭髮。）

　　　＜比較＞ *Is* his *hair* red or blond?

　　　　　　（他的頭髮是紅的，還是金黃色的？）

3. 抽象名詞 ➡ 普通名詞

(1) 表示具體的行爲或人

【例】 He showed me *a lot of kindness* (= kind acts).
（他廣施恩惠於我。）

He was *a success* (= a successful person) as
a doctor. (他是個成功的醫生。)

(2) 表示種類

【例】 Courage is *a virtue*. (勇氣是種美德。)

She has *a* strong *will*. (她有堅強的意志。)

4. 抽象名詞 ➡ 形容詞或副詞

(1) of + 抽象名詞 = 形容詞
of + no + 抽象名詞 = not + 形容詞
of + great + 抽象名詞 = very + 形容詞

【例】 He's a man *of learning*. (他是個有學問的人。)
= He's a *learned* man.

The matter is *of no importance*. (這件事不重要。)
= The matter is *not important*.

It's *of great importance*. (這件事非常重要。)
= It's *very important*.

(2) 介系詞 ＋ 抽象名詞 ＝ 副詞

【例】 *with* care (小心地)   *with* ease (容易地)
on purpose (故意地)   *by* chance (偶然地)
in haste (匆忙地)   *in* excitement (興奮地)

4. 名詞的複數形

1. 規則的複數變化

(1) 一般是在單數名詞的字尾加上 s，而字尾若是 s, z, x, sh, ch，則加 es，但若字尾的 ch 發音為〔k〕時，只須加 s；(e)s 的發音有〔s〕〔z〕〔ɪz〕三種。

　① 無聲子音時，s 唸〔s〕：book*s*, cap*s*, cat*s*, month*s*

　② 有聲子音時，s 唸〔z〕：cow*s*, dog*s*, hole*s*, bed*s*

　③ 字尾發音為〔s〕〔z〕〔ʃ〕〔ʒ〕〔tʃ〕〔dʒ〕時，(e)s 唸〔ɪz〕：

　　【例】 hors*es*, ros*es*, bridg*es*, ag*es* <比較> hous*es*〔′hauzɪz〕bus*es*, box*es*, dish*es*, bench*es*

(2) 「子音＋o」時，字尾加 es：

　　【例】 echo*es*（回聲），hero*es*（英雄），potato*es*（馬鈴薯），tomato*es*（蕃茄）

　　<例外> piano*s*（鋼琴），photo*s*（照片）

　　「母音＋o」時，只加 s：radio*s*（收音機），studio*s*（畫室）

(3) 「子音＋y」時，將 y 改為 i，再加 es：baby → bab*ies*, lady → lad*ies*, city → cit*ies*

　　「母音＋y」時，只加 s：boy → boy*s*, key → key*s*, toy → toy*s*

(4) 字尾為 f(e) 時，變為 ves：life → li*ves*, thief → thie*ves*（小偷），wolf → wol*ves*（狼），knife → kni*ves*（刀子）

　　<例外> roof → roof*s*（屋頂），grief → grief*s*（悲傷）

2. 不規則的複數變化

(1) *母音字母的變化*：man → m*e*n, tooth → t*ee*th, foot → f*ee*t, goose → g*ee*se（鵝），mouse → m*i*ce（老鼠）

(2) 字尾加 en 或 ren：ox → ox*en*（公牛）, child → child*ren*

(3) 單複數同形：dear（鹿）, fish（魚）, sheep（羊）,
Chinese, Japanese（日本人）, Swiss（瑞士人）

---

3. 注意複合名詞、外來名詞的複數形

(1) 複合名詞的複數形：

　【例】 *sons*-in-law（女婿）　　*passers*-by（過路人）

　　　　girl *students*（女學生）　step-*mothers*（繼母）

　＜比較＞ 有 man 或 woman 的複合名詞，前後兩個字都要變
複數形：

　　　【例】 m*e*n servant*s*（男僕）

　　　　　　m*e*n student*s*（男學生）

　　　　　　wom*e*n writer*s*（女作家）

　　　　　　wom*e*n driver*s*（女司機）

(2) 外來名詞的複數形：

　【例】

alumna → alumn*ae*（女校友）　　alumnus → alumn*i*（男校友）

antenna → $\begin{cases} \text{antenna}s（天線） \\ \text{antenna}e（觸角） \end{cases}$　datum → dat*a*（資料）

　　　　　　　　　　　　　　　basis → bas*es*（基礎）

　　　　　　　　　　　　　　　crisis → cris*es*（危機）

(3) 字母、文字、數字、符號、縮寫字的複數形，以加 's 為原則，
如無誤解的可能，也常只加 s。

　【例】 three R'*s* (R*s*)（三個 R）

　　　　two UFO'*s* (UFO*s*)（兩個不明飛行物體）

　　　　Your 3'*s* (3*s*) look like 8'*s*(8*s*).

　　　　（你寫的 3 看起來像 8。）

(4) 下列名詞常用複數形：

【例】 trouser*s*（褲子）, pant*s*（褲子）, scissor*s*（剪刀）

glass*es*（眼鏡）【用複數動詞】

new*s*（消息）, mathematic*s*（數學）, physic*s*（物理學）

the United State*s*（美國）【用單數動詞】

(5) 下列名詞單複數的意義不同：

arm（手臂）　　custom（習慣）　　manner（態度；方法）
arm*s*（武器）　custom*s*（海關）　manner*s*（禮貌）

scale（規模）　　quarter（四分之一）
scale*s*（天平）　quarter*s*（軍營）

5. 名詞的格

名詞分主格、受格、所有格三種。

1. 主格可以做主詞、主詞補語、同位語、形容詞、稱呼用

【例】 ***Tom*** is kind.【主詞】

Tom and I are ***friends***.【補語】

Tom, my ***friend***, is very happy.【同位語】

Tom has many ***gold*** watches.【形容詞】

Tom, come here.【稱呼】

2. 受格可以做動詞及介詞的受詞、受詞補語

【例】 I like ***Tom*** very much.【動詞的受詞】

I went hiking with ***Tom***.【介詞的受詞】

We call him ***Tom***.【受詞補語】

---

3. 名詞所有格的形成和用法

⑴ 「人」或「動物」名詞，在字尾加 ('s) 或 (')。

【例】

Tom's watch	my dog's legs【單數名詞】
a girls' school	birds' nests（鳥巢）【複數名詞字尾有 s】
men's hats（男帽）	children's books【複數名詞字尾無 s】

⑵ 字尾為 s 的單數專有名詞，二音節或二音節以上，在字尾加 (')，
單音節則加 ('s)。

【例】 Mr. *Jones's* mistake Mr. *James's* help
Mr. *Williams'* house Mr. *Hopkins'* friend

⑶ 複合名詞或名詞片語的所有格，在最後一個字的字尾加 ('s)。

【例】 my father-in-*law's* house（我岳父的房子）
somebody *else's* bag（別人的袋子）

⑷ 無生命名詞的所有格，用 of 表示。

【例】 the door *of* the room
the legs *of* the chair

☞ 無生物名詞中 (a) 表時間、距離、長度、重量、價格的名詞
(b) 人格化的名詞之所有格，用 ('s)。

【例】 (a) *today's* paper（今天的報紙）【單數加('s)】
a *mile's* distance（一哩之遙）
a *boat's* length（一艘船的長度）
two *pounds'* weight（二磅重）【複數加(')】
ten *dollars'* debt（十元的債務）

(b) the *earth's* surface（地球表面）
Heaven's will（天意）

⑸ 名詞之後有同位語表示所有格時，把 ('s) 加在同位語的字尾。

【例】 Have you seen my brother *John's* bicycle?
（你有沒有看到我弟弟約翰的腳踏車？）

⑹ 表個別所有，每個名詞字尾都加 ('s)。

【例】 *Paul's* and *Mary's* schools
= Paul's school and Mary's school

表共同所有，在最後的名詞字尾加 ('s)。

【例】 Paul and *Mary's* school【二人在同一所學校】

6. 所有格後面名詞的省略

1. 所有格後面的名詞，因重複而被省略

【例】 This doll is my daughter's (*doll*).
（這個洋娃娃是我女兒的。）

2. 下列建築物，習慣上予以省略

house, home, shop, store, church, hospital, college,
theater, hotel, restaurant, office

【例】 He stays at his uncle's (*house*).
（他待在舅舅家。）

You must go to the dentist's (*office*).
（你必須去看牙醫。）

3. 雙重所有格時，省略所有格後面的名詞

當 a(n), this, that, these, those, some, another, every, such,
any, no 與所有格修飾同一名詞時，兩者不能同時放在該名詞前
面，應用雙重所有格，即：

a 〔**this, that,**⋯ 〕+ 名詞 + **of** + 所有格名詞

He is *a my father's friend.*【誤】

He is *a* friend *of my father's.*【正】

【例】 That's *no* fault *of John's.*（那不是約翰的錯。）

7. 注意下列名詞的用法

> 1. 做形容詞用：名詞 + 名詞

【例】 our *school* building（我們學校的建築物）

family tree（家譜）

☞ a. 修飾名詞的名詞，要用單數形。

【例】 I need some *ten-dollar* stamps.

（我需要一些十元的郵票。）

＜例外＞*sales* tax（貨物稅）

weapons system（武器系統）

b. 由名詞和形容詞所構成的名詞修飾語，其名詞不可用複數形。

【例】 a three-*year*-old boy（三歲的男孩）

a 200-*foot* high hill（二百呎高的山）

> 2. 做副詞用，修飾動詞、形容詞、副詞

【例】 *Wait a minute*, please.（請等一下。）

She is *sixteen years old.*（她十六歲。）

He went to England *three years* ago.

（他三年前去英國。）

He lives *two miles* from the station.

（他住在離車站二哩遠的地方。）

歷屆聯考試題

(　) 1. Because <u>of ill</u> Andy <u>canceled</u> his trip <u>to</u> Europe. (改錯)
　　　　　　(A)(B)　　　　(C)　　　　　(D)

(　) 2. 字典對學生是很有幫助的。
　　　(A) Dictionary is very helpful to a student.
　　　(B) A dictionary is very helpful to student.
　　　(C) A dictionary is very help to students.
　　　(D) A dictionary is very helpful to a student.

(　) 3. _____ have many friends in the park.
　　　(A) Gibson　　　　(B) Gibsons
　　　(C) the Gibsons　　(D) The Gibson
　　　(E) The Gibsons

(　) 4. Machines are _____ no use without the power to
　　　run them.
　　　(A) at　　(B) by　　(C) in　　(D) of　　(E) on

(　) 5. 他的建議沒有用處。(選錯的)
　　　(A) His suggestion was of no use.
　　　(B) His suggestion was useless.
　　　(C) His suggestion was not useful.
　　　(D) His suggestion was of no useful.

(　) 6. My major is accounting but he majors in _____.
　　　(A) economy　　　(B) economical
　　　(C) economics　　　(D) economic

( ) 7. You have to fill out this _____ form before you see the manager.
    (A) applicable   (B) application
    (C) apply   (D) applicant

8. 他是一位愛迪生。(他是一位發明家)〔 中翻英 〕

_____

( ) 9. Peter is going to the _____ for a haircut.
    (A) baker's   (B) butcher's
    (C) barber's   (D) banker's

【 歷屆聯考試題解答 】

1. (**B**) → illness   2. (**D**)   3. (**E**)   4. (**D**)   5. (**D**)
6. (**C**)   7. (**B**)   8. He is an Edison.   9. (**C**)

【 解析 】

1. 「*because of* + 名詞」表「因為~」。
  ill 是形容詞，應改成名詞 illness。   cancel〔'kænsl〕*v.* 取消

2. 「a〔an〕+ 單數普通名詞」代表名詞的全體（ 總稱 ）。

4. 5. *of no use* 沒有用處 (= *not useful* = *useless*)

6. 我的主修科目是會計學，但他主修經濟學。
  major〔'medʒɚ〕*n.* 主修科目   *v.* 主修 < *in* >
  accounting〔ə'kauntıŋ〕*n.* 會計學
  economics〔,ikə'namıks〕*n.* 經濟學

7. *application form* 申請書

9. *barber's* 理髮店 (= *barber's shop*)

精選模擬考題

(　　) 1. My father never gave me ＿＿＿＿.
　　(A) many advice　　　　(B) much advice
　　(C) many advices　　　 (D) a lot of advices

(　　) 2. Mary had only three ＿＿＿＿.
　　(A) baggages　　　　　(B) pieces of baggage
　　(C) pieces of baggages

(　　) 3. ＿＿＿＿ were found in the room.
　　(A) Two furnitures
　　(B) Two pieces of furniture
　　(C) Two pieces of furnitures
　　(D) Two furniture

(　　) 4. The police ＿＿＿＿ looking for a small boy.
　　(A) is　　(B) are　　　(C) has　　(D) have

(　　) 5. The audience ＿＿＿＿ deeply impressed by his speech.
　　(A) had　(B) were　　(C) has　　(D) have

(　　) 6. The lecture was attended by ＿＿＿＿ audience.
　　(A) many　　　　　　(B) a large
　　(C) much　　　　　　(D) a lot

(　　) 7. Shakespeare wrote ＿＿＿＿.
　　(A) a number of poems　(B) a number of poetry
　　(C) a piece of poem　　　(D) a number of poetries

(   ) 8. You will never be _____ in astronomy.

      (A) Newton   (B) a Newton

      (C) Newtons   (D) an Newton

(   ) 9. We bought several French _____.

      (A) wine   (B) wines

      (C) Wines   (D) bottle of wine

(   ) 10. The gentleman has two _____.

      (A) son-in-laws   (B) sons-in-law

      (C) son-ins-law   (D) son-in-law

(   ) 11. These boys are waiting for their _____.

      (A) girls friends   (B) girlfriends

      (C) girls friend   (D) girls' friend

(   ) 12. _____ is very high.

      (A) The books price

      (B) The book price

      (C) The book of the price

      (D) The price of the book

(   ) 13. I met a friend of my _____ at the _____.

      (A) brother, barber

      (B) brother's, barber's

      (C) brother's, barber

      (D) brother, barbers

(　) 14. He bought two _____ worth of sugar at the grocer's.

    (A) dollar   (B) dollar's

    (C) dollars   (D) dollars'

(　) 15. He puts two _____ of sugar in his coffee.

    (A) spoonfuls   (B) spoonful

    (C) spoon   (D) spoons

(　) 16. My sister doesn't eat much. She usually eats two

    _____ for breakfast.

    (A) slices of bread   (B) slice of breads

    (C) loaves of bread   (D) loaf of breads

(　) 17. I'd like to make _____ with you.

    (A) friend   (B) friends

    (C) a friend   (D) the friend

(　) 18. He takes great _____ in educating his children.

    (A) pain   (B) efforts

    (C) pains   (D) effort

(　) 19. That is _____.

    (A) no John's fault   (B) no John of fault

    (C) no faults of John   (D) no fault of John's

(　) 20. The class _____ listening to the teacher

    attentively.

    (A) be   (B) has   (C) are   (D) have

( ) 21. Do you like _____ for breakfast?

    (A) tea   (B) a tea   (C) teas   (D) the tea

( ) 22. The cart was drawn by two _____.

    (A) oxen (B) oxes   (C) oxs   (D) ox

( ) 23. They raise thousands of _____ on their ranch.

    (A) cattles   (B) ball

    (C) cow   (D) cattle

( ) 24. Do you know the difference between _____?

    (A) childs and babys

    (B) childs and babies

    (C) children and babies

    (D) children and baby

( ) 25. The French _____.

    (A) are very polite peoples

    (B) is a very polite people

    (C) are a very polite people

    (D) is a very polite persons

( ) 26. You will see many _____ in Richmond Park.

    (A) deers, sheeps and goats

    (B) deer, sheep and goats

    (C) deer, sheeps and goats

    (D) deers, sheep and goat

(　) 27. I met some ＿＿＿＿＿ at the museum.

    (A) Japaneses and Germans

    (B) Japanese and Germen

    (C) Japaneses and Germen

    (D) Japanese and Germans

(　) 28. There is not ＿＿＿＿＿ in the bottle.

    (A) some wines   (B) a few wine

    (C) much wine   (D) many wines

(　) 29. I live at ＿＿＿＿＿ from the town.

    (A) a mile distant   (B) a mile's distant

    (C) a mile distance   (D) a mile's distance

(　) 30. My house is within a few ＿＿＿＿＿ walk of the station.

    (A) minute   (B) minute's

    (C) minutes'   (D) minutes

(　) 31. ＿＿＿＿＿ school stands at the corner of the road.

    (A) Harry's and Tom's

    (B) Harry's and Tom

    (C) Harry and Tom's

    (D) Harry and Tom

(　) 32. I took ＿＿＿＿＿ hat by mistake.

    (A) somebody else'   (B) somebody's else

    (C) somebodys' else   (D) somebody else's

【精選模擬考題解答】

1. (**B**)	2. (**B**)	3. (**B**)	4. (**B**)	5. (**B**)	6. (**B**)
7. (**A**)	8. (**B**)	9. (**B**)	10. (**B**)	11. (**B**)	12. (**D**)
13. (**B**)	14. (**D**)	15. (**A**)	16. (**A**)	17. (**B**)	18. (**C**)
19. (**D**)	20. (**C**)	21. (**A**)	22. (**A**)	23. (**D**)	24. (**C**)
25. (**C**)	26. (**B**)	27. (**D**)	28. (**C**)	29. (**D**)	30. (**C**)
31. (**C**)	32. (**D**)				

【解析】

1. 2. advice「忠告」、baggage「行李」,都是不可數名詞。

3. furniture「傢俱」,雖是集合名詞,但在用法上卻相當於物質名詞,故沒有複數形,而以 a piece of,two pieces of 表其數。

6. a large〔small〕audience 很多〔很少〕觀衆

7. poem〔'po‧ɪm〕*n.* 詩 (普通名詞)
   poetry〔'po‧ətrɪ〕*n.* 詩 (集合名詞)

8. 你永遠不會成爲天文學方面的牛頓。
   astronomy〔ə'strɑnəmɪ〕*n.* 天文學

9. 我們買了幾種法國酒。
   wine 表示酒的種類時,可以數。

18. *take great pains* 非常努力

2. 代 名 詞 (1)

分爲人稱代名詞、指示代名詞、不定代名詞、
疑問代名詞，及關係代名詞。

1. 人稱代名詞

1. 人稱代名詞的格應注意要點

⑴ 在比較時，若 than 或 as 前面的子句中，動詞爲不及物動詞，則
than、as 後面的代名詞，須用**主格**。

【例】 I *am* taller than *he* (is). (我比他高。)
I *run* faster than *she* (does). (我跑得比她快。)

⑵ than 或 as 前的主要子句，動詞爲及物動詞時，其後的代名詞做
主詞時用主格，做受詞時用受格。

【例】 He *likes* Mary better than *I* (*like he*).
(他比我更喜歡瑪麗。)
He *likes* Mary better than (*he likes*) *me*.
(他喜歡瑪麗甚於喜歡我。)

⑶ be junior to （較年輕）
be senior to （較年長）
be superior to （較優秀） ＋ 受格
be inferior to （較低劣）
He is junior to *me*. (他比我年輕。)
I am superior to *him*. (我比他優秀。)

⑷ 人稱代名詞當補語時，與不定詞 "to be" 前面的代名詞或名詞的格一致。

> *I* was taken to be *he*.（我被誤認爲是他。）【主格】
>
> They took *me* to be *him*.（他們誤以爲我是他。）【受格】

2. 人稱代名詞的排列順序

⑴ **單數時：**通常按 **2, 3, 1** 或 **3, 2, 1** 人稱排列。

【例】 *You*, *he*, and *I* are of the same age.

（你、他和我，年齡相同。）

⑵ **複數時：**按 **1, 2, 3** 人稱排列。

【例】 *We*, *you*, and *they* are all good boys.

（我們、你們和他們，都是好孩子。）

⑶ 第三人稱男女兩性並用時，**男先女後**。

【例】 Everyone agrees to Jim's plan except *him* and *her*.

（除了他和她之外，每個人都同意吉姆的計畫。）

3. 非人稱代名詞 It 的用法

⑴ 做天氣、時間、季節、距離的主詞。

【例】 *It* is cloudy〔rainy, windy〕.（多雲〔下雨、刮風〕。）

How far is *it* from here to the station?

（從這裡到車站有多遠？）

⑵ **做形式主詞或受詞**，以代替後面的不定詞、動名詞，或名詞子句。

【例】 *It* is wrong *to tell a lie*.【做形式主詞，代替不定詞】

（說謊是不對的。）

It is nice *talking with you*.【做形式主詞，代替動名詞】

（和你談話眞好。）

I think *it* true *that he's a hypocrite*.【做形式受詞，代替子句】

（我認爲他的確是個偽君子。）

(3) it 代替前面已經提過的名詞、片語，或子句，以避免重複。

　　【例】 He bought *a watch* and gave *it* to me.

　　　　　（他買了一只錶，並把它給了我。）

　　　　　He's an honest man; I know *it* well.

　　　　　（他是個誠實的人；這點我知道得很清楚。）

(4) 加強語氣：**It is (was)** + 強調部份 + **that** + 其餘部份

　　【例】 *It was I that* bought a guitar yesterday.

　　　　　（昨天買吉他的是我。）

　　　　　It was a guitar that I bought yesterday.

　　　　　（我昨天買的是吉他。）

---

4. 所有代名詞

(1) 代替「所有形容詞（代名詞的所有格）+ 名詞」，以避免名詞的重複。

　　【例】 His car is larger than *mine* (= *my car*).

　　　　　（他的車子比我的大。）

　　　　　His shoes are expensive, but *mine* (= *my shoes*) are cheap. （他的鞋子很貴，但我的很便宜。）

(2) 做雙重所有格：a〔that, this, any, no…〕+ 名詞 + of + 所有代名詞。

　　【例】 That doll of *yours* is lovely. （你的那個洋娃娃很可愛。）

---

5. 反身代名詞

反身代名詞的第一、二人稱，是由**所有格** + **self (selves)** 所形成。第三人稱則由**受格** + **self (selves)** 而成：myself, ourselves, yourself, yourselves, himself, herself, itself, themselves

⑴ 主詞和受詞為同一人或物時，要用反身代名詞。

【例】 Please make *yourself* at home.（請不要拘束。）

　　　 He killed *himself*.（他自殺了。）

⑵ 加強語氣的用法

【例】 I made the cake *myself*.（蛋糕是我自己做的。）

　　　 Jane told me that *herself*.（珍親自告訴我那件事。）

⑶ 反身代名詞的慣用語

① 動詞 + **oneself**

【例】 abandon *oneself* to　沉迷於　　enjoy *oneself*　玩得愉快

　　　 accustom *oneself* to　習慣於

　　　 lose *oneself*　迷失　　avail *oneself* of　利用

　　　 help *oneself* to　自行取用　　come to *oneself*　甦醒

　　　 make *oneself* at home　不要拘束

　　　 devote *oneself* to　致力於

② 介詞 + **oneself**

【例】 beside *oneself*　發狂　　of *oneself*　自行

　　　 by *oneself*　獨自地　　in *itself*　在本質上；本身

　　　 for *oneself*　親自

③ 抽象名詞 + **itself** = **all** + 抽象名詞 = **very** + 形容詞

　　　 She is beauty *itself*.（她很漂亮。）

　　　 = She is *all* beauty. = She is *very beautiful*.

2. 指示代名詞

⑴ this, that 可代替前面所提過的片語、子句，或句子，以避免重複。

【例】 He told her *to see a doctor*. **This** she did at once.

　　　　（他告訴她去看醫生，她立刻照做。）

　　　 She went to a dance. **That** is an unusual thing.

　　　　（她去參加舞會，那是件不尋常的事。）

that (those) 可代替前面所提過的名詞，以避免重複。

【例】 The *climate* of Taiwan is hotter that *that* of England.

（台灣的氣候比英國的氣候炎熱。）

(2) **that ~ this…**
those ~ these… } = the former ~ the latter… 前者～後者…

【例】 Health is above wealth, for *this* (= *the latter*) cannot give so much happiness as *that* (= *the former*).

（健康重於財富，因後者〔財富〕不如前者〔健康〕能給我們那麼多幸福。）

(3) **those who** + **複數動詞** 凡是…的人 (= one who + 單數動詞)

【例】 Heaven helps *those who help* themselves.

（天助自助者。）

(4) so 可做下列動詞的受詞：do, call, say, tell, think, hope, suppose, imagine, see, hear, notice… 。

【例】

A: Will he come? （他會來嗎？）

B: { I think *so*. （我想他會來。）
So he says. （他說他會來。）
I hope *so*. （我希望他會來。）

☞ so 可以放在句首或句尾，但做 see, hear, notice 三個動詞之受詞時，只能放在句首。如：*So* I hear. （聽說如此。）

(5) so 可做 be 動詞的補語，不過要注意字序及意義之不同。

【例】 A: He is wise. （他很聰明。）

B: *So he* is. （他的確很聰明。）(= Yes, he is.)

A: He is wise. （他很聰明。）

B: *So* is *she*. （她也聰明。）

歷屆聯考試題

一、人稱代名詞

(　) 1. He is a much better teacher than _____.
  (A) her   (B) she
  (C) himself   (D) herself

(　) 2. This made _____ easier for him to understand his patients.
  (A) there (B) one (C) it   (D) that

(　) 3. We think _____ our duty to pay taxes to our government.
  (A) that (B) this (C) its   (D) it

(　) 4. They made _____ to have a picnic on Sunday.
  (A) it a custom   (B) it is a custom
  (C) it was a custom (D) custom of it
  (E) it as a custom

(　) 5. I think _____ a good habit to get up early.
  (A) this (B) it   (C) that (D) its

(　) 6. It was _____ that came here at midnight.
  (A) him (B) them (C) her (D) they

(　) 7. 昨天我所買的是一本字典。

    (A) It was a dictionary that I bought yesterday.

    (B) It is a dictionary that I bought yesterday.

    (C) It is a dictionary which I bought yesterday.

    (D) It was a dictionary that I bought it yesterday.

(　) 8. The lens gathers and focuses the light rays as _____ come into the camera.

    (A) it   (B) they   (C) its   (D) them

(　) 9. 她很漂亮。(選錯的)

    (A) She is beauty itself.

    (B) She is very beautiful.

    (C) She is all beauty.

    (D) She is much beautiful.

(　) 10. The telephone makes _____ possible to get in touch with people quickly.

    (A) he   (B) his   (C) its   (D) it

(　) 11. After Lincoln became a lawyer, there were many stories
      (A)   (B)
about how he intelligence helped him to win important
         (C)   (D)
cases. (改錯)

(　) 12. A friend of _____ came to see you.

    (A) you   (B) your

    (C) your's   (D) yours

( ) 13. A friend of _____ came to see you yesterday.

    (A) me   (B) I   (C) my   (D) mine

( ) 14. The watch Helen <u>bought</u> yesterday <u>is</u> <u>much</u> more
                   (A)   (B) (C)

    expensive than <u>you</u>. (改錯)
             (D)

( ) 15. I hurt _____.

    (A) myself   (B) himself

    (C) themselves   (D) me

( ) 16. Don't leave her by herself.

    (A) Don't let her go home.

    (B) Don't let her do it on her own.

    (C) Don't make her do it without help.

    (D) Stay with her so she isn't alone.

( ) 17. That's no business of _____.

    (A) yours   (B) your

    (C) you   (D) yourself

( ) 18. Do you think the chief to be _____?

    (A) his   (B) he   (C) I   (D) me

( ) 19. Do you think _____ difficult to answer these
    questions?

    (A) it   (B) this   (C) very   (D) much

( ) 20. I have a dog. _____ tail is very short.

    (A) It's   (B) Its   (C) Itself   (D) Dog's

(　) 21. It is not a tree of _____ planting.
    (A) he　　　　　(B) his
    (C) one　　　　　(D) himself

22. _____ was yesterday that I bought a book.

二、指示代名詞

(　) 1. The eyes of a dog are bigger than _____ of a cat.
    (A) these　　　　(B) that
    (C) this　　　　　(D) those

(　) 2. The climate of Taichung is better than _____ of Taipei.
    (A) that　　　　　(B) it
    (C) which　　　　(D) what

(　) 3. The cars made in Taiwan are generally cheaper than
    _____ imported.
    (A) that　　　　　(B) which
    (C) them　　　　(D) those

(　) 4. The tail of a fox is longer than _____ of a hare.
    (A) this　　　　　(B) these　　　　(C) it
    (D) that　　　　　(E) those

(　) 5. The <u>average</u> speed of <u>cars</u> <u>is</u> <u>much</u> greater than <u>those</u>
       (A)　　　　　　(B) (C) (D)　　　　　(E)
    of motorcycles. (改錯)

【歷屆聯考試題解答】

一、

1.（**B**）	2.（**C**）	3.（**D**）	4.（**A**）	5.（**B**）	6.（**D**）
7.（**A**）	8.（**B**）	9.（**D**）	10.（**D**）	11.（**C**）→ his	
12.（**D**）	13.（**D**）	14.（**D**）→ yours		15.（**A**）	16.（**D**）
17.（**A**）	18.（**D**）	19.（**A**）	20.（**B**）	21.（**B**）	22. It

二、

1.（**D**）	2.（**A**）	3.（**D**）	4.（**D**）	5.（**E**）→ that

【解析】

一、

4. *make it a custom to* + *V.* 使～成爲習慣

8. they 代替 the light rays（光線）。

14. 應將 you 改成 yours（＝ *your watch*）。

15. hurt（受傷）接反身代名詞做受詞，須與主詞一致，主詞爲 I，故選 (A) myself。

16. *by oneself* 獨自（＝ *alone*）

17. 原句 = Mind your own business.（少管閒事。）

18. 你認爲首領是我嗎？
此處 to be 後面要用 me，做 think 的受詞補語。

21. *of one's* + *V-ing* 某人自己～的
a tree of his planting 他自己種的樹

二、

4. that 代替 the tail（尾巴）。

5. 汽車的平均速度比機車的平均速度快得多。
those 改成 *that*，代替 the average speed。

精選模擬考題

( ) 1. We think _____ our duty to pay taxes to our government.
   (A) that (B) this (C) its (D) it

( ) 2. Was _____ you who sent me the box?
   (A) it (B) he (C) which (D) what

( ) 3. There were no objections on the part of _____ who were present.
   (A) that (B) this (C) these (D) those

( ) 4. The legs of a dog are longer than _____ of a rabbit.
   (A) that (B) ones (C) which (D) those

( ) 5. She makes mistakes, and _____ very often.
   (A) which (B) that (C) then (D) this

( ) 6. This is _____.
   (A) the book of me (B) a my book
   (C) a book of mine (D) a book of my

( ) 7. I had a pleasant time last evening. I enjoyed _____ last evening.
   (A) myself (B) me
   (C) mine (D) I

( ) 8. I saw _____ reflected in the mirror.
    (A) me   (B) I
    (C) myself   (D) one

( ) 9. He flatters _____ that we shall have need of his
    help.
    (A) himself   (B) him
    (C) ourselves   (D) us

( ) 10. I found _____ impossible to go on with my work.
    (A) that   (B) it   (C) one   (D) which

( ) 11. I make _____ a rule to get up at seven every
    morning.
    (A) that   (B) it   (C) one   (D) which

( ) 12. My view differed widely from _____.
    (A) him   (B) he   (C) his   (D) himself

( ) 13. Is she as tall as _____?
    (A) him   (B) he
    (C) himself   (D) his

( ) 14. He is by three inches taller than _____.
    (A) me   (B) I
    (C) myself   (D) mine

【精選模擬考題解答】

1.(**D**)　　2.(**A**)　　3.(**D**)　　4.(**D**)　　5.(**B**)　　6.(**C**)

7.(**A**)　　8.(**C**)　　9.(**A**)　　10.(**B**)　　11.(**B**)　　12.(**C**)

13.(**B**)　　14.(**B**)

【解析】

2. 直述句 "It was you who〔that〕sent me the box." 改為疑問句，則為 "Was it you…?"

3. 在出席的人這方面沒有異議。
   on the part of~ 在~方面

5. 「***and that*** ＋副詞或副詞片語」，作「而且…」解；其中 that 代替前面提過的整個句子（she makes mistakes），以避免重複，而且有加強語氣的作用。this 不可用在此一句型中。

9. flatter〔ˊflætɚ〕*v.* 奉承；使得意
   flatter oneself that~ 自以為~；自誇~

11. ***make it a rule to*** ＋ *V.* 經常~；照例要做~

14. 「他比我高三吋。」在比較級句子中，「by ＋數詞＋名詞」，指兩者間的差距。

2. 代 名 詞 (2)

1. 不定代名詞

指不定數量的人或物的代名詞；假如後面有名詞，即成為不定形容詞。

1. one 可指一般人，或代替前面已提過的單數名詞

複數為 ones，所有格為 one's，反身代名詞為 oneself。

【例】 ***One*** should keep *one's* promise. （人應該信守諾言。）

Please give me two white *tulips* and three red ***ones***.
（請給我兩朵白色鬱金香和三朵紅色的。）

<比較>

I don't have a pen. Can you lend me ***one***
(= *a pen*)? 【不定，同類但不是同一個】
（我沒有筆，你能借我一支嗎？）

He had a pen and lent *it* (= *the pen*) to me.
（他有一支筆，他把那支筆借給我。）【特定，同一物】

The pen I bought is cheaper than ***that*** you
bought. 【特定，同類但不是同一個】
（我買的筆比你買的便宜。）

☞ one 不可代替不可數名詞（即物質名詞和抽象名詞）。

If you need money, I'll lend you $\begin{cases} \textbf{\textit{one}}. （誤） \\ \textbf{\textit{some}}. （正） \end{cases}$
（如果你需要錢，我可以借你一些。）

2. another, other 有形容詞的用法

(1) another 是不特定的「另一個」。

【例】 May I have ***another*** cup of coffee?
（我可以再喝一杯咖啡嗎？）

　　　If I am a fool, you are *another*.

　　　（如果我是傻瓜，你也是。）

<比較> ⎰ I don't like *the watch*. Show me *another*.
　　　⎱ I don't like *these shoes*. Show me *some others*.

⑵ **one thing…another**　～是一回事，…又是另一回事

【例】 *To say* is **one thing**, *to do* is *another*.

　　　（說是一回事，做又是另一回事。）

⑶ ⎧ 二人或二物時：**one…the other**
　 ⎨ 三人或三物時：**one…another…the other**
　 ⎩ 三者以上時：**some…others**（…others）

【例】 He has two dogs; *one* is white, and *the other* is black.

　　　（他有兩隻狗；一隻白色，一隻黑色。）

　　　There are three men; *one* is blind, *another* is deaf
　　　and *the other* is lame.

　　　（有三個人；一個是瞎子，一個是聾子，另一個是跛子。）

　　　Some said yes, *others* said no.

　　　（有些人說是，有些則說不。）

⑷ **the one…the other**　前者…後者
　 = the former…the latter
　 = that…this

⑸ 有關 another, other 的慣用語：

【例】 ⎧ another day　改天
　　　 ⎨ the other day　前幾天
　　　 ⎩ every other day　每隔一天

　　　 ⎰ each other　互相（強調各個之間）
　　　 ⎱ one another　互相（強調全體之間）

$$\begin{cases} \text{one after the other （二者）相繼地} \\ \text{（指特定數的東西，依次地）} \\ \text{one after another （三者以上）相繼地} \\ \text{（指不定數的東西，陸陸續續地）} \end{cases}$$

3. some, any 也有形容詞的用法

some 通常用於肯定句，any 用於疑問句、否定句，或條件句。

(1) 在期望對方回答 Yes 時，問句也用 "some"。

【例】 Will you have *some* more coffee?

（要不要再來點咖啡？）

(2) 若 any 特指「任何」或「任何一個」時，也可用在肯定句裡。

【例】 *Any* food is better than none.

（任何食物都比沒有來得好。）

(3) $\begin{cases} \textbf{some} + 單數名詞　某一 \\ \textbf{some} + 數詞　大約…（= \textit{about}） \end{cases}$

【例】 I have read the story in *some* book.

（我在某本書裡讀過這個故事。）

I waited for her *some* twenty minutes.

（我等了她大約二十分鐘。）

4. each, every, all 的用法

(1) each 是不定代名詞，也是不定形容詞，every 則只能作不定形容詞。each, every 之後都用單數動詞。

<比較> $\begin{cases} \textbf{\textit{Each}} \text{ of us } \textit{has} \text{ to do his best.　【不定代名詞】} \\ \textbf{\textit{Each}} \text{ girl } \textit{has} \text{ her own doll.　【不定形容詞】} \\ \textbf{\textit{Every}} \text{ one } \textit{loves} \text{ his own country.　【不定形容詞】} \end{cases}$

(2) every 之後可接數詞，但 each 不可以。

【例】 every two days 每兩天；每隔一天 (= *every other day*)

every four days 每四天；每隔三天

(3) all 指人時用複數動詞，指**事物**時用單數動詞。

【例】 *All are* happy in my family.

（我的家人全都很高興。）

All is well with him. (他一切順利。)

All men *are* equal before the law.

（法律之前人人平等。）

He lost *all* his money. (他弄丟了所有的錢。)

(4) all 的慣用語：

【例】 all in 很疲倦   all at once 突然地

all but 幾乎 (= *almost*) all the same 仍然

---

5. no one, nobody, none 的用法

(1) no one, nobody 用單**數**動詞。

【例】 *No one*〔*Nobody*〕 *believes* the story.

（沒有人相信這個故事。）

(2) none 指可數名詞時，用複**數**動詞，指不可數名詞時，用單數動詞。

【例】 *None* of the students *are* absent.

（學生中沒有人缺席。）

None of the money *was* wasted.

（錢一點也沒浪費。）

6. both, either, neither 的用法

both 用複數動詞，either 及 neither 用單數動詞。

【例】 *Both* (of) his parents *are* good at golf.

（他的雙親都擅長打高爾夫。）

Either of the boys *knows* her address.

（這兩個男孩中，任何一個都知道她的地址。）

Neither of the stories *is* interesting.

（這兩篇故事都很乏味。）

Neither picture *is* beautiful. 【接單數名詞】

（這兩幅畫都不好看。）

2. 疑問代名詞

1. who 代替 whom 的法則

whom 做動詞或介詞的受詞，放在句首時，可以用 "who" 代替。
但是，如果疑問代名詞前面有介詞，則不可用 who 代替 whom。

【例】 *Whom*〔*who*〕did you go to school with?

With whom did you go to school?

2. 間接問句的形式：主詞＋動詞…

<比較> $\begin{cases} \textbf{\textit{What}} \text{ time } \textit{is it}? \\ \text{I don't know } \textbf{\textit{what}} \text{ time } \textit{it is}. \end{cases}$

$\begin{cases} \text{Have you heard } \textbf{\textit{what}} \textit{ he wanted}? （你曾聽說他要什麼嗎？）\\ \text{Yes, I } \textit{have}. \text{ 或 No, I } \textit{haven't}. \end{cases}$

（是的，我聽說過。）或（不，我沒聽說。）

☞ ① 可以用 yes, no 回答者，接在主要子句之後：

$\left. \begin{array}{l} \text{Do you } \textbf{\textit{know, hear}} \\ \text{Did you } \textbf{\textit{ask, tell}} \end{array} \right\} + 疑問詞 + \begin{cases} 動詞？\\ 主詞 + 動詞？ \end{cases}$

② 不可以用 yes, no 回答者，疑問詞必須放在句首：

$$疑問詞 + do \ you \begin{Bmatrix} \textbf{\textit{think, believe}} \\ \textbf{\textit{suppose, guess}} \\ \textbf{\textit{imagine}} \end{Bmatrix} + （主詞）+ 動詞 ？$$

【例】 *Do you know **who** he is?* — Yes, I do.

　　　***Who** do you think* he is? — I think he is Jack.

---

3. What do you say to + （動）名詞 ? = What about~ ?

【例】 ***What do you say to*** *the plan*?

　　　（你覺得這項計劃如何？）

　　　What do you say to *visiting* the museum?

　　　（我們去參觀博物館，你覺得怎麼樣？）

3. 關係代名詞

關係代名詞 = 代名詞 + 連接詞，故兼有代名詞及連接詞的作用。

【例】 This is the hat ***that*** I bought yesterday.

　　　（這就是我昨天買的帽子。）

　　　【在上句中，that 代替前面的 the hat，同時又連接 This is the hat

　　　和 I bought yesterday 兩個部分，具有兩種作用。】

1. 關係代名詞的格及用法

先行詞 ＼ 格	主　格	所有格	受　格
人	who	whose	whom
動物、事	which	of which whose	which
人、動物、事	that	—	that
無	what	—	what

【例】 This is *the girl **whom*** I saw yesterday.
（這就是我昨天看到的女孩。）

There stands *a house* $\left\{\begin{array}{l}\textbf{\textit{whose roof}}\\ \text{the roof } \textbf{\textit{of which}}\end{array}\right\}$ is red.

（那裡有間紅屋頂的房子。）

Can you see *a lady and a dog **that*** are crossing the bridge? (你看得到正在過橋的女士和狗嗎？)

【先行詞有「人」和「非人」時，關係代名詞要用 that】

What he said is true. (他所說的是眞話。)【無先行詞】

---

2. 關係代名詞必須與先行詞的「人稱」與「數」一致

【例】 *I, **who am*** blind, advise you to use your eyes well.

（ 我這個盲人勸告你們，要善用眼睛。 ）【第一人稱單數】

I want to read ***books that are*** interesting.

（ 我要讀的是有趣的書。 ）【第三人稱複數】

歷屆聯考試題

一、不定代名詞

(　) 1. Some cities seem to be strangling in their own traffic
jams. _____ are almost buried under a mountain of
collected garbage and trash.
(A) Other　　　　　　(B) Others
(C) Another　　　　　(D) Every other

(　) 2. I usually go to the movies once _____ two weeks.
(A) each　　(B) every　　(C) of　　　(D) during

(　) 3. Each of them _____ own idea.
(A) have their　　　　(B) has their
(C) has his　　　　　 (D) have his
(E) has one's

(　) 4. I think it is human nature for everyone to want
_____ own way.
(A) their　　(B) his　　　(C) its　　　(D) one's

(　) 5. He doesn't want to be a professor because his father
happens to be _____.
(A) it　　　　　　　　(B) one
(C) the one　　　　　 (D) another

(　) 6. Everyone <u>was</u> in <u>their</u> place <u>when</u> the bell <u>rang</u>. (改錯)
　　　　　　　　 (A)　　 (B)　　　　 (C)　　　　　 (D)

( ) 7. Those pencils are expensive. Show me cheaper _____.
    (A) one   (B) ones   (C) one's   (D) them

8. 屋子裡有兩隻貓。一隻是黑的，另一隻是白的。(中翻英)
_____

二、疑問代名詞、關係代名詞

( ) 1. Students are <u>supposed</u> to <u>pay</u> attention to <u>that</u> their
                (A)   (B)   (C)
    teacher says <u>in</u> class. (改錯)
                (D)

( ) 2. Do you know _____?
    (A) who is he   (B) who he is
    (C) he is who   (D) who is him

( ) 3. The best way to make people like you is to show an
    active interest in _____ is said.
    (A) what   (B) that
    (C) where   (D) whom

( ) 4. _____ came to see me?
    (A) Who you think
    (B) Do you think who
    (C) Who do you think
    (D) Whom do you think

( ) 5. I don't know _____.
    (A) for why you do it   (B) what you do it for
    (C) what for you do it   (D) do it what for you

( ) 6. I don't know _____.
    (A) whom is he   (B) whom he is
    (C) who is he   (D) who he is
    (E) which is he

( ) 7. Do you have any idea _____?
    (A) when will Ann arrive
    (B) when do Ann arrive
    (C) when Ann will arrive
    (D) when Ann arrive

( ) 8. 我想要知道她長相如何。
    I wanted to know _____.
    (A) what she looked like
    (B) what appearance she looked
    (C) what look she was
    (D) how she looked like
    (E) how she looked to

( ) 9. I am not sure _____.
    (A) whether he will leave tomorrow
    (B) how old is he
    (C) where he come from
    (D) that he is sick or not

( ) 10. Do you know _____?
    (A) where he lives   (B) where does he live
    (C) where is he living   (D) where he live

( ) 11. I'd like to know _____

  (A) why do you want to work for us?

  (B) why do you do want to work for us?

  (C) why do you want to work for us.

  (D) why you want to work for us.

【歷屆聯考試題解答】

一、

 1. (**B**) 2. (**B**) 3. (**C**) 4. (**B**) 5. (**B**)

 6. (**B**) → his   7. (**B**)

 8. There are two cats in the house. One is black and the
  other is white.

二、

 1. (**C**) → what 2. (**B**) 3. (**A**) 4. (**C**) 5. (**B**)

 6. (**D**) 7. (**C**) 8. (**A**) 9. (**A**) 10. (**A**) 11. (**D**)

【解析】

一、

 1. 有些城市似乎因交通阻塞而窒息，有些城市幾乎淹沒在垃圾
  堆下。

  strangle〔ˈstræŋgḷ〕*v.* 使窒息 ***traffic jams*** 交通阻塞

 5. one 代替 a professor（教授）。

精選模擬考題

( ) 1. He is one of the greatest poets that _____ ever lived.
  (A) has (B) was (C) have (D) were

( ) 2. He is the only one of my friends who really _____ me.
  (A) understands   (B) understanding
  (C) understanded   (D) understand

( ) 3. He is the man _____ I believe can help me.
  (A) whom   (B) that
  (C) who   (D) as

( ) 4. Give the book to anyone _____ wants it.
  (A) whoever   (B) whomever
  (C) whom   (D) who

( ) 5. _____ was reading the book aloud?
  (A) Do you think whom
  (B) Do you think who
  (C) Whom do you think
  (D) Who do you think

( ) 6. There are plenty of people _____ we know are ignorant of this crime.
  (A) whom   (B) them
  (C) which   (D) who

(　　) 7. Thank you very much for _____ you have done for
　　　　 my brother.
　　　　(A) that　　　　　　(B) what
　　　　(C) which　　　　　(D) it

(　　) 8. This is the same man _____ I saw on the train.
　　　　(A) whom　　　　　(B) as
　　　　(C) that　　　　　　(D) what

(　　) 9. We visited Mito Park, _____ is noted for its plum
　　　　 blossoms.
　　　　(A) which　　　　　(B) that
　　　　(C) where　　　　　(D) as

(　　) 10. He has the same dictionary _____ you have.
　　　　(A) which　　　　　(B) this
　　　　(C) what　　　　　　(D) as

(　　) 11. This is all _____ I know about the matter.
　　　　(A) what　　　　　　(B) that
　　　　(C) hat　　　　　　(D) as

(　　) 12. Is that the lady _____ you are waiting?
　　　　(A) for who　　　　(B) for whom
　　　　(C) who　　　　　　(D) whom

(　　) 13. This is the house _____ he was born.
　　　　(A) that　　　　　　(B) in that
　　　　(C) in which　　　　(D) which

( ) 14. Swimming, _____ is a good sport, makes us strong and healthy.

    (A) it   (B) what   (C) which (D) that

( ) 15. I cannot tell _____.

    (A) what she wants   (B) what does she want

    (C) what she want   (D) what did she want

( ) 16. To do is one thing and to teach is _____.

    (A) the other   (B) another

    (C) others   (D) other

( ) 17. Don't speak ill of _____ behind their back.

    (A) the other   (B) anothers

    (C) others   (D) another

( ) 18. Mary can borrow a pencil if she needs _____.

    (A) one   (B) it   (C) that   (D) which

( ) 19. This is the same man _____ I saw in the train.

    (A) what (B) whom (C) that   (D) which

( ) 20. This is the most difficult problem _____ I've ever had to face.

    (A) this (B) that   (C) it   (D) what

( ) 21. Your coat, a button of _____ is missing, needs mending.

    (A) which (B) that   (C) it   (D) what

( ) 22. The doctor will speak to _____ comes in first.
    (A) whom   (B) whomever
    (C) who   (D) whoever

( ) 23. He has two brothers. One is in America and _____ is in China.
    (A) another   (B) the other
    (C) other   (D) one

( ) 24. The construction work will be finished in _____ three weeks.
    (A) other   (B) another
    (C) the other   (D) other's

( ) 25. Some went on foot and _____ went by bus.
    (A) another   (B) others
    (C) else   (D) other

( ) 26. You should try to be kind to _____.
    (A) other   (B) another
    (C) others   (D) the other

( ) 27. We could hardly see _____ around here after dark.
    (A) anybody   (B) nobody
    (C) somebody   (D) everybody

( ) 28. _____ of the three boys are diligent.
    (A) Both   (B) Neither
    (C) None   (D) Each

(　) 29. You can't have ＿＿＿＿＿ of these books—not this one,
　　　　nor that one.
　　　　(A) either　(B) both　　(C) all　　(D) any

(　) 30. I picked up a man ＿＿＿＿＿ I thought was honest.
　　　　(A) who　　　　　　(B) whose
　　　　(C) whom　　　　　(D) which

(　) 31. I picked up a man ＿＿＿＿＿ I thought to be honest.
　　　　(A) who　　　　　　(B) whose
　　　　(C) which　　　　　(D) whom

(　) 32. Have you seen a live eagle?　Yes, I have seen
　　　　＿＿＿＿＿ once.
　　　　(A) it　　(B) one　　(C) an　　(D) that

(　) 33. In ＿＿＿＿＿ two hours, he will be home again.
　　　　(A) other　　　　　(B) the other
　　　　(C) others　　　　(D) another

(　) 34. She doesn't care what ＿＿＿＿＿ people think of her.
　　　　(A) other　　　　　(B) another
　　　　(C) it　　　　　　(D) does

(　) 35. I said nothing, ＿＿＿＿＿ made him still more angry.
　　　　(A) that　　(B) and　　(C) which　　(D) it

【精選模擬考題解答】

1. (**C**)	2. (**A**)	3. (**B、C**)	4. (**D**)	5. (**D**)	6. (**D**)
7. (**B**)	8. (**C**)	9. (**A**)	10. (**D**)	11. (**B**)	12. (**B**)
13. (**C**)	14. (**C**)	15. (**A**)	16. (**B**)	17. (**C**)	18. (**A**)
19. (**C**)	20. (**B**)	21. (**A**)	22. (**D**)	23. (**B**)	24. (**B**)
25. (**B**)	26. (**C**)	27. (**A**)	28. (**C**)	29. (**A**)	30. (**A**)
31. (**D**)	32. (**B**)	33. (**D**)	34. (**A**)	35. (**C**)	

【解析】

1. 先行詞為「one of ＋ 複數名詞」時，其後子句用複數動詞。
   先行詞為「the only one of ＋ 複數名詞」時，其後子句用單數動詞。

4. anyone who ＝ whoever，其中 who 做子句的主詞，故不可以選 (C) whom。

5. 答案 (B) 中，用 Do you think 開頭的問句，其回答為 Yes, I do. 或 No, I don't. 而本句是問「你認為誰正在大聲唸書呢？」，回答時不能是 Yes 或 No，故 (B) 不可選。

6. we know 是插入語，解題時可省略不看，由 are ignorant… 得知，本題需要當主格的關代，故選 (D) who。
   ***be ignorant of*~** 不知道～

7. what ＝ all that which，用於前無先行詞的子句中。

8. 先行詞之前有 the same，關係代名詞用 that。

13. in which ＝ where。

14. which is a good sport 是補述用法的形容詞子句，關代 which 不能用 that 代替。

20. 先行詞有最高級形容詞修飾時，關係代名詞用 that。有關 that 用法，請參照 Part 2 中之關係詞。

22. 子句中需要主詞，且前無先行詞，故選 (D) whoever（= any one who）。

24. 這項建築工程再過三個星期就會完工。

27. hardly（幾乎不）為否定副詞，故不可以用 nobody，而 somebody 則不可用在否定句中。everybody 用在否定句中，表部分否定。

28. none 用於三者以上，用單、複數動詞皆可。

30. I thought 是插入語，解題時可省略不看，由 was honest 可知，本題需要當主詞的關代，故選 (A) who。

31. 由 to be honest 是受詞補語可知，子句中的關代，是做 thought 的受詞，故選 (D) whom。

35. 由逗點（,）可知，後面的子句是補述用法的形容詞子句，故關代選 (C) which, 而 which 的先行詞是子句 I said nothing。

3. 形 容 詞 (1)

> 1. **代名形容詞**：由代名詞轉換而來的形容詞。
> 2. **數量形容詞**：用來表示數、量，或程度的形容詞。
> 3. **修飾形容詞**：用來描述人或事物的性質或狀態。

1. 形容詞的用法與位置

1. 限定用法：緊跟在名詞前或後

(1) 數個形容詞修飾名詞時，其順序為：「序數 → 數量 → 大小、長短 → 形狀 → 新舊 → 顏色 → 材料、國籍」。

【例】 These *two beautiful young American* ladies are famous novelists.

（這兩位漂亮年輕的美國小姐是有名的小說家。）

(2) 形容詞片語，或修飾 anything, nothing 等代名詞的形容詞，須放在名詞後面，做後位修飾。

【例】 She had a *basket full of flowers*.

（她有一個裝滿花朵的籃子。）

Is there *anything interesting* in today's paper?
（今天的報紙有任何有趣的事嗎？）

2. 敘述用法：做補語

She looks very **happy**. （她看起來非常快樂。）【主詞補語】

The news makes *him sad*. （這消息使他難過。）【受詞補語】

☞ 下列形容詞只有限定用法，而無敘述用法，只能放在名詞前：

only 唯一的	woolen 毛質的	inner 裡面的
wooden 木製的	latter 後半的	very 正是；就是

former 以前的	utmost 最大限度的	elder 年長的
certain 某一	main 主要的	drunken 喝醉的
mere 僅僅	golden 金色的	outer 外面的

☞ 下列形容詞只有敘述用法，而無限定用法，不可放在名詞前：

afraid 害怕的	drunk 喝醉的	alone 單獨的
asleep 睡著的	unable 不能的	aware 知道的
content 滿足的	alive 活的	sunk 沉沒的
sure 確實的	awake 醒著的	worth 值得的
alike 相像的	ill 生病的	ashamed 羞愧的
alive 活的		

2. 數量形容詞

1. many, (a) few 修飾複數可數名詞

(1) many + 複數名詞 + 複數形動詞

= many a + 單數名詞 + 單數形動詞

【例】 *Many prisoners have* been set free.

（許多犯人已經被釋放。）

= *Many a prisoner has* been set free.

(2) a great〔good〕many $\left\{\begin{array}{l}+ \text{複數名詞} \\ + \text{of} + \text{代名詞} \\ + \text{of} + \text{所有形容詞} + \text{複數名詞}\end{array}\right.$

【例】 *A great many planes* were shot down.

（許多飛機被擊落。）

A great many of them surrendered.

（他們之中有許多人投降。）

A great many of my friends went abroad.

（我有許多朋友出國了。）

(3) as〔so〕many = the same number of（同樣數目的）

【例】 We waited about *ten* minutes; it seemed to me
as many hours.

（我們等了十分鐘左右；那對我而言好像是十個小時。）

(4) few = only a few（很少）

a few（一些）

not a few = quite a few（不少；很多）= many

【例】 I have *few* friends.（我的朋友很少。）

There are *a few* mistakes in his composition.
（他的文章有一些錯誤。）

Not a few boys go to school by bus.
（不少男孩搭公車上學。）

---

2. much, (a) little 修飾不可數名詞

much, little + $\begin{cases} 物質名詞 → 表示量（much money　很多錢）\\ 抽象名詞 → 表示程度（little patience　耐心不夠）\end{cases}$

(1) as much = the same amount of（同樣數量的）

【例】 He buys *two* pounds of sugar and *as much* tea.
（他買兩磅糖和兩磅茶葉。）

(2) not so much～as… 與其說是～不如說是…

【例】 He is *not so much* a scholar *as* a writer.
（與其說他是學者，倒不如說他是作家。）

(3) little = only a little（很少）

a little（一些）

not a little = quite a little（不少；很多）= much

【例】 He made *not a little* contribution to our town.
（他對我們鎮上做了不少的貢獻。）

3. a lot of, lots of, plenty of 的用法

(1) 肯定時，a lot of, lots of, plenty of 等於 *many* 或 *much*，但否
定或疑問句，則只能用 many, much。

此外，肯定句中 how, too, so, as 之後，也只能用 many 或 much。

【例】

> We have *a lot of* rain in June.（此地六月多雨。）
> Do you have *much* rain in June?（貴地六月多雨嗎？）

A: *Did* he take *many* pictures?（他拍了很多照片嗎？）

B: Yes, he took *lots of* pictures.

> （是的，他拍了許多照片。）

No, he did*n't* take *many* pictures.

> （不，他沒拍許多照片。）

There are *so many* strangers in the room; therefore,
he dares not enter.

（房間裡有這麼多陌生人，因此他不敢進去。）

3. 數詞

數詞包括：(1)基數詞，如 one, two, three…；(2)序數詞，如 first,
second…；(3)倍數詞，如 half, double…。

1. 數字的讀法

(1) 基數

【例】　243 = two hundred (and) forty-three

5,678 = five thousand six hundred (and) seventy-eight

57,914 = fifty-seven thousand nine hundred and
　　　　 fourteen

(2) 年、月、日

【例】 1901－1966 = nineteen hundred (and) one *to*
                         nineteen sixty-six

      May 21, 1927 = May twenty-first〔the twenty-
                         first〕, nineteen twenty-seven

(3) 電話號碼

【例】 733-3074 = seven, double three, three, o, seven, four
      102-1055 = one, o, two, one, o, double five
               = one, o, two, ten, fifty-five

(4) 住址

【例】 426 Maple Avenue = four twenty-six Maple Avenue
      1400 16th St. = fourteen hundred, sixteenth street

(5) 貨幣

【例】 $ 7.35 = seven dollars thirty-five cents
             = seven thirty-five
      $ 20 = twenty dollars even（二十元整）
      £ 2 = two pounds（兩英鎊）
      NT$ 123 = one hundred and twenty three (N.T.)
                   dollars（新台幣一百二十三元）

(6) 分數、小數

【例】 $\dfrac{1}{2}$ = a half; one-half $\dfrac{1}{3}$ = a third; one-third

      $\dfrac{1}{4}$ = a quarter; one quarter; one-fourth

      $\dfrac{3}{4}$ = three quarters; three-fourths $\dfrac{2}{5}$ = two-fifths

$$2\frac{5}{6} = \text{two and five-sixths}$$

2.54 cm = two point five four centimeters

0.9144 m = point nine one four four meters

1.609 km = one point six naught [zero] nine
　　　　　　　 kilometers

2. 含數詞的慣用法

【例】 ***Dozens of*** people attended the party.

（數十人出席宴會。）

Hundreds of houses were washed away.

（數以百計的房屋被沖走。）

Thousands of students took part in the demonstration.

（數以千計的學生參加這次的示威活動。）

4. 修飾形容詞

用於描述人或事物的性質、狀態的形容詞，稱作修飾形容詞。如：
diligent（勤奮的），kind（仁慈的），glad（高興的），green
（綠色的），round（圓的），deep（深的）……

1. 包括由動詞轉變而成的形容詞

(1) 現在分詞：

a ***flying*** bird（飛鳥），***running*** water（流動的水）

(2) 過去分詞：

a ***broken*** leg（跌斷的腿），***lost*** treasure（遺失的珍寶）

(3) 動名詞：

a ***diving*** board（跳水板），a ***swimming*** pool（游泳池）

2. 由物質名詞轉變而成的形容詞

(1) 物質名詞做形容詞者

【例】 a *gold* watch（金錶）

　　　a *rain* coat（雨衣）

(2) 物質名詞＋en 或 y 者

【例】 a *golden* opportunity（千載難逢的機會）

　　　a *rainy* day（下雨天）

3. 由專有名詞轉變而成的形容詞

由人名、地名或國名等專有名詞轉變而成的形容詞，**起首字母要大寫**。

【例】 *Buddhist* temple（佛寺）

　　　Peiping dialect（北平話）

　　　Japanese houses（日本式房子）

　　　Arabian horses（阿拉伯馬）

歷屆聯考試題

一、形容詞的用法及位置

(　) 1. You may learn ＿＿＿＿ from everyone.
　　　(A) useful thing
　　　(B) something useful
　　　(C) somethings useful
　　　(D) useful something

(　) 2. She is a ＿＿＿＿.
　　　(A) beautiful girl young
　　　(B) young beautiful girl
　　　(C) beautiful young girl
　　　(D) girl young beautiful

(　) 3. I never read ＿＿＿＿ book before.
　　　(A) a such　　(B) X　　(C) such　　(D) such a

二、數量形容詞

(　) 1. They ate ＿＿＿＿ loaves of bread.
　　　(A) a little　　　　　(B) a lot of
　　　(C) a great deal of　(D) very much

(　) 2. Since they are moving to a new house, they have to buy ＿＿＿＿ furniture.
　　　(A) many　　　　　(B) quite a few
　　　(C) a lot of　　　　(D) a few

( ) 3. A senior official has ＿＿＿＿＿ jobs to do.
    (A) much more
    (B) very much
    (C) a number of
    (D) a great deal of

( ) 4. She was desperate because there was ＿＿＿＿＿ hope.
    (A) a little   (B) a few
    (C) few   (D) little

( ) 5. There are ＿＿＿＿＿ homes in Taiwan today that do not
    have ＿＿＿＿＿ a radio or a television set.
    (A) little, neither
    (B) a few, both
    (C) little, either
    (D) few, either
    (E) a few, neither

( ) 6. There was hardly ＿＿＿＿＿ money left in my pocket.
    (A) no   (B) some   (C) not
    (D) few   (E) any

三、數詞

( ) 1. About three ＿＿＿＿＿ of the students were present.
    (A) fifth   (B) five
    (C) fifths   (D) fives

【歷屆聯考試題解答】

一、1. (**B**) 2. (**C**) 3. (**D**)

二、1. (**B**) 2. (**C**) 3. (**C**) 4. (**D**) 5. (**D**) 6. (**E**)

三、1. (**C**)

【解析】

二、

1. a great deal of (= very much) + 不可數名詞

2. furniture〔'fɜnɪtʃɚ〕*n.* 傢俱，爲集合名詞，不可數，故只能選 (C) a lot of 來修飾。

3. 資深的職員有很多的工作要做。
   a number of + 可數名詞；a great deal of + 不可數名詞。
   official〔ə'fɪʃəl〕*n.* 官員；職員

4. little 作「少到幾乎沒有」解，表否定。
   desperate〔'dɛspərɪt〕*adj.* 絕望的

5. 現今在台灣，很少有家庭沒有錄音機，或沒有電視機。

三、

1. *three fifths* 五分之三

精選模擬考題

( ) 1. These two _____ ladies are famous.
 (A) beautiful American young
 (B) beautiful young American
 (C) American beautiful young
 (D) young beautiful American

( ) 2. The superstition is still _____ among the natives.
 (A) alive　(B) living　(C) lived　(D) live

( ) 3. There were only a _____ number of pupils on the playground.
 (A) few　　　　　(B) little
 (C) small　　　　(D) large

( ) 4. Do you have _____ chalk?
 (A) many　(B) much　(C) few　　(D) little

( ) 5. There is _____ time for argument, I'm afraid.
 (A) a few　(B) few　　(C) a little　(D) little

( ) 6. She has a great _____ of money.
 (A) plenty　　　　(B) number
 (C) deal　　　　　(D) lot

( ) 7. There is _____ tea left in the pot.
 (A) little　(B) any　　(C) a few　　(D) small

(　) 8. I have _____ money with me right now.
(A) a few　(B) a little　(C) many　(D) few

(　) 9. I am glad that you have made _____ mistakes in the examination.
(A) a few　　　　　(B) quite a few
(C) few　　　　　(D) little

(　) 10. There are _____ books on the desk.
(A) a little　　　　(B) little
(C) a few　　　　(D) much

(　) 11. I feel lonely, as I have _____ friends here.
(A) little　(B) a little　(C) few　(D) a few

(　) 12. We must hurry. We have _____ time left.
(A) little　(B) few　(C) much　(D) many

(　) 13. He is a very _____ swimmer.
(A) badly　　　　(B) good
(C) well　　　　(D) strongly

(　) 14. She works hard in the office for a _____ salary.
(A) little　(B) few　(C) cheap　(D) small

(　) 15. It was _____ to see you.
(A) pleased　　　　(B) pleasant
(C) pleasure　　　　(D) happily

( ) 16. My house is so small that I have _____ furniture in it.
    (A) few   (B) little
    (C) many   (D) much

( ) 17. I have never seen _____ children before.
    (A) such a   (B) such
    (C) a such   (D) a so

( ) 18. I am very busy now; I have _____ time for writing.
    (A) little   (B) a little
    (C) few   (D) fewer

( ) 19. The book is worth _____.
    (A) read   (B) reading
    (C) buy   (D) to reading

( ) 20. I have nothing _____ to talk about.
    (A) special   (B) specially
    (C) strangely   (D) newer

( ) 21. He is a _____ painter.
    (A) fame   (B) famous
    (C) famousness (D) famer

( ) 22. How _____ mistakes did you make in your composition?
    (A) little   (B) much
    (C) many   (D) a little

(　　) 23. My uncle told us many ＿＿＿＿＿ stories.

    (A) interest   (B) interesting

    (C) interested   (D) interfere

(　　) 24. We must be ＿＿＿＿＿ not to catch cold.

    (A) careful   (B) careless

    (C) care   (D) care about

(　　) 25. My father gave me ＿＿＿＿＿ advice when I was confronted with a difficulty.

    (A) a good   (B) good

    (C) a few   (D) many

(　　) 26. The last few games in the pennant race were ＿＿＿＿＿.

    (A) excited   (B) exciting

    (C) excite   (D) excitement

(　　) 27. Pedro seemed ＿＿＿＿＿ when I last saw him.

    (A) happily   (B) happy

    (C) happiness   (D) sadly

(　　) 28. The tea tastes too ＿＿＿＿＿ for me.

    (A) sweet   (B) sweetly

    (C) hotter   (D) coldly

(　　) 29. This point is very ＿＿＿＿＿.

    (A) important   (B) well

    (C) badly   (D) better

( ) 30. There aren't _____ plates on the shelf.
     (A) any   (B) some
     (C) no   (D) a

( ) 31. I have _____ money with me.
     (A) a few   (B) a little
     (C) many   (D) few

( ) 32. He is the _____ man we'd like to have as a guide.
     (A) same as   (B) just
     (C) true   (D) very

( ) 33. _____ food is better than none.
     (A) Any   (B) Every
     (C) Few   (D) Big

( ) 34. He had _____ reason to be satisfied.
     (A) all   (B) any
     (C) each   (D) every

( ) 35. By nine o'clock in the evening, I always find myself falling _____.
     (A) in sleep   (B) asleep
     (C) sleep   (D) sleeping

【精選模擬考題解答】

1. (B)	2. (A)	3. (C)	4. (B)	5. (D)	6. (C)
7. (A)	8. (B)	9. (C)	10. (C)	11. (C)	12. (A)
13. (B)	14. (D)	15. (B)	16. (B)	17. (B)	18. (A)
19. (B)	20. (A)	21. (B)	22. (C)	23. (B)	24. (A)
25. (B)	26. (B)	27. (B)	28. (A)	29. (A)	30. (A)
31. (B)	32. (D)	33. (A)	34. (D)	35. (B)	

【解析】

3. *a small number of* 少數的；不多的
   playground (ˈpleˌgraʊnd) *n.* (主要指兒童的) 遊戲場；運動場

4. chalk (tʃɔk) *n.* 粉筆 (物質名詞，不可數)

5. argument (ˈɑrgjəmənt) *n.* 爭論

14. salary (ˈsælərɪ) *n.* 薪水   *a small salary* 薪水很少

15. 原句 = It was a pleasure to see you.
    pleasant (ˈplɛznt) *adj.* 愉快的
    pleasure (ˈplɛʒə) *n.* 愉快；樂趣

23. interesting (有趣的) 修飾事物，interested (感興趣的) 修飾人。

25. advice (ədˈvaɪs) *n.* 建議 (為不可數名詞)

26. excited (興奮的) 修飾人，exciting (刺激的) 修飾事物。
    pennant (ˈpɛnənt) *n.* 錦標   *the pennant race* 錦標賽

32. 「他正是我們要的嚮導人選。」very 作「正是；就是」解。

34. *have every reason to* + *V.* 有充分的理由~

35. 到了晚上九點，我老是覺得自己就要睡著了。
    fall asleep 睡著

3. 形容詞 (2) — 冠詞

> a, an 泛指一般普通名詞，稱為不定冠詞；
> the 則指一特定名詞，故稱之為定冠詞。

---

1. 不定冠詞 a, an 的用法

> 1. 用於代表全體的單數名詞之前

【例】 *A* dog is a faithful animal. (狗是忠實的動物。)
= *The* dog is a faithful animal.
= *Dogs are* faithful animals.

> 2. a = one

【例】 She went away without saying *a* word.
(她一句話也沒說就走了。)
He will be back in *a* day or two.
(他將在一兩天之內回來。)

> 3. a = per

【例】 She wrote to her parents twice *a* month.
(她每個月寫兩封信給父母。)

> 4. a = the same

【例】 Those shoes are all of *a* size.
(那些鞋子都是同一個尺寸。)
Birds of *a* feather flock together. (物以類聚。)

5. 不定冠詞 ＋ 專有名詞

(1)　「像～那樣的人」

【例】 I wish to become **an Edison**.

（我想成爲像愛迪生那樣的科學家。）

(2)　「一個叫～的人」

【例】 **A John Smith** came to see you this morning.

（今天早上有個叫約翰・史密斯的人來看你。）

2. 定冠詞 the 的用法

在子音之前讀作〔ðə〕，在母音之前讀作〔ðɪ〕；通常用以指示前面已提過或已知的名詞。

1. 限定用法

【例】 He is **the** principal *of our school*.

（他是我們學校的校長。）

She is not **the** Mrs. Smith *that I know*.

（她不是我所認識的史密斯太太。）

2. 用於最高級形容詞及序數之前

【例】 He is **the** *fastest* swimmer in our class.

（他是我們班上游得最快的人。）

Tuesday is **the** *third* day of the week.

（星期二是一星期的第三天。）

3. 用以指示獨一無二的天體名稱、方向

【例】 **the** moon, **the** earth, **the** sun, **the** east, **the** west……

---

4. 專有名詞與定冠詞

(1) 有**性質形容詞**所修飾的人名要加 the。

【例】 *the ambitious* Caesar（野心勃勃的凱撒）
　　 the dauntless Sun Yat-sen（不屈不撓的孫逸仙）

(2) 表全體國民的專有名詞要加 the。

【例】 *the* Chinese, *the* English, *the* Americans
　　 the Japanese（日本人），*the* French（法國人）

(3) 姓氏的複數之前要加 the，用以表示全家人。

【例】 *The* Williams*es* live next door.
　　（威廉斯一家住在隔壁。）

(4) 帝國名、朝代名等，前面要加 the。

【例】 *the* Ming Dynasty（明代）
　　 the British Commonwealth of Nations（大英國協）

(5) 機關、學校、醫院、商店，或其他公共建築物名稱，要加 the。

【例】 *the* White House（白宮）
　　 the National Central University（國立中央大學）

(6) 複數形（字尾有 s）的專有名詞要加 the。

【例】 *the* United Nations（聯合國）
　　 the Alps（阿爾卑斯山脈）
　　 the Philippine Islands *or the* Philippines（菲律賓群島）

(7) 江河、海洋、運河、半島、森林、沙漠、海峽、港灣的名稱要加 the。

【例】 *the* Yellow River（黃河）
　　 the Pacific Ocean（太平洋）
　　 the Suez Canal（蘇伊士運河）
　　 the Malay Peninsula（馬來半島）

　　　　　the Black Forest（黑森林）
　　　　　the Sahara Desert（撒哈拉沙漠）
　　　　　the Taiwan Strait（台灣海峽）
　　　　　the Persian Gulf（波斯灣）

(8) 書籍、報紙、雜誌名稱要加 the。

　　【例】 *the* Bible（聖經）　　　*the* Reader's Digest（讀者文摘）
　　　　　the Central Daily News（中央日報）

　☞ 車站、公園、湖、橋的名稱不加 the。

　　　　　Taipei Station（台北車站）
　　　　　Central Park（中央公園）
　　　　　Lake Michigan（密西根湖）
　　　　　London Bridge（倫敦橋）

3. 定冠詞的特殊用法

1. the ＋ 形容詞 ＝ 複數名詞

　　【例】 *The rich* are not always happy.（有錢人未必快樂。）
　　　　　You should be kind to *the old* and *the weak*.
　　　　　（你應該善待老人及弱者。）

2. the ＋ 形容詞 ＝ 抽象名詞

　　【例】 We search for *the true*（ = truth ）.（我們尋求眞理。）
　　　　　He has an eye for *the beautiful*（ = beauty ）.
　　　　　（他有審美的眼光。）

3. the ＋ 普通名詞 ＝ 抽象名詞

　　【例】 *The pen* is mightier than *the sword*.（文勝於武。）
　　　　　She felt *the mother* rise in her heart.
　　　　　（她感到母愛自心底湧現。）

4. 定冠詞的慣用法

【例】 I took him by *the* hand. (我抓著他的手。)

He looked me in *the* face. (他看著我的臉。)

I tapped her on *the* shoulder. (我拍她的肩膀。)

4. 冠詞的位置

1. so 〔as, too〕+ 形容詞 + a(n) + 名詞

【例】 I have never seen *so kind a* girl (as she).
(我從未看過 (像她) 這麼仁慈的女孩。)

This is *too difficult a* book for me.
(這本書對我而言太難了。)

2. such 〔quite, what〕+ a(n) + 形容詞 + 名詞

【例】 We haven't had *such a* good time for years.
(我們已經很多年沒玩得這麼開心了。)

He was *quite a* rich man. (他是個很有錢的人。)

What a cute girl she is! (她是個多麼可愛的女孩啊！)

3. all 〔both, half, double〕+ the + 名詞

【例】 You must answer *all the* questions.
(你必須回答所有的問題。)

She paid *double the* price for his work.
(她付給他雙倍於工作的價錢。)

He saved *half the* money for Mary.
(他省下一半的錢給瑪麗。)

<比較> He ran *half a* mile [*a half* mile]. (他跑了半哩路。)

5. 冠詞的省略

1. 稱呼語之前不用冠詞

【例】 *Waiter*, give me a glass of orange juice, please.
（服務生，請給我一杯柳橙汁。）
Come, *boys*.　Let's play soccer.
（來呀！孩子們，我們來踢足球。）

2. 建築物或場所指原有的用途時不用冠詞

【例】 He seldom *goes to church*.（他很少上教堂。）
School begins in September.（九月開學。）

3. 表示官職地位的名詞當做補語時不用冠詞

【例】 He was elected *President* of the United States.
（他當選爲美國總統。）
He was appointed *principal* of this school.
（他奉派爲該校校長。）

4. 交通工具及運動名稱前不用冠詞

【例】 by bus, by car, by train, by plane, by bicycle
play baseball, play basketball, play football,
play tennis

5. 兩個名詞相對並用時不用冠詞

【例】 Butterflies flew *from flower to flower*.
（蝴蝶在花叢中飛舞。）
We stood *face to face* with death.（我們面對著死亡。）

歷屆聯考試題

一、不定冠詞

(   ) 1. "Is he an American?"

      "No, he is _____ European."

      (A) a   (B) an   (C) the   (D) much

(   ) 2. He is _____.

      (A) a honest man   (B) an honest man

      (C) a man honest   (D) an man honest

  3. Birds of a feather flock together. (英翻中)

_____

二、定冠詞

(   ) 1. They sell meat by _____.

      (A) a pound   (B) pounds

      (C) pound   (D) the pound

(   ) 2. Mr. Lee is _____ one-eyed man you mentioned.

      (A) an   (B) the   (C) a   (D) each

(   ) 3. Aristotle, the famous Greek philosopher, believed that the brain was an organ that cooled _____.

      (A) heart   (B) a heart

      (C) the heart   (D) hearts

(　　) 4. A most important developments in air transportation
　　　　(A)　　　　　　　　　　　　　　　(B)

have been with airplanes. (改錯)
(C)　　　　(D)

三、冠詞的省略

(　　) 1. _____ is a very fashionable place in Taipei City.
　　(A) Taipei Park
　　(B) The Taipei Park
　　(C) A Taipei Park
　　(D) An Taipei Park

(　　) 2. What kind of _____ do you want?
　　(A) book　　　　　　(B) the books
　　(C) the book　　　　(D) an book

(　　) 3. They are playing _____.
　　(A) basketball
　　(B) one basketball
　　(C) the basketball
　　(D) a basketball

(　　) 4. _____ of our club is Mr. Jones.
　　(A) Secretary and treasurer
　　(B) The secretary and treasurer
　　(C) The secretary and the treasurer
　　(D) Both secretary or treasurer
　　(E) A secretary and treasurer

【歷屆聯考試題解答】

一、1. (**A**)　　2. (**B**)　　3. 物以類聚。

二、1. (**D**)　　2. (**B**)　　3. (**C**)　　4. (**A**) → The

三、1. (**A**)　　2. (**A**)　　3. (**A**)　　4. (**B**)

【解析】

一、　1. European〔͵jurə'piən〕以子音開始，故冠詞用 a。

　　　2. honest〔'ɑnɪst〕以母音開始，故冠詞用 an。

二、　1. *by the pound*　以磅計

　　　3. 「希臘著名的哲學家亞里斯多德認為，大腦是使心靈冷靜的器官。」由 the brain 可知，空格內應填入相對的名詞 the heart。

三、　2. *what kind of* + 單數可數名詞　哪一種的～

　　　4. 我們俱樂部的秘書兼會計是瓊斯先生。

　　　　由 is Mr. Jones 可知，秘書和會計是指同一人，故用一個冠詞。

　　　　treasurer〔'trɛʒərə〕*n.* 會計

精選模擬考題

(　) 1. She went away without saying _____ word.
  (A) any   (B) a   (C) some   (D) the

(　) 2. Birds of _____ feather flock together.
  (A) an   (B) the   (C) X   (D) a

(　) 3. She wrote her parents twice _____ month.
  (A) a   (B) the   (C) for   (D) in

(　) 4. We hired the boat by _____ hour.
  (A) every   (B) an   (C) the   (D) one

(　) 5. He earns 100 pounds _____ month.
  (A) last   (B) any   (C) the   (D) a

(　) 6. _____ Mr. Armstrong is waiting for you at the gate.
  (A) A   (B) The   (C) This   (D) Any

(　) 7. This is _____ excellent tea.
  (A) a   (B) any   (C) an   (D) the

(　) 8. I had _____ lunch with _____ old friend of mine.
  (A) a, an   (B) X, an   (C) a, X   (D) the, an

(　) 9. A black and white dog _____ running after the cat.
  (A) were   (B) have   (C) was   (D) has

( ) 10. The poet and the statesman _____ dead.
(A) were   (B) have   (C) was   (D) has

( ) 11. _____ gives us milk.
(A) A cow   (B) The cows
(C) Cows   (D) Every cows

( ) 12. Two of _____ trade can never agree.
(A) X   (B) a
(C) the   (D) an

( ) 13. Will you please pass me _____ salt?
(A) one   (B) a   (C) the   (D) X

( ) 14. The educated _____ always gentle.
(A) be   (B) are   (C) is   (D) act

( ) 15. He is _____ principal of our school.
(A) a   (B) the   (C) an   (D) one

( ) 16. He was elected _____ Mayor of London.
(A) a   (B) an   (C) X   (D) one

( ) 17. They elected him _____ president.
(A) as   (B) a   (C) an   (D) X

( ) 18. Washington D.C., is _____ capital of _____ United States.
(A) the, the   (B) X, the
(C) the, X   (D) a, the

(　) 19. We call the islands _____ West Indies.

　　(A) the　　(B) X　　　(C) that　　(D) a

(　) 20. _____ Greeks were _____ first nation of
antiquity that became civilized.

　　(A) X, X　　(B) X, the　　(C) The, X　　(D) The, the

(　) 21. _____ pen is mightier than _____ sword.

　　(A) The, X　　　　　　(B) X, the

　　(C) X, X　　　　　　(D) The, the

(　) 22. I am _____ only son in my family.

　　(A) an　　(B) a　　(C) the　　(D) X

(　) 23. I took him by _____ hand.

　　(A) her　　(B) my　　(C) the　　(D) X

(　) 24. He looked his mother in _____ eye.

　　(A) X　　(B) the　　(C) that　　(D) her

(　) 25. I tapped her on _____ shoulder.

　　(A) X　　(B) the　　(C) that　　(D) his

(　) 26. I have never seen _____.

　　(A) a so good film　　(B) so a good film

　　(C) such good a film　　(D) so good a film

(　) 27. This is _____ for me.

　　(A) too difficult a book　　(B) a too difficult book

　　(C) a so difficult book　　(D) so a difficult book

( ) 28. It is comfortable to travel by _____ air.

     (A) an   (B) X   (C) the   (D) way of

( ) 29. In America _____ school begins in September.

     (A) a   (B) the   (C) X   (D) one

( ) 30. Butterflies flew _____.

     (A) from flower to flower

     (B) from one flower to flower

     (C) from the flower to another

     (D) from flower to flowers

【精選模擬考題解答】

1.(B)	2.(D)	3.(A)	4.(C)	5.(D)	6.(A)
7.(C)	8.(B)	9.(C)	10.(A)	11.(A)	12.(B)
13.(C)	14.(B)	15.(B)	16.(C)	17.(D)	18.(A)
19.(A)	20.(D)	21.(D)	22.(C)	23.(C)	24.(B)
25.(B)	26.(D)	27.(A)	28.(B)	29.(C)	30.(A)

【解析】

4. *by the hour* 按小時計

8. 三餐前面不加冠詞，have lunch〔breakfast, dinner〕。

9. a black and white dog 是「一隻黑白相間的狗」，故用單數動詞。

10. 用兩個冠詞，表示詩人和政治家不是同一個人，故用複數動詞。

12. 「同行相忌。」句中的 a = the same。

14. the + 形容詞 = 複數名詞，故用複數動詞。

    the educated 有教養的人

4. 副 詞

副詞修飾動詞、形容詞或其他副詞，

有時也修飾片語、子句或整個句子。

---

1. 副詞的用法

1. 副詞修飾動詞

【例】 He *walked slowly*.【放在不及物動詞之後】

H *crossed* the street *carefully*.　【放在及物動詞前後】
He *carefully crossed* the street.

2. 副詞修飾形容詞

【例】 It is *very hot* today. (今天天氣非常熱。)

We had *too much* snow last year.

(此地去年雪下得太多。)

3. 副詞修飾其他副詞

【例】 She spoke *so fast*. (她講話的速度很快。)

4. 副詞修飾片語、子句

【例】 He came here *just at ten o'clock*.

(他剛好在十點整來到這裡。)

She failed *only because she was careless*.

(她只因為粗心而失敗。)

> **5. 修飾整個句子：可置於句首或主詞與動詞之間**

【例】 ***Fortunately***, *the child arrived home safe.*

（所幸，孩子平安回到家。）

He, ***foolishly***, *told me the secret.*

（他傻傻地告訴我這個秘密。）

> **6. 副詞修飾名詞、代名詞**

【例】 ***Only*** *he* solved the problem.

（只有他解決了這個問題。）

The *climate **here*** is mild.

（這裡的氣候很溫和。）

2. 頻率副詞的位置

頻率副詞有：always, usually, often, sometimes, seldom, never。

頻率副詞的位置：①在 be 動詞之後 ②在一般動詞前 ③在助動詞與動詞之間。

【例】 She *is **seldom*** late for school. （她上學很少遲到。）

He ***usually*** *goes* to bed at ten-thirty.

（他通常十點半上床睡覺。）

The job *will **never*** be finished.

（這工作永遠做不完。）

注意下列特殊的位置：

⑴ very〔so〕often, very seldom 置於句末

【例】 I go to the movies ***very often***. （我常去看電影。）

She attends our meeting ***very seldom***.

（她很少參加我們的會議。）

(2) 簡答句中，頻率副詞必須放在助動詞或 be 動詞前。

　【例】　A: Have you always lived in Taipei?
　　　　　　（你們一直都住在台北嗎？）

　　　　　　B: Yes, we *always* have.（是的，我們一直住在台北。）

　☞ 頻率副詞在「主詞 + 助 (be) 動詞」的省略式對話中，也必須放在助 (be) 動詞前。

　【例】　A: He is late.（他遲到了。）

　　　　　　B: He *always* is.（他一向如此。）

3. 副詞並列時的順序

1. 同類副詞，由小單位到大單位

　【例】　He lives in *San Francisco*, *California*, *U.S.A.*
　　　　　（他住在美國加州舊金山。）

　　　　　He usually gets up *at eight* in the morning *in the summer*.（他夏天通常在早上八點起床。）

　☞ away, out, up, down, over, here 為不確定的地方副詞，兩個地方副詞並列時，**不確定的地方副詞在前面**，確定的在後面。

　【例】　Thousands of stars were twinkling *up in the sky*.
　　　　　（數以千計的星星在天空上閃耀。）

　　　　　We do not shake hands so often *here in Taiwan*.
　　　　　（在台灣我們不那麼常握手。）

2. 不同類副詞按「地點、狀態（方法）、次數、時間」的順序排列

　【例】　He went *to the library* twice a day *last week*.
　　　　　（他上週一天去圖書館兩次。）

　　　　　He arrived in *Taipei safely the other day*.
　　　　　（他前幾天平安抵達台北。）

4. 注意下列副詞的用法

1. 容易混淆的副詞

【例】

hard 努力地
hardly 幾乎不

late 遲；晚
lately 最近

near 靠近
nearly 幾乎

high 高
highly 極；很

pretty 相當地
prettily 漂亮地

He studies very **hard**. (他非常努力用功。)
He **hardly** studied before. (他以前幾乎沒讀書。)

The eagle flies **high**. (老鷹飛得很高。)
He spoke very **highly** of her. (他極讚揚她。)

2. very 與 much 的用法

⑴ very 修飾原級形容詞及副詞，(very) much 修飾比較級、動詞。

【例】 I am **very glad** to see you. (很高興見到你。)【修飾形容詞】

He walks **very fast**. (他走得很快。)【修飾原級副詞】

He walks **much faster** than you. 【修飾比較級】
(他走得比你快多了。)

I **enjoyed** the concert **very much**. 【修飾動詞】
(我非常喜歡這場音樂會。)

⑵ the very + 最高級 (形容詞、副詞) = much the + 最高級

【例】 This is **the very best** of all. (這是所有當中最好的。)
= This is **much the best** of all.

⑶ very 修飾現在分詞，much 修飾過去分詞

【例】 I heard some **very surprising** news.
(我聽到一些非常驚人的消息。)

He is *much exhausted* after the long journey.

（長途旅行後他非常疲憊。）

☞ tired, learned（有學問的）為純粹形容詞，用 very 修飾。

【例】He's a *very learned* man.（他是一個很有學問的人。）

☞ 限定用法的過去分詞（即 p.p. ＋ n.），常用 very 來修飾。

【例】He's a *very experienced English teacher.*

（他是個很有經驗的英文老師。）

⑷ 只能作敘述用法的形容詞，多以 a- 起頭者，只能用 much 修飾，
如 afraid, alone, alike, alive⋯

【例】The twins look *much alike.*（這對雙胞胎很相像。）

She is *much afraid* of dogs.（她非常怕狗。）

3. ago 及 before 的差別

ago —只能與過去簡單式連用，前面必須有表示期間的字。

before —① 前面**有**表示期間的字時，須與過去完成式連用。

② 前面**無**表示期間的字時，可用過去式、現在完成式，
或過去完成式。

【例】I *met* him *two days ago.*（我兩天前遇到他。）

She said she *had met* him *two days before.*

（她說她兩天前曾遇到他。）

It never *happened before.*（那件事以前從未發生過。）

4. so 與 neither 的用法

⑴ **So ＋ S. ＋ V.** → 某人**的確**～；某人**真的**～

【例】He can play the flute. — *So he* can.

（他會吹笛子。—— 他的確會吹。）

She went to the party. — *So she* did.

（她去參加宴會。—— 她的確去了。）

(2) **So** + **V.** + **S.** → 某人也~

【例】 He can play the guitar. — *So* can I.

（他會彈吉他。— 我也會。）

She went to the party. — *So* did I.

（她去參加宴會。— 我也去參加了。）

(3) **Neither**〔**Nor**〕+ **V.** + **S.** → 某人也不~

【例】 He *can't* play soccer. — *Neither* can I.

（他不會踢足球。— 我也不會。）

She *didn't* go to the concert. — *Neither* did I.

（她沒去聽音樂會。— 我也沒去。）

---

5. too 用於肯定句，either 用於否定句

【例】 He plays the guitar, and I *play*, *too*.

（他彈吉他，我也彈。）

If you *don't* go to the party, I *won't*, *either*.

（如果你不去參加宴會，我也不去。）

---

6. still, already 及 yet 的區別

already 用於肯定句，yet 用於疑問句、否定句；肯定句時表示「還；仍然」，則用 still。

【例】 Let's begin now; it is *already* too late.

（我們現在開始吧；已經太晚了。）

He has *not* finished the work *yet*.（他工作還沒做完。）

Has she returned *yet*?（她回來了沒？）

The matter is *still* unsettled.（那件事尚未解決。）

7. far 及 a long way 的用法

口語中 far 用於否定句或疑問句，a long way 則用於肯定句。

【例】 The university is *not far* from here.

（那所大學離這裡不遠。）

How far is it from here to the station?

（從這裡到車站有多遠？）

It's *a long way* to Spain.（到西班牙非常遠。）

8. so 與 such 的區別

so 是副詞，後接形容詞或副詞；such 是形容詞，後接名詞。

【例】 He is not *so stupid as to* do that.

（他不會笨到去做那種事。）

She's *so lovely* a girl *that* everybody likes her.

= She's *such* a *lovely* girl *that* everybody likes her.

（她是個如此可愛的女孩，每個人都喜歡她。）

9. 形容詞、副詞 + enough

【例】 He's not *old enough* to smoke.（他還沒到抽煙的年齡。）

= He's *too young to* smoke.（他太年輕，不能抽煙。）

10. cannot…too~　無論再怎麼~也不為過

【例】 You *cannot* be *too* careful.

（你再怎麼小心也不為過。）

You *cannot* study *too* hard.

（不論你多用功也不為過。）

歷屆聯考試題

一、副詞的用法及位置

(   ) 1. He _____.
    (A) badly was wounded
    (B) was badly wounded
    (C) wounded badly was
    (D) wounded was badly

(   ) 2. He had loved her and he had been, _____, good to her.
    (A) accord   (B) according
    (C) accorded   (D) accordingly

(   ) 3. I tried to wake up my wife by ringing the doorbell, but she was _____ asleep.
    (A) fast   (B) quick   (C) rapid   (D) quickly

(   ) 4. Are you _____ three sandwiches?
    (A) enough hungry eat
    (B) enough hungry to eat
    (C) hunger enough eat
    (D) hunger enough to eat
    (E) hungry enough to eat

(   ) 5. _____ he planned to come but then he changed his mind.
    (A) Origin   (B) Original
    (C) Origination   (D) Originally

(　) 6. The young man has always worked _____ (ambition).

(　) 7. When Mrs. Brown <u>appeared</u> at the party, all <u>of</u> us were
　　　　　　　　　　　　　(A)　　　　　　　　　　　　　(B)
　　　　attracted <u>by</u> her <u>special</u> designed gown. (改錯)
　　　　　　　　(C)　　　(D)

(　) 8. If we can work <u>fast</u> and <u>steady</u>, we can <u>finish</u> it by
　　　　　　　　　　　　　(A)　　　　(B)　　　　　　　　(C)
　　　　<u>noon</u>. (改錯)
　　　　(D)

(　) 9. Two thieves slipped <u>quick</u> through the dark <u>bushes</u>
　　　　　　　　　　　　　　　(A)　　　　　　　　　　　　(B)
　　　　which <u>surrounded</u> the house. (改錯)
　　　　　　　(C)

二、副詞應注意事項

(　) 1. I can't come now. I haven't finished my homework
　　　　_____.

(A) already　　　(B) before　　　(C) yet
(D) just　　　　　(E) now

(　) 2. We _____ see the road in the rain.
(A) could hard　　　(B) couldn't hardly
(C) could hardly　　(D) couldn't hard

(　) 3. _____ I was told that I passed the examination.
(A) Happily　　　　(B) Happy
(C) Happiness　　　(D) For happiness
(E) Be happy

( ) 4. He cannot type, and you cannot, _____.
  (A) too (B) either
  (C) neither (D) started

( ) 5. He doesn't play baseball, and I don't, _____.
  (A) either (B) neither
  (C) too (D) also

( ) 6. Jack: I've never sent a telegram before.
  Peter: I haven't, _____.
  (A) neither (B) too (C) either
  (D) also (E) so

( ) 7. He is _____ changed since I last saw him.
  (A) much (B) very
  (C) many (D) more

( ) 8. She is _____ taller than her sister.
  (A) very (B) much
  (C) more (D) less

( ) 9. Betty: I like honest friends.
  Linda: _____
  (A) So am I. (B) Neither does she.
  (C) Are you? (D) So do I.
  (E) Don't you?

(   ) 10. Character cannot be counterfeited, _____ be put on
     and cast off as if it were a garment to meet the whim
     of the moment.
     (A) nor it can   (B) can it nor
     (C) not can it   (D) nor can it
     (E) no can it

(   ) 11. You cannot fly, nor _____ make the distance shorter.
     (A) you can   (B) you cannot
     (C) can you   (D) can't you

(   ) 12. Mary will not come, _____ will her brother.
     (A) nor   (B) or   (C) either

(   ) 13. He worked so hard _____ to go home.
     (A) that forgot   (B) forgot
     (C) that he forgets   (D) that he forgot

(   ) 14. The book is _____ I cannot read it.
     (A) such difficult that
     (B) so difficulty that
     (C) such difficult as
     (D) such difficulty that
     (E) so difficult that

(   ) 15. It's too late _____ there.
     (A) that we walk   (B) for us walking
     (C) us to walk   (D) for us to walk

(　) 16. (A) I talked with him for a long time over the telephone.
　　　　(B) You should study hardly to improve your English.
　　　　(C) The satellite travels in space very fast.
　　　　(D) You have the wrong number. (選錯的)

(　) 17. Mary is ＿＿＿＿ clever ＿＿＿＿ she understands everything.
　　　　(A) such a, that　　(B) such an, that　　(C) so, that
　　　　(D) so, as　　(E) as, so

(　) 18. She is ＿＿＿＿ a nice girl that she is liked by all.
　　　　(A) so　　(B) as　　(C) such　　(D) how

(　) 19. His father writes him ＿＿＿＿.
　　　　(A) in regular　　(B) of regularly
　　　　(C) with regularity　　(D) of regular
　　　　(E) by regularity

(　) 20. The children ran ＿＿＿＿.
　　　　(A) to upstair　　(B) to upstairs　　(C) fastly
　　　　(D) upstair　　(E) upstairs

(　) 21. Mr. Wang <u>dropped</u> in to see us <u>on</u> his <u>home way</u> from
　　　　　　　　(A)　　　　　　　　(B)　　　　(C)
　　　　the <u>theater</u>. (改錯)
　　　　　　(D)

(　) 22. He is not <u>so</u> <u>a</u> dishonest man <u>as</u> you <u>think</u>. (改錯)
　　　　　　　　(A)(B)　　　　　　　(C)　　　　(D)

(　) 23. If you do not take part in the game, he will not take part in the game, _____.

(　) 24. No <u>other</u> girl in her class <u>dances</u> as <u>beautiful</u> as she
　　　　　　　(A)　　　　　　　　　　(B)　　　　　(C)
<u>does</u>. (改錯)
(D)

三、疑問副詞

(　) 1. He taught me _____.
　　(A) how should I speak English
　　(B) how spoke English
　　(C) how speak English
　　(D) how to speak English
　　(E) how can I speak English

(　) 2. Where did the thief hide? _____
　　(A) He tried to run away.
　　(B) I caught him.
　　(C) Under the bed.
　　(D) No policeman came.

(　) 3. No matter _____ hard it may be, I must try.
　　(A) what　　　　　　(B) how
　　(C) any way　　　　(D) some way

(　) 4. How far is it to Taichung?
　　(A) By train.　　　　　(B) In three hours.
　　(C) For three hours.　(D) Three hours by train.

(   ) 5. The way you should <u>write</u> a letter depends on <u>how good</u>
                           (A)   (B)

        you know the person <u>to whom</u> you are writing.（改錯）
                                    (C)

(   ) 6. "<u>How long</u> do you go to the theater?"

        "Twice a week."（改錯）

【歷屆聯考試題解答】

一、   1.（**B**）   2.（**D**）   3.（**A**）   4.（**E**）   5.（**D**）

      6. ambitiously   7.（**D**）→ specially   8.（**B**）→ steadily

      9.（**A**）→ quickly

二、   1.（**C**）   2.（**C**）   3.（**A**）   4.（**B**）   5.（**A**）   6.（**C**）

      7.（**A**）   8.（**B**）   9.（**D**）   10.（**D**）   11.（**C**）   12.（**A**）

     13.（**D**）   14.（**E**）   15.（**D**）   16.（**B**）   17.（**C**）   18.（**C**）

     19.（**C**）   20.（**E**）   21.（**C**）→ way home   22.（**A**）→ such

     23. either   24.（**C**）→ beautifully

三、   1.（**D**）   2.（**C**）   3.（**B**）   4.（**D**）

      5.（**B**）→ how well   6 How often

【解析】

一、

   1. wound〔wund〕*v.* 使受傷

   2. accordingly〔ə'kɔrdɪŋlɪ〕*adv.* 因此

   3. *fall asleep* 睡著了

   4. enough 放在所修飾的形容詞之後。

   5. 起初，他打算要來，但後來他改變主意了。

      空格應填一副詞，修飾一整句，且依句意，選(D) Originally

     〔ə'rɪdʒənl̩〕*adv.* 起初

6. ambitiously〔æmˈbɪʃəslɪ〕*adv.* 野心勃勃地

7. 因修飾過去分詞 designed 要用副詞，故 (D) 須改成 specially（特別地）。

二、

1. already「已經」，用於肯定句；yet「尚（未）」，用於疑問句和否定句。

2. hardly（幾乎不）表否定，所以本題不需要再加 not。

7. 過去分詞用 much 修飾。

8. 修飾比較級可用 much, even, still, far。

9. 前面的子句爲肯定時，則後面子句用「so＋助動詞＋主詞」，表示「…也是」。

10. 個性不能假裝，也不能爲滿足一時的衝動，而把它當成衣服一樣，任意穿上或脫掉。
    counterfeit〔ˈkaʊntəˌfɪt〕*v.* 假裝　　meet〔mit〕*v.* 滿足
    whim of the moment 一時的衝動；偶發的念頭

13. *so ~ that*… 如此～以致於…

15. *too ~ to* + V. 太～而不能…

16. (B) 中 hardly（幾乎不）應改爲 hard（辛苦地；努力地）。
    (C) satellite〔ˈsætlˌaɪt〕*n.* （人造）衛星
    (D) 你打錯電話了。

18. such＋a＋形容詞＋名詞＋that…
    ＝ so＋形容詞＋a＋名詞＋that… 如此～以致於…

19. *with regularity* 定期地（＝ *regularly*）

21. 王先生離開戲院，他在回家的路上順道來看我們。
    on one's way home 在某人回家的路上

23. *take part in* 參加

精選模擬考題

(　) 1. I _____ to the museum.
    (A) have often been
    (B) often have been
    (C) have been often

(　) 2. She _____ late for school.
    (A) seldom is   (B) is seldom
    (C) seldom   (D) often

(　) 3. He could _____ work after a long illness.
    (A) hardly   (B) hard
    (C) not hardly   (D) possible

(　) 4. The boy came _____ me.
    (A) nearly   (B) near
    (C) quick   (D) straight

(　) 5. He is _____ exhausted after the long journey.
    (A) very   (B) much   (C) such   (D) to

(　) 6. He was _____ loved by the boys of his school.
    (A) much   (B) very   (C) such   (D) too

(　) 7. If you don't go to the party, I won't, _____.
    (A) too   (B) either
    (C) neither   (D) so

(　　) 8. When I saw Mary last year, she had returned from France only two days _____.

      (A) ago   (B) before   (C) after   (D) since

(　　) 9. Have you finished your homework _____?

      (A) still   (B) just now

      (C) already   (D) soon

(　　) 10. If you do not go, I will not go, _____.

      (A) either   (B) neither

      (C) too   (D) so

(　　) 11. He is _____ smart to do such a foolish thing.

      (A) too   (B) to   (C) so   (D) such

(　　) 12. I think that you are _____ that shelf.

      (A) enough tall to reach

      (B) tall to reach enough

      (C) tall to enough reach

      (D) tall enough to reach

(　　) 13. I have not heard from him _____.

      (A) late   (B) lately   (C) latter   (D) later

(　　) 14. I am _____ afraid that it will rain tomorrow.

      (A) some   (B) much   (C) great   (D) pretty

(　　) 15. I've looked _____ for my new pen.

      (A) every where   (B) everywhere

      (C) at everywhere   (D) for where

( ) 16. I didn't go there, _____.

      (A) too   (B) also   (C) either   (D) both

( ) 17. He spoke English _____ quickly for me to follow him.

      (A) so   (B) such   (C) too   (D) as

( ) 18. I haven't visited the museum and _____.

      (A) he has   (B) so has he

      (C) neither does he   (D) has he

( ) 19. He doesn't speak French, and I don't speak it _____.

      (A) also   (B) either

      (C) likewise   (D) too

( ) 20. They are all men of high position, so they should be treated _____.

      (A) respectfully   (B) respectively

      (C) respectably   (D) in respect

( ) 21. If you speak too _____, most of us will not understand what you are saying.

      (A) rapid   (B) rapidly

      (C) quick   (D) slowly

( ) 22. I think it happened about two years _____.

      (A) late   (B) ago

      (C) latter   (D) from now

(　) 23. It is _____ hot to go out today.

      (A) very   (B) so   (C) too   (D) much

(　) 24. He is _____ taller than his father.

      (A) very   (B) much   (C) a few   (D) some

(　) 25. He likes watching TV _____.

      (A) very much   (B) all time

      (C) some time   (D) as much

(　) 26. I _____ him act in Hamlet.

      (A) enjoy always watching

      (B) always enjoy watching

      (C) enjoy watching always

      (D) always enjoy watch

(　) 27. The weather was _____ pleasant.

      (A) very   (B) much   (C) too   (D) some

(　) 28. He spoke so quietly that we could _____ hear him.

      (A) almost   (B) rarely

      (C) hardly   (D) little

(　) 29. I'm _____ fond of apples.

      (A) some   (B) like   (C) very   (D) much

(　) 30. We arrived in London a few days _____.

      (A) ago   (B) then

      (C) passed   (D) since

( ) 31. His grades aren't _____ for a scholarship.

    (A) enough good   (B) good enough

    (C) well enough   (D) enough well

( ) 32. The work is _____ finished.

    (A) near   (B) nearly

    (C) so near   (D) so quick

( ) 33. You are young and _____.

    (A) so am I   (B) so do I

    (C) so have I   (D) so I am

( ) 34. I have never seen _____ large a peach before.

    (A) such   (B) too

    (C) so   (D) very

( ) 35. "How often do you go to the theater?"

    "_____."

    (A) Twice a week   (B) By bus

    (C) With friends   (D) Probably Monday

【精選模擬試題解答】

1. (A)	2. (B)	3. (A)	4. (B)	5. (B)	6. (A)
7. (B)	8. (B)	9. (C)	10. (A)	11. (A)	12. (D)
13. (B)	14. (B)	15. (B)	16. (C)	17. (C)	18. (D)
19. (B)	20. (A)	21. (B)	22. (B)	23. (C)	24. (B)
25. (A)	26. (B)	27. (A)	28. (C)	29. (C)	30. (A)
31. (B)	32. (B)	33. (A)	34. (C)	35. (A)	

【解析】

8. 過去完成式 had returned 與 two days before 連用。

12. shelf〔ʃɛlf〕*n.* 架子

13. (B) lately〔'letlɪ〕*adv.* 最近

　　(C) latter〔'lætɚ〕*adj.* 後者的

　　(D) later〔'letɚ〕*adj.*（時間）更遲的　*adv.* 以後

　　　　hear from ＋ 人　得知某人的消息；收到某人的來信

14. afraid 用 much 修飾。

15. everywhere〔'ɛvrɪ,hwɛr〕*adv.* 到處

18. museum〔mju'ziəm〕*n.* 博物館

20. (A) respectfully〔rɪ'spɛktfəlɪ〕*adv.* 恭敬地

　　(B) respectively〔rɪ'spɛktɪvlɪ〕*adv.* 個別地

　　(C) respectably〔rɪ'spɛktəblɪ〕*adv.* 高尚地

　　(D) 無此用法。

26. 頻率副詞 ＋ enjoy ＋ V-ing。

31. 他的成績不夠好，得不到獎學金。

　　grade〔gred〕*n.* 成績

　　scholarship〔'skɑlɚ,ʃɪp〕*n.* 獎學金

5. 動 詞

① 不及物動詞 ⎰ 完全不及物 → 沒有受詞
⎱ 不完全不及物 → 沒有受詞，但有主詞補語

② 及物動詞 ⎧ 完全及物 → 有受詞
⎨ 不完全及物 → 有受詞及受詞補語
⎩ 授與動詞 → 有兩個受詞，一為直接受詞，
一為間接受詞

1. 及物動詞與不及物動詞

1. 不及物動詞 + 介系詞 + 受詞

【例】 They *decided on* a different plan.
(他們決定改變計劃。)

She's always *complaining of* high prices.
(她總是抱怨價錢太高。)

He *graduated from* college last year.
(他去年大學畢業。)

She *apologized to* him for being late.
(她因遲到向他道歉。)

2. 有些動詞只能做及物動詞

【例】 I *discussed* the matter with Joe.
(我和喬討論這件事。)

<比較> I *talked about* the matter with Joe.

【例】 He *married* a pretty girl.

（他娶了一位美嬌娘。）

<比較> He *got married to* a pretty girl.

【例】 We are *approaching* the town.

（我們走近這城鎮。）

<比較> We are *coming near* the town.

3. 不完全不及物動詞 + 形容詞（做補語）

不完全不及物動詞：

(1) be 動詞 —— 用來表狀態

(2) seem, appear, look（看起來像…）

(3) keep, remain（保持；依然）—— 用來表態度、狀態

(4) smell, feel, taste, sound —— 連綴動詞

(5) become, get, grow, come, go, turn, fall（漸漸變成…）

(6) prove, turn out（證實；變成）

She *kept* silent.（她保持沉默。）

The rumor *proved* true.（這謠言證實是真的。）

4. 不完全及物動詞 + 受詞 + 受詞補語

不完全及物動詞：

(1) 「想；認爲」型：think, believe, suppose, find, consider

(2) 「呼叫」型：call, name, declare, admit

(3) 「使」型：keep, leave, make, have, compel

(4) 「希望」型：want, wish

(5) 「感官」型：see, hear, feel

【例】 We *considered* him (to be) *honest*. 【to be 經常被省略】

（我們認爲他很誠實。）

I will *leave* the door *open*.（我會讓門開著。）

> 5. 授與動詞＋間接受詞（人）＋直接受詞（物）
> ＝授與動詞＋直接受詞＋介詞＋間接受詞

(1) 介詞用 **to** 的授與動詞：give, lend, bring, show, tell, write, send, hand, teach, offer, sell, promise, pass。

【例】 He *writes me a letter* every other week.
He *writes a letter to me* every other week.
（他每隔一週寫一封信給我。）

(2) 介詞用 **for** 的授與動詞：buy, make, leave, do, choose, order, sing。

【例】 She *sang me a song*.（她爲我唱一首歌。）
She *sang a song for me*.

(3) 介詞用 **of** 的授與動詞：ask。

【例】 He *asked the teacher a question*.
（他問老師一個問題。）
He *asked a question of the teacher*.

2. 動詞片語

> 1. 動詞＋副詞

put off 延期	give up 放棄
turn off 關掉	put on 穿；戴
cut down 砍倒	see off 送行
take off 脫掉	put down 記下
speak up (out) 大聲說	call up 打電話
leave out 遺漏	come about 發生
clear up 放晴	make out 了解
look up 查閱	bring up 養育
turn on 打開（開關）	

【例】　We'll **put off** (= *postpone*) the meeting till next week.

（我們將把會議延至下週。）

He hasn't **turned up** (= *appeared*) yet.

（他還沒出現。）

☞ 動詞的受詞為名詞時,「動詞＋副詞＋**名詞**＝動詞＋**名詞**＋
副詞」。若受詞為代名詞,只能放在二者中間,「動詞＋**代名詞**
＋副詞」。

【例】　He *took off his coat*. (他脫下外套。)

He *took his coat off*.

He *took it off*.

---

2. 動詞＋介系詞

look for　尋找	come across　偶然遇到
cope with　應付	take after　像
look into　調查	get in　上車
get off　下車	get to　到達
call on (＋人)　拜訪	call at (＋地)　拜訪
run over　輾過	stand for　代表
get through　完成	look after　照顧
run into　撞到	break into　插嘴;闖入

【例】　Who will **look after** the children?

（誰將照顧小孩子?）

She **takes after** (= *resembles*) her mother.

（她像她媽媽。）

<比較>
{ I **called on** *my uncle* yesterday. 【正】
{ I *called* my uncle *on* yesterday. 【誤】

3. 動詞＋副詞＋介系詞

catch up with　趕上	speak ill of　講壞話
keep away from　遠離	look forward to　期待
speak well of　稱讚；講好話	look down up(on)　輕視
put up with　忍受	get out of　放棄；避免
look up to　尊敬	make much of　特別強調
get along with　與（人）相處；進步	
do away with　廢除	keep up with　趕上

【例】 You should ***get out of*** bad habits.

（你應該戒除壞習慣。）

I can't ***put up with*** the noise. （我無法忍受噪音。）

You shouldn't ***speak ill of*** your neighbors.

（你不應該講鄰居的壞話。）

精選模擬考題

(　　) 1. She looks _____.
   - (A) angry
   - (B) angrily
   - (C) anger
   - (D) angried

(　　) 2. May I ask a favor _____ you?
   - (A) to
   - (B) for
   - (C) of
   - (D) on

(　　) 3. I found my vase _____ into pieces.
   - (A) break
   - (B) breaking
   - (C) to break
   - (D) broken

(　　) 4. When will you have the house _____?
   - (A) paint
   - (B) painted
   - (C) to paint
   - (D) painting

(　　) 5. Don't _____ the willow tree; it will fall by itself.
   - (A) fall
   - (B) fell
   - (C) fall down
   - (D) lie

(　　) 6. He _____ to live on his wife's earnings.
   - (A) enables
   - (B) manages
   - (C) are able
   - (D) can

(　　) 7. Where did you _____ your bicycle _____?
   - (A) have, repair
   - (B) have, repaired
   - (C) get, repair
   - (D) get, to repair

(　　) 8. I am sorry to _____ you waiting so long.
     (A) keeped   (B) be kept
     (C) have kept   (D) have been kept

(　　) 9. Would you please _____ me a favor?
     (A) make (B) do   (C) get   (D) let

(　　) 10. She can't _____ right from wrong.
     (A) say   (B) speak   (C) tell   (D) get

(　　) 11. The medicine will _____ you better.
     (A) do   (B) make   (C) cause (D) let

(　　) 12. They _____ at the skill of the man at the game.
     (A) alarmed   (B) amazed
     (C) astonished   (D) marvelled

(　　) 13. If you had _____ home five minutes earlier, you could have caught the train.
     (A) gone to   (B) left
     (C) arrived   (D) delivered

(　　) 14. Mr. Watson _____ Miss Brown.
     (A) married with   (B) married to
     (C) married   (D) be married

(　　) 15. If I can't put up with something, I can't _____ it.
     (A) stand (B) enjoy (C) love (D) understand

(　　) 16. Please _____ yourself to the cake.
     (A) have (B) help (C) let   (D) make

【精選模擬考題解答】

1. (**A**)　　2. (**C**)　　3. (**D**)　　4. (**B**)　　5. (**B**)　　6. (**B**)

7. (**B**)　　8. (**C**)　　9. (**B**)　　10. (**C**)　　11. (**B**)　　12. (**D**)

13. (**B**)　　14. (**C**)　　15. (**A**)　　16. (**B**)

【解析】

1. look（看起來）為不完全不及物動詞，須接形容詞做為主詞補語，look at（看）則視為及物動詞，須用副詞修飾。

2. *ask a favor of~*　請（某人）幫忙

3. 本題以過去分詞做受詞補語，因為受詞 vase（花瓶）**不會主動破裂**。

4. 使役動詞＋物＋過去分詞（表被動）
   <比較> 使役動詞＋人＋原形動詞（表主動）

5. fall〔fɔl〕*v.* 落下；下降（三態變化為：fall, fell, fallen）
   fell〔fɛl〕*v.* 砍伐（樹木）（三態變化為：fell, felled, felled）

6. *manage to ＋ V.* 設法~
   而 (A) 的用法應為「*enable* ＋人＋ *to* ＋ V.」表「使某人能~」。
   live on 以~維生；靠~過活

9. *do sb. a favor* 幫某人一個忙

10. *tell right from wrong* 分辨是非

12. *marvel at* 對…驚嘆
    (A) (B) (C) 則要改成被動語態，才能表示「感到吃驚」。

14. marry（結婚）為及物動詞，用主動與被動意義相同。
    原句 = Mr. Watson was married to Miss Brown.

15. *put up with* 忍受（= *stand*）

16. *help* oneself *to* 自行取用

6. 助 動 詞

1. can, could 的用法

⑴ can 用以表示**能力**、**許可**，及**推測**。

【例】 He *can* speak Spanish, but he *can't* speak French.
(他會說西班牙文，但不會說法文。)【表能力】

You *can* (= *may*) have the book if you like it. 【表許可】
(如果你喜歡這本書的話，可以拿走。)

Can the rumor be true? 【表推測】
(這傳言會是眞的嗎？)

☞ can 表示推測時，只用於**否定句**和**疑問句**中。

$$\begin{cases} \text{can (not)} + 原形動詞 \to 表對\textbf{現在}的推測 \\ \text{can (not)} + \text{have} + 過去分詞 \to 表對\textbf{過去}的推測 \end{cases}$$

【例】 The rumor *cannot be* true. (那傳言不可能是眞的。)

Can he *have done* such a thing? (他會做這種事嗎？)

⑵ **未來式**、**完成式**時，以 **be able to** 代替。

【例】 She will *be able to* come tomorrow. 【未來式】
(她明天能來。)

No one has ever *been able to* solve the puzzle. 【完成式】
(從來沒有人能夠解開這個謎。)

⑶ **could** 除了是 can 的過去式，也表示**客氣的請求**。

【例】 She told me that she *could* type.
(她告訴我她會打字。)

Could you come and see me next Sunday? 【客氣的請求】
(你下週日能來看我嗎？)

(4) **cannot but + V**. 不得不
　　= **cannot help + V-ing**

　【例】 I *cannot but tell* him the truth.
　　　　　（我不得不告訴他實情。）

　　　　　I *cannot help* admiring his courage.
　　　　　（我不得不佩服他的勇氣。）

2. **may, might** 的用法

(1) may 用以表示**許可、推測、祈願**。

　【例】 *May* I come in? — No, you *may* not. 【表許可】
　　　　　（我可以進來嗎？— 不，你不可以。）

　　　　　It *may* rain in the afternoon. 【表推測】
　　　　　（下午可能會下雨。）

　　　　　May you both be happy!（祝你們倆快樂！）【表祈願】

　☞ may 用以表示推測時，**不用在疑問句中**。

$$\begin{cases} \text{may + 原形動詞} \rightarrow \text{表對現在或未來的推測} \\ \text{may + have + p.p.} \rightarrow \text{表對過去的推測} \end{cases}$$

　【例】 He *may* not *be* sick.（他不可能會生病。）

　　　　　She *may have been* beautiful once, but she is not
　　　　　anymore.（她從前可能很漂亮，但現在已不再漂亮了。）

(2) may 可用在**表目的的副詞子句**中。

$$\left.\begin{array}{l} \text{so that} \\ \text{in order that} \end{array}\right\} \cdots \text{may} \quad \ulcorner 爲了，以便 \lrcorner$$

　【例】 I open the window *so that* I *may* see the moon.
　　　　　（我打開窗戶，以便能看到月亮。）

　　　　　He'll go abroad *in order that* he *may* continue his
　　　　　studies.（他要出國，以便能繼續求學。）

⑶ might 可以表示「**責備**」或「**忠告**」。

might 表示責備或忠告時,只能用在肯定句中,且不可用 may,因 might 是假設法助動詞,**表示可做而未做**。

【例】 You *might have let* us know beforehand.

（你可以事先讓我們知道嘛！）

You *might* at least *have said* hello to me.

（你至少可以和我打個招呼啊！）

⑷ may 的三種慣用法

① **may well** ＋ 原形動詞 「大可以；很有理由…」

【例】 She *may well be* proud of her son.

（她大可以她的兒子爲榮。）

② **may as well** 「最好；不妨」(＝ *had better*)

【例】 We *may as well stay* where we are.

（我們最好留在原處。）

③ **may as well** ＋ V. (原) ～ **as** ＋ V. 「與其…不如～」

【例】 You *may as well know* nothing at all *as know* imperfectly. (與其一知半解,你還不如全然不知。)

3. must 的用法

⑴ 表示**必須、義務**,及**肯定的推測**。

【例】 Time is up. We *must go*. 【表義務】

（時間已到,我們必須走了。）

You *must obey* the traffic law. 【表強烈的勸告】

（你必須遵守交通規則。）

You *must be* joking. 【表肯定的推測】

（你一定是在開玩笑。）

☞　{ **must** + 原形動詞 → 表示對**現在**肯定的推測
　　{ **must have** + **過去分詞** → 表示對**過去**肯定的推測

【例】　What he says *must be* true. (他說的一定是眞的。)

　　　　He *must have received* my letter mailed a week ago.

　　　　(他一定早就收到我一週前寄的那封信。)

(2) **must** + **not** 表示禁止。

【例】　You *must not* smoke in class. (上課時不准抽煙。)

　　　　You *must not* walk on the grass. (不可踐踏草地。)

☞　回答 must 的疑問句，肯定用 must (必須)，否定用 need
　　not (不必)。

【例】　A: *Must* I rewrite the report? (我必須重寫這份報告嗎？)

　　　　B: Yes, you *must*. / No, you *need not*.

(3) **未來式、過去式**用 have 〔had〕 to 代替。

【例】　You *will have to* pay the money tomorrow.

　　　　(你明天得付錢。)

　　　　She *had to* sit and wait for the news.

　　　　(她得坐著等這個消息。)

4. need 的用法

　　need 有助動詞和本動詞兩種功能，當助動詞時，只能用於疑問句、
否定句中。

【例】　A: *Need* you *finish* the work today?

　　　　　(你今天必須把工作做完嗎？)

　　　　B: No, I *need not*. / Yes, I *must*.

　　　　　You *need not* come again. (你不必再來。)【助動詞】

　　<比較> You *don't need to come* again. 【本動詞】

5. dare 的用法

dare 也有助動詞和本動詞兩種功能，當助動詞時，只能用於疑問句、否定句中。

【例】 How ***dare*** you *say* such a thing to me?【助動詞】
（你怎麼敢對我說這種話？）

He ***dared*** not oppose his father.
（他不敢反抗他父親。）

<比較> He *didn't* ***dare*** *to oppose* his father. 【本動詞】

6. ought to 的用法

⑴ 表義務、勸告，或推測。

【例】 You ***ought to*** follow his advice.
（你應該聽從他的勸告。）

You ***ought*** not *to* visit such a place alone.
（你不應該獨自參觀這種地方。）

Ought I *to* see a doctor at once?
（我應該立刻去看醫生嗎？）

Your new suit ***ought to be*** ready on Tuesday.
（你的新西裝週二應該就做好了。）

⑵ **ought to** + **have** + **p.p.** → 過去該做而未做

【例】 He ***ought to*** *have graduated* from the university.
（他早就該大學畢業了。）

My sister ***ought to*** *have arrived* home by now.
（我妹妹這時候早就該到家了。）

☞ 除表示推斷之外，還可以對過去不當行為表示**指責**之意。

【例】 You ***ought to*** *have studied* harder while young.
（你年輕時早就該用功一點了。）

7. should 的用法

⑴ 表**義務**、**勸告**，或**推測**（ = *ought to* ）。

【例】 You *should* obey traffic rules.
（你應該遵守交通規則。）

You *should* drink your coffee while it's hot.
（你應該趁熱喝咖啡。）

He *should* come by eight.（他應該會在八點前來。）

⑵ **should** + **have** + **p.p.** → 過去該做而未做

【例】 I *should have mailed* the letter, but I forgot.
（我早該寄這封信，但我忘了。）

⑶ 用於表**提議**、**命令**、**決定**、**主張**、**要求**的名詞子句中。

$$S. + \begin{cases} \textbf{suggest} & \text{command} \\ \textbf{insist} & \text{order} \\ \text{demand} & \text{propose} \\ \text{require} & \textbf{arrange} \\ \text{request} & \vdots \end{cases} + \text{that} + S_2 + (\textbf{should}) + V.$$

＊should 可以省略

【例】 He *suggested* that we (*should*) go on a picnic.
（他提議我們去野餐。）

I *insisted* that my son (*should*) come home early.
（我堅持要兒子早點回家。）

⑷ 用於表達**主觀意見**而非**陳述事實**的名詞子句中。

$$\text{It's} \begin{cases} \text{no wonder} & \text{a pity} \\ \text{necessary} & \text{surprising} \\ \text{natural} & \text{right} \\ \text{strange} & \text{wrong} \\ \text{wonderful} & \text{good} \\ & \vdots \end{cases} + \text{that} + S. + (\textbf{should})$$

$$+ \begin{cases} \text{原形 V.【表現在或未來】} \\ \text{完成式【表過去】} \end{cases}$$

【例】 It is ***natural*** that he (***should***) say so.【表現在】
（他會這麼說是很自然的。）

It's ***no wonder*** that he (***should***) have succeeded.
（難怪他會成功。）【表過去】

<比較> It's ***no wonder*** that he ***didn't*** come.【陳述事實】
（難怪他沒來。）

8. would 的用法

⑴ 表過去的習慣及反覆的動作。

【例】 He ***would often*** play soccer when young.
（他年輕時常常踢足球。）

Sometimes they ***would*** play tricks on their teacher.
（他們有時會跟老師開玩笑。）

⑵ 表示客氣的請求。

【例】 ***Would*** you mind opening the door?
（你介意打開門嗎？）

⑶ would 的慣用語

① **would rather**「寧願」(= *would sooner*)

【例】 I ***would rather*** *not* go to school.（我寧願不上學。）

②
would $\begin{Bmatrix} \textbf{rather} \\ \textbf{sooner} \end{Bmatrix}$ + **V~than** + **V…**「寧可…而不願」

【例】 I ***would rather*** *stay* here ***than*** go dancing.
（我寧可留在這裡，而不願去跳舞。）

③ **would like**「想要」(= *should like*)

【例】 I ***would like*** to talk about my plan.
（我想要談談我的計劃。）

9. used to 的用法

「used to + 原形動詞」：表以前的習慣或狀態。

【例】 He *used to* smoke, but now he doesn't.
（他以前抽煙，但現在不抽。）

He *used to* live in Tainan, but now he lives in Taipei.
（他以前住在台南，但現在住在台北。）

> *Used* you *to* go to school by bus?
> （你以前搭公車上學嗎？）
> *Did* you *use to* go to school by bus?【口語】

> He *used not* (= usedn't) *to* eat onion.（他以前不吃洋蔥。）
> He *didn't use to* eat onion.【口語】

☞ *be used to* + *V-ing*「習慣於～」

【例】 He *is used to* *driving* a car.（他習慣開車。）

10. do 的用法

⑴ 加在原形動詞前 — 加強語氣

【例】 I *do* want to be rich and famous.（我真想有錢又有名。）
Do be quiet, boys.（孩子們，務必要安靜。）

⑵ 用於倒裝句中

形成倒裝句的副詞有：never, seldom, little, rarely, well, so, only, happily。

【例】 *Never did* I see him playing the piano.
（我從沒看過他彈鋼琴。）

Rarely do we see him recently.（我們最近很少見到他。）

⑶ 簡單答話時，代替動詞，以避免重複。

【例】 *Read* just as I *do*.（照我所唸的唸。）
I *like* apples, and so *does* she.（我喜歡蘋果，她也喜歡。）

歷屆聯考試題

一、can, could 的用法

( ) 1. We cannot but _____.
    (A) laugh   (B) laughing
    (C) to laugh   (D) laughed

( ) 2. By 1978, the new airport will _____ handle five million passengers and 200,000 tons of air freight annually.
    (A) can   (B) able to
    (C) be able   (D) be able to
    (E) able

_____ 3. I shall can buy myself a new dress. (改錯)

4. You cannot be too careful. (英翻中)

_____

二、may, might 的用法

( ) 1. May you _____!
    (A) success   (B) successful
    (C) succeed   (D) successfully

( ) 2. You have good reason to rely on him.
    = You may _____ rely on him.
    (A) very   (B) well   (C) full

(　) 3. He may be out.

    (A) He can't be at home.

    (B) Perhaps he isn't at home.

    (C) He might be in the garden.

    (D) Perhaps he has left the country.

三、must 的用法

(　) 1. When <u>a</u> man loses <u>all</u> hope, or falls <u>into</u> despair, he
         (A)   (B)   (C)

    <u>must dead</u>. (改錯)
      (D)

(　) 2. I can't find my bag. It _____ stolen just now.

    (A) has   (B) must have been

    (C) will have been   (D) had

四、need 的用法

(　) 1. We know that a housewife does not need _____ for
    food every day.

    (A) going shoping

    (B) to go shoping

    (C) to going shopping

    (D) to go shopping

五、助動詞＋have＋p.p.

(　) 1. You _____ that letter for him, but you didn't.

    (A) should copy   (B) would copy

    (C) will have copied (D) should have copied

(　) 2. You _____ your lessons over the weekend, but you didn't.
- (A) would study
- (B) did not study
- (C) had not studied
- (D) should have studied

六、ought to 的用法

(　) 1. You ought _____ your homework last night.
- (A) do
- (B) to do
- (C) did
- (D) to have done

七、should 的用法

(　) 1. I propose that he _____ chairman.
- (A) be elected
- (B) electing
- (C) elected
- (D) elects

(　) 2. I run fast lest I should miss the train.
- (A) 我跑得很快，以免誤了火車。
- (B) 我跑得很快，以便坐上火車。
- (C) 火車慢下來的速度，和我跑的速度一樣快。
- (D) 火車的速度最慢也比我跑的快。
- (E) 我跑得很快，我將及時趕上火車。

(　) 3. It is important that you _____ smoking.
- (A) stop
- (B) were stopped
- (C) stopping
- (D) to stop

(　) 4. His father insisted that he _____ abroad.
- (A) went
- (B) goes
- (C) go
- (D) was going

(　　) 5. Our teachers asked that right ＿＿＿＿ distinguished from wrong.

    (A) be　(B) were　(C) being (D) been　(E) was

(　　) 6. He suggested that she <u>meets</u> her daughter the <u>next</u>
                       (A)　 (B)
     week, but she <u>flatly</u> <u>rejected</u> this suggestion. (改錯)
                 (C)　 (D)

八、would 的用法

(　　) 1. I ＿＿＿＿ to read the newspaper now but I haven't time.
    (A) would like　　　(B) like
    (C) am liking　　　(D) will like

(　　) 2. Which would you rather ＿＿＿＿, go to the cinema or stay at home?
    (A) do　　　(B) doing　　　(C) to do
    (D) did　　　(E) to be done

(　　) 3. Radio used <u>to be</u> the <u>most popular</u> kind of home
                (A)　 (B)
     entertainment, but now most people would rather
     <u>watching</u> television. (改錯)
     (C)

九、used to 的用法

(　　) 1. I don't like him because he usually ＿＿＿＿ ill of others.
    (A) tells　　　(B) says
    (C) calls　　　(D) speaks

( ) 2. 她過去常患頭痛。

She used to _____ a headache.

(A) having   (B) have pain

(C) suffer from   (D) painful with

(E) pained

十、do 的用法

( ) 1. Mary likes the flowers and Jane _____.

(A) does too   (B) likes too

(C) is too   (D) is like too

( ) 2. I don't know whether he speaks Chinese or not, but he might _____.

(A) be   (B) do

(C) have   (D) speak

( ) 3. He said he didn't take the money, but I am sure he _____.

(A) does   (B) did   (C) is   (D) was

【歷屆聯考試題解答】

一、 1.（**A**）   2.（**D**）   3. be able to   4. 你愈小心愈好。

二、 1.（**C**）   2.（**B**）   3.（**B**）

三、 1.（**D**）→ must die   2.（**B**）   四、 1.（**D**）

五、 1.（**D**）   2.（**D**）   六、 1.（**D**）

七、 1.（**A**）   2.（**A**）   3.（**A**）   4.（**C**）   5.（**A**）

     6.（**A**）→ meet

八、 1.（**A**）   2.（**A**）   3.（**C**）→ watch

九、 1. (**D**)   2. (**C**)

十、 1. (**A**)   2. (**B**)   3. (**B**)

【解析】

一、 2. 「在一九七八年之前，新的機場將能夠每年處理二百萬的乘客和二十萬噸的空運貨物。」一個句子不可以有兩個助動詞，所以 will 之後不可用 can，須以 be able to 代換。annually〔ˈænjʊəlɪ〕 *adv.* 每年地

　　 4. *cannot~too*… 再…也不為過

二、 2. *rely on* 依賴；信賴　　*may well* + *V.* 很有理由；大可以
　　 (B) relative〔ˈrɛlətɪv〕 *n.* 親戚

三、 2. 我找不到我的袋子。它一定是剛才被偷了。
　　 「must have + 過去分詞」，表示對過去肯定的推測。

五、 1. should〔ought to〕+ have + 過去分詞，表「過去該做而未做」。

七、 1. propose(提議)後面的子句，必須用 that + S. + (should) + V. 的形式。其中 should 可以省略，that 不可省。

　　 5. 我們的老師要求正確的應與錯誤的區分開來。

　　 6. flatly〔ˈflætlɪ〕 *adv.* 斷然地　　reject〔rɪˈdʒɛkt〕 *v.* 拒絕

八、 1. would like = want，此處 would 不表示過去式。

　　 3. would rather + 原形動詞 「寧願~」

九、 1. *speak ill of others* 說別人的壞話
　　 2. *suffer from* 受~之苦；罹患

精選模擬考題

(   ) 1. It is quite natural that he _____ take care of his old parents.
(A) should (B) shall
(C) will (D) had

(   ) 2. He was very stubborn and _____ not listen to reason.
(A) should (B) would
(C) could (D) might

(   ) 3. You _____ go in; the notice says "Keep out".
(A) may (B) must not
(C) need not (D) might not

(   ) 4. I don't think you _____ take a walk at this hour alone.
(A) can (B) should (C) ought (D) must

(   ) 5. Why _____ come tonight?
(A) need he to (B) needs he
(C) does he need to (D) needed he

(   ) 6. You may read this book, but you _____ read that one.
(A) don't need (B) mustn't
(C) should (D) can

(   ) 7. You won't forget our appointment, _____?
(A) will you (B) won't you
(C) do you (D) shall you

(　　) 8. How _____ say such a thing to me?

    (A) dare he   (B) dare he to

    (C) dares he   (D) he dare

(　　) 9. I don't smoke any more, but I _____.

    (A) am used to   (B) used to

    (C) used to it   (D) am used it

(　　) 10. You _____ read this book.

    (A) hadn't better   (B) had not better

    (C) not had better   (D) had better not

(　　) 11. I _____ attend the meeting yesterday.

    (A) ought to   (B) must

    (C) had to   (D) should

(　　) 12. I _____ the book, but I hardly remember if I have.

    (A) cannot have read (B) may read

    (C) may have read   (D) am reading

(　　) 13. She _____ here by now.

    (A) must arrive   (B) can arrive

    (C) may arrive   (D) ought to have arrived

(　　) 14. I _____ telephoned you last night.

    (A) can   (B) should

    (C) should have   (D) should had

(   ) 15. It is necessary that every member _____ inform himself of the rules of the club as soon as possible.

      (A) would   (B) might

      (C) should   (D) could

(   ) 16. Not only _____ he refuse to help me but he also scolded me.

      (A) should   (B) could

      (C) did   (D) must

(   ) 17. You _____ come tomorrow if you have something else to do.

      (A) needn't   (B) don't need

      (C) needn't to   (D) don't have

(   ) 18. Painters _____ be too careful in their choice of colors.

      (A) may not   (B) must not

      (C) ought not   (D) cannot

(   ) 19. He _____ have arrived there yet, because he just left.

      (A) couldn't   (B) mustn't

      (C) need not   (D) have not

(   ) 20. You _____ as well seek a fish in a tree as try to do that.

      (A) should   (B) would

      (C) might   (D) could

(   ) 21. He _____ well be proud of his son.

      (A) has   (B) may

      (C) have   (D) was

(　) 22. You _____ better not have gone with him.
- (A) had
- (B) should
- (C) might
- (D) would

(　) 23. You _____ as well go abroad to study as not.
- (A) can　(B) may　(C) have　(D) could

(　) 24. You _____ as well throw away your money as spend it gambling.
- (A) could
- (B) might
- (C) should
- (D) may

(　) 25. You _____ as well not know anything at all as know it imperfectly.
- (A) might
- (B) may
- (C) would
- (D) had

(　) 26. He who _____ search for pearls must dive deep.
- (A) should
- (B) could
- (C) would
- (D) likes

(　) 27. It is a pity that he _____ give up his studies halfway through.
- (A) could
- (B) had
- (C) would
- (D) should

(　) 28. I _____ rather not do it.
- (A) had
- (B) should
- (C) would
- (D) could

( ) 29. He is not friendly, nor _____ he wish to be.
     (A) do   (B) does   (C) will   (D) could

( ) 30. You _____ do what you are told, man!
     (A) may   (B) need   (C) would   (D) should

( ) 31. It _____ have rained last night, because the ground is wet.
     (A) must   (B) should   (C) can   (D) would

( ) 32. He is as poor as poor _____ be.
     (A) may   (B) must   (C) can   (D) might

( ) 33. _____ you return home safe and sound!
     (A) May   (B) Should
     (C) Might   (D) Would

( ) 34. "Did John lose his book?" "He doesn't think so, but he _____."
     (A) didn't   (B) must
     (C) must have   (D) did have

( ) 35. You cannot call him a genius, but you _____ call him a man of the world.
     (A) ought   (B) need
     (C) rather   (D) could

( ) 36. I do not drink coffee now, but I _____.
     (A) am used to   (B) used to
     (C) used to it   (D) used to have

(   ) 37. I remember rushing home after school and shouting
for Mother as every child _____, and then running
upstairs.

     (A) has   (B) do   (C) doing   (D) does

(   ) 38. We _____ go in there. The notice says, "Entrance
Forbidden."

     (A) don't have to   (B) may
     (C) mustn't   (D) needn't

(   ) 39. You _____ not take an umbrella. It is not likely to rain.

     (A) must   (B) can   (C) need   (D) may

(   ) 40. "Have you sent the telegram?" "No, but _____ to."

     (A) I should   (B) I must
     (C) I ought   (D) I can

(   ) 41. When I was a child, I _____ to go to the seashore
every summer.

     (A) was used   (B) was using
     (C) was used to   (D) used

(   ) 42. I don't think we should wait any longer. They
_____ that we are expecting them.

     (A) may forget   (B) might forget
     (C) might be forgetting   (D) may have forgotten

(   ) 43. The maid worked hard lest she _____ scolded.

     (A) should be   (B) would be
     (C) should not be   · (D) will be

(   ) 44. Something was wrong with my radio, it _____ not work.

    (A) will   (B) would   (C) shall   (D) should

(   ) 45. How _____ you like to have your eggs cooked, soft-boiled or hard-boiled?

    (A) will   (B) can   (C) should   (D) would

(   ) 46. We _____ be too careful in the choice of our friends.

    (A) cannot   (B) may not

    (C) ought not   (D) must not

(   ) 47. We _____ not help laughing at the idea.

    (A) could   (B) did   (C) should   (D) may

(   ) 48. I would like to buy that dictionary, but I _____ have enough money.

    (A) did not   (B) do not

    (C) had not   (D) would not

(   ) 49. "Will you help me with my homework?" "I _____ but I don't know how."

    (A) will   (B) cannot

    (C) like to   (D) would like to

(   ) 50. He _____ rather sleep than eat.

    (A) might   (B) would   (C) will   (D) was

(   ) 51. He is a man of few words; but when he _____ speak, he is very eloquent.

    (A) is   (B) may   (C) can   (D) does

(　) 52. Yesterday a friend of mine met with an accident and
I _____ him to a hospital.
(A)　should take　　　　(B)　had to take
(C)　must have taken　　(D)　must taken

【精選模擬考題解答】

1. (**A**)　　2. (**B**)　　3. (**B**)　　4. (**B**)　　5. (**C**)　　6. (**B**)

7. (**A**)　　8. (**A**)　　9. (**B**)　　10. (**D**)　　11. (**C**)　　12. (**C**)

13. (**D**)　14. (**C**)　15. (**C**)　16. (**C**)　17. (**A**)　18. (**D**)

19. (**A**)　20. (**C**)　21. (**B**)　22. (**A**)　23. (**B**)

24. (**B、D**)　　25. (**A、B**)　26. (**C**)　27. (**D**)　28. (**C**)

29. (**B**)　30. (**D**)　31. (**A**)　32. (**C**)　33. (**A**)　34. (**C**)

35. (**D**)　36. (**B**)　37. (**D**)　38. (**C**)　39. (**C**)　40. (**C**)

41. (**D**)　42. (**D**)　43. (**A**)　44. (**B**)　45. (**D**)　46. (**A**)

47. (**A**)　48. (**B**)　49. (**D**)　50. (**B**)　51. (**D**)　52. (**B**)

【解析】

1. natural 後面的名詞子句必須用助動詞 should。
   take care of 照顧

2. stubborn (ˈstʌbən) *adj.* 頑固的

3. must + not 表示「禁止」。

5. 原句 = Why need he come tonight?
   need 可以做本動詞或助動詞。

10. *had better* + *V*. 「最好」，否定為 *had better not* + *V*.。

12. 我可能讀過這本書，但是我幾乎記不得是否讀過。
    「may + have + p.p.」表示對過去的推測。

16. 句首為否定副詞（not only）時，須把助動詞 did 放在主詞 he
    前面，形成倒裝。
    refuse〔rɪ'fjuz〕v. 拒絕　　scold〔skold〕v. 責罵

20. 你嘗試做那件事，無疑是緣木求魚。

21. *may well* 很有理由；大可以　　*be proud of* 以～為榮

23. 與其不出國留學，你還不如出國的好。

24. 與其把錢花在賭博上，你還不如把它扔了。
    may〔*might*〕*as well* + V.～*as* + V.…「與其…不如～」，
    其中用 might 語氣比較委婉。

26. 凡是想要尋找珍珠的人，必須潛到深水裡去。
    would 表示「想做…」的意思。

32. *as～as*（～）*can be* 非常～

34. 原句 =…, but he *must have lost* his book.
    「must + 完成式」表示對過去事實肯定的推測。

38. *Entrance Forbidden.* 禁止進入。

39. *need not*「不需要」；*must not*「不可以」，表示「禁止」。

40. telegram〔'tɛlə,græm〕n. 電報

43. maid〔med〕n. 女傭
    lest + S. + *should* + V. 以免～會…

45. soft-boiled〔'sɔft'bɔɪld〕adj.（蛋等）煮得半熟的
    hard-boiled〔'hɑrd'bɔɪld〕adj.（蛋等）煮得很硬的

48. would like = want 是現在式，故後面子句的時態用現在式。

51. 他很少說話；不過一旦開口說話，卻很善辯。
    此處 does 用來加強語氣，when he *does speak* = when he
    really speaks。
    eloquent〔'ɛləkwənt〕adj. 善辯的；口才好的

7. 連 接 詞

用來連接單字、片語、子句，或句子的詞類，稱
為連接詞，分為對等連接詞及從屬連接詞兩種。

1. 對等連接詞

對等連接詞的作用，是連接**文法作用相同**的單字、片語或子句，連接
兩個子句時，其前面有無逗點均可。

1. and 型累積連接詞的用法

(1) and 連接兩個物品被視為一物，或同一人有兩種身份時，第二個
名詞不加冠詞，做主詞時，用**單數動詞**。

【例】 *A needle and thread was* found on the floor.
（在地板上找到一根穿著線的針。）

The poet and novelist is dead.
（這位詩人兼小說家死了。）

(2) 祈使句之後接 and，有條件句的作用。

【例】 *Hurry up, and* you'll catch the bus.
= *If you hurry up*, you'll catch the bus.
（你如果快一點，就趕得上公車。）

(3) 形容詞 + and = 副詞（very, quite）。

nice and　　fine and　　　good and
big and　　　rare and

【例】 It was *good and* (= *very*) dark, so we started for
home. （天色非常暗了，因此我們動身回家。）

(4) **not only ~ but (also)**…「不但～而且…」，若連接兩個主詞時，動詞要配合第二個主詞。

【例】 *Not only* you *but also* he *has* to go there.

（不僅是你，他也必須去那裡。）

---

2. but 型反義連接詞的用法

(1) **never ~ but**…「沒有～不…；每～必…」

【例】 It *never* rains *but* pours.

（不雨則已，一雨傾盆。）

(2) $\left\{ \begin{array}{l} \textbf{indee}d \textbf{~ but}\cdots \\ \textbf{it's true ~ but}\cdots \end{array} \right\}$ 「的確～不過…」

【例】 *Indeed* he tried hard, *but* he did not succeed.

（他的確很努力，不過沒有成功。）

It's true he is old, *but* he is still strong.

（他的確老了，但依然很強壯。）

(3) **not ~ but**… 「不～而…」

【例】 *Not* money *but* wisdom *is* what we want.

（我們所需要的不是錢，而是智慧。）

---

3. or 型連接詞的用法

(1) or 作「否則」解，與 else, otherwise 同義。

【例】 Hurry up, *or* you will miss the bus.

（快點，否則你會錯過公車。）

You must study hard, *else* you'll fail.

（你必須努力用功，不然就會失敗。）

Leave the room; *otherwise* you'll be caught.

（離開這房間，否則你會被捕。）

(2) or 用於相對意思之結合，表讓步。

【例】 *Rain or shine*, I'll go. (不論晴雨，我都會去。)

(3) either~or… 「不是~就是…」；如果連接兩個主詞時，動詞的
人稱與數和第二個主詞一致。

【例】 *Either* he *or* I *am* to blame.

(不是他就是我該受責備。)

---

4. 連接詞 so 的用法

【例】 The shops were closed, (*and*) *so* I couldn't get any
food. (店都關門了，所以我買不到食物。)

☞ 但是像 therefore, thus, consequently, accordingly, then ,
hence 等作「因此；所以」解的轉承語，是副詞，並不是連
接詞。

【例】 He studied hard; *thus* he got high marks.

(他用功讀書，因此獲得高分。)

It's very late; *hence* you must go to bed.

(時間很晚了，所以你得上床睡覺。)

---

5. 連接詞 for 的用法

(1) for 引導的子句不能放在句首 (because 引導的可以)

【例】 He felt no fear, *for* he's a brave man.

(他不害怕，因為他很勇敢。)

(2) for 表示附加的理由 (because 表示直接的理由)

He must be honest, *for* he's loved by all. 【表推斷的理由】

He is loved by all, *because* he is honest. 【表直接的理由】

(3) for 不可用以回答問題（because 可以）

【例】 Why did you beat him?（你為什麼打他？）

I beat him $\left\{ \begin{array}{l} \textit{for}（誤） \\ \textit{because}（正） \end{array} \right\}$ I was angry.

（我打他是因為我生氣了。）

2. 從屬連接詞

> 1. 引導名詞子句的從屬連接詞

(1) that 子句做主詞時，that 不可省略；做受詞時可以省略。

【例】 It is certain *that he will come.*（他一定會來。）

I don't think (*that*) he will come.（我想他不會來。）

☞ 在「**S. + V.** + *it* + 受詞補語 + **that 子句**」的句型中，that 不可省略。

【例】 I found *it* strange *that she hasn't come yet.*

（她到現在還沒來，我覺得很奇怪。）

(2) that 子句不可做下列動詞的受詞：

ask, doubt（懷疑）, see, hear, help, let, love, like, hate, want, refuse（拒絕）, admire（欽佩）, allow（允許）

【例】 Please *ask* $\left\{ \begin{array}{l} \textit{that}（誤） \\ \textit{when}（正） \end{array} \right\}$ she will be back.

（請問問她何時會回來。）

I *doubt **whether*** he will come.

（我懷疑他是否會來。）

☞ 但 do not doubt 和疑問句中的 doubt，可接 that 子句做受詞。

【例】 I do not *doubt **that*** he'll come.（我相信他會來。）

Do you *doubt **that*** he'll succeed?

（你不相信他會成功嗎？）

⑶ 　{ **whether**⋯(**or** *not*) = **if**「是否」
　　{ **whether or** *no*「無論如何；必定」

【例】 Let me know *whether* you're coming (*or not*).
　　　（你來不來都要讓我知道。）

　　　 I'll go *whether or no*.（我無論如何都會去。）

☞ whether 子句做主詞且置於句首時，不可用 if 代替。

【例】 { *If*（誤）
　　　{ *Whether*（正） } *we need it* is a different matter.
　　　（我們是否需要它是另一回事。）

⑷ 疑問代名詞 who, whom, whose, which, what；疑問副詞
　 when, where, why, how 可引導名詞子句。

【例】 I don't know *who she is*.
　　　（我不知道她是誰。）

　　　 She asked me *which I liked best*.
　　　（她問我最喜歡哪一個。）

　　　 Do you know *when and where she was born*?
　　　（你知道她何時何地出生的嗎？）

　　　 That's *where you are mistaken*.
　　　（那就是你的錯誤所在。）

---

2. 引導形容詞子句的從屬連接詞

⑴ 關係代名詞 who, whom, whose, which, that 可用以引導形容
　 詞子句。

【例】 We found the boy *who was lost in the forest*.
　　　（我們找到那個在森林裡迷路的小孩。）

⑵ 關係副詞 when, where, why, how 可引導形容詞子句。

【例】 The day *when he was born* remains unknown.
（仍然沒有人知道他出生在哪一天。）

Tell me the reason *why you didn't come*.
（告訴我你沒來的理由。）

⑶ 準關係代名詞 as, but, than 可引導形容詞子句。

【例】 This is *the same* book *as* I lost yesterday.
（這本書和我昨天遺失的那本一樣。）

There is *no* one *but* admires her.
（沒有人不欽佩她。）

He got *more* money *than* he asked for.
（他得到比他所要求的更多的錢。）

---

3. 引導副詞子句的從屬連接詞

⑴ 表**時間**的從屬連接詞：when, while, as（當～時候），till, until, whenever（無論何時），since（自從），after, before, as long as（只要），as soon as（一…就），no sooner…than（一…就）。

【例】 I will come *when I am at leisure*. （我有空就會來。）

I shall *not* start *till he arrives*.
（直到他到達，我才要開始。）

As long as I live, you shan't want for anything.
（只要我還活著，你就不虞匱乏。）

⑵ 表**地點**的從屬連接詞：where, wherever（任何地方），everywhere, anywhere。

【例】 Apricots won't grow *where the winters are cold*.
（杏樹不會長在冬天很冷的地方。）

He is welcomed *wherever he goes*.
（他無論到哪裡都很受歡迎。）

⑶ 表**狀態**的從屬連接詞：as（依照），(just) as～so…（像～那樣；
猶如），as if〔though〕（就好像）。

【例】 Do in Rome *as the Romans do.*（入境隨俗。）

As you sow, so will you reap.

（要怎麼收穫，先怎麼栽；種瓜得瓜，種豆得豆。）

The child talks *as if he were a man.*

（那孩子說起話來，就像是個大人一樣。）

⑷ 表**比較**的從屬連接詞：than, as～as（像～一樣），not so (as)～
as（不像～那樣）。

【例】 Tom is taller *than I.*（湯姆比我高。）

Mary is *as* beautiful *as* (*she is*) *kind.*

（瑪麗既漂亮又仁慈。）

The work is *not so* easy *as you think.*

（這工作不如你想像的那樣容易。）

⑸ 表**原因**的從屬連接詞：as（因為），because, seeing that（既然），
since（既然）。

【例】 *As I am busy*, I cannot go with you.

（因為我很忙，所以不能陪你去。）

Since you said so, I believed it to be true.

（既然你這麼說，我相信那是真的。）

⑹ 表**目的**的從屬連接詞：(in order) that〔so that〕～may（為了～；
以便～），lest～(should)（以免～），for fear that～(should)
（惟恐～）。

【例】 Betty got up early *so that she might* catch the early
train.（為了趕上早班火車，貝蒂起得很早。）

He hid it *lest I* (*should*) see it.

（他把它藏起來，以免被我看到。）

(7) 表**結果**的從屬連接詞：so＋形容詞、副詞＋that（如此～以致於），
such＋名詞＋that

【例】 He ran *so fast that* I couldn't catch him.
（他跑得這麼快，以致於我捉不到他。）

He was *such a good runner that* I couldn't catch him.

＜比較＞ **but (that)** 或 **but what** 引導表示結果的副詞子句，
but 含有**否定**的意思（but＝that…not），通常前面
的主要子句必須有否定的字（如 no, never, hardly…），
構成雙重否定。

【例】 *Nothing* is *so* hard *but* it becomes easy by practice.
↔ *Nothing* is *so* hard *that* it does *not* become easy
by practice.（無論多麼困難的事，經由練習都變得容易。）

(8) 表**條件**的從屬連接詞：if＝in case, unless（除非），as〔so〕
long as（只要），once（一旦）

【例】 The baby won't cry *unless he is hungry*.
（除非是餓了，不然那個嬰兒不會哭。）

You can't get out, *once you are in*.
（你一旦進去了，就出不來。）

(9) 表**讓步**的從屬連接詞：whether～or（無論），(al)though（雖然），
even though〔if〕（即使），no matter＋疑問詞＋may（無論～）

【例】 *Even if I were starving*, I would not ask a favor of
him.（即使會餓死，我也不會求他幫忙。）

No matter what you (*may*) *do*, do it well.
（無論你做什麼，都要好好地做。）

歷屆聯考試題

一、對等連接詞

( ) 1. (A) For two days as well as the electricity was the water cut off.
　　(B) The water for two days as well as the electricity was cut off.
　　(C) For two days the water as well as the electricity was cut off.
　　(D) As well as the electricity the water for two days was cut off.

( ) 2. Tom had a headache, _____ he didn't go to the party.
　　(A) why　(B) how　(C) but　(D) or　(E) so

( ) 3. Respect yourself _____ people will respect you.
　　(A) then　(B) if　(C) and　(D) or

( ) 4. It is not what you think _____ what you do that makes the difference.
　　(A) but　(B) and
　　(C) although　(D) unless

( ) 5. This is not imagination, _____ reality.
　　(A) and　(B) for　(C) also　(D) so　(E) but

( ) 6. Work hard, _____ you will succeed.
　　(A) or　(B) nor　(C) and　(D) but

(   ) 7. My brother couldn't go; _____, I went instead.

      (A) so as   (B) consequently

      (C) rather   (D) accordingly

(   ) 8. He would rather go to work by car; _____, the train is cheaper and faster.

      (A) furthermore   (B) therefore

      (C) however   (D) similarly

(   ) 9. Some countries are rich _____ others are poor.

      (A) who   (B) while   (C) where

      (D) why   (E) which

(   ) 10. To know a person's language is to understand his culture _____ language grows out of and reflects culture.

      (A) because of   (B) therefore

      (C) though   (D) for

(   ) 11. We must get up early tomorrow, _____ we'll miss the first bus to Taichung.

      (A) so   (B) or   (C) but

      (D) however   (E) because

(   ) 12. When I returned <u>home</u>, I couldn't find my keys. So I
                                 (A)

      got a ladder, <u>put</u> it against the wall, and <u>begin</u> <u>climbing</u>
                 (B)   (C)   (D)

      towards my bedroom window. (改錯)

(　) 13. <u>Avoid</u> <u>doing</u> and <u>say</u> things that <u>hurt</u> <u>others</u>. (改錯)
　　　　　(A)　　(B)　　　(C)　　　　(D)　　(E)

(　) 14. It is not the object of any sport or game to damage an
　　　　　opponent, <u>and</u> rather to <u>defeat</u> him <u>by</u> a higher degree
　　　　　　　　　　　(A)　　　　　　　(B)　　　(C)
　　　　　of skill—<u>with</u> the feet in soccer and greater mental
　　　　　　　　　　(D)
　　　　　ability in chess. (改錯)

二、從屬連接詞

(　) 1. ＿＿＿＿ it was raining, we decided to go out.
　　　　(A) If　　　　　　　　(B) Despite
　　　　(C) Unless　　　　　　(D) Though

(　) 2. (A) This is a very beautiful dress except that it does
　　　　　　　not go well with my shoes.　　　　(選對的)
　　　　(B) This is a very beautiful dress except if it does not
　　　　　　　go well with my shoes.
　　　　(C) This is a very beautiful dress except which it does
　　　　　　　not go well with my shoes.
　　　　(D) This is a very beautiful dress except for it does
　　　　　　　not go well with my shoes.

(　) 3. You can use my car as long as you drive carefully.
　　　　(A) 你可以永遠使用我的車子。
　　　　(B) 如果你常開車，你可以使用我的車子。
　　　　(C) 你要永遠小心地開我的車就像開你自己的車。
　　　　(D) 當你使用我的車時，要小心地開。
　　　　(E) 只要你小心地開車，你就可以使用我的車。

( ) 4. I will not arrive until everyone has left.

    (A) 我不會來，因為每個人都已經離開了。

    (B) 每個人離開前，我會來。

    (C) 我不等每個人離開就來。

    (D) 直到每個人離開，我才來。

    (E) 等到每個人都已經離開了，我還是不想來。

( ) 5. The noise <u>made</u> by his neighbor was <u>too</u> loud that John
               (A)   (B)

    could not <u>fall</u> <u>asleep</u>. (改錯)
           (C)   (D)

( ) 6. He was so friendly _____ to write to me.

    (A) so   (B) that   (C) as   (D) man

( ) 7. At the interview, he was so impressed by her analytical
    and linguistic abilities _____ he sent her to the
    editor-in-chief.

    (A) that   (B) which

    (C) what   (D) where

( ) 8. War is avoidable _____ people use their heads and
    are willing to talk things out.

    (A) though   (B) but

    (C) as long as   (D) nevertheless

( ) 9. As far as I _____, I don't think it is wise to stand
    by them.

    (A) concern   (B) am concerned

    (C) am concerning (D) have concerned

(　) 10. The doctor sent her <u>to</u> the hospital <u>in order to</u> she could
　　　　　　　　　　　　　(A)　　　　　　　　　　(B)

　　　　take <u>a series of</u> tests. (改錯)
　　　　　　　(C)

(　) 11. Water is to fish _____ air is to man.
　　　　(A) that 　　(B) which 　　(C) what 　　(D) so

(　) 12. 書本之於人類，猶如記憶之於個人。
　　　　(A) As books are 　　　　　（選出 3 項，組成一個句子）
　　　　(B) Books are
　　　　(C) to mankind
　　　　(D) so is memory to the individual
　　　　(E) memory is what to the individual

(　) 13. Courtesy is to business _____ oil is to machinery.
　　　　(A) which 　　　　　　(B) at which
　　　　(C) in which 　　　　　(D) what

(　) 14. He succeeded _____ all the difficulties.
　　　　(A) for 　　　　　　　(B) despite
　　　　(C) in spite of 　　　　(D) with

(　) 15. No budget can succeed _____ it is carefully followed.
　　　　(A) how 　　(B) unless 　　(C) what 　　(D) why

(　) 16. 他雖然有那麼多錢，他並不快樂。
　　　　_____ all his money, he is not happy.
　　　　(A) Though 　　　　　　(B) In spite
　　　　(C) For 　　　　　　　 (D) But
　　　　(E) In

( ) 17. He loves his cousins, _____ they are neither kind nor generous.
(A) although　　　(B) unless
(C) because　　　(D) if

( ) 18. I made up my mind to tell my father as soon as I returned home.
(A) 我回家後，會儘快告訴我父親。
(B) 我不介意告訴我父親，只要我回到家。
(C) 當我回家時，我不敢告訴我父親。
(D) 如果我早回家的話，我一定會記得告訴我父親。
(C) 當我一回到家，我就決定要告訴我父親。

( ) 19. _____ as the book is, I don't like it at all.
(A) Interesting　　(B) Interested
(C) Interest　　　(D) Interests

( ) 20. I doubt _____ it will rain.
(A) how　　　(B) that
(C) what　　　(D) about

( ) 21. 我很想知道他現在是否在家。
I _____ he is at home.
(A) no matter
(B) wonder if
(C) might to know
(D) must to understand
(E) wander from

(　) 22. 他說得如此快，以致於我聽不懂。

He spoke _____ quickly _____ I could not understand him.

(A) more, than　　(B) such, and　　(C) so, that

(D) too, to　　(E) enough, to

(　) 23. I haven't seen him _____ he was a little boy.

(A) since　　(B) when　　(C) for

(D) as　　(E) that

(　) 24. "Are you ready?" Frank asked me.

= Frank asked me _____ I was ready.

(　) 25. _____ it rained, the boys still decided to continue the game.

(A) Although　　(B) Because

(C) And　　(D) Ever since

(　) 26. They became so interested in their discussion <u>as</u> they forgot the lunch. (改錯)

(　) 27. Though he is <u>wealthy,</u> <u>but</u> he is not <u>happy.</u> (改錯)
　　　　　　　　　　(A)　　(B)　　　　　　(C)

【 歷屆聯考試題解答 】

一、

1. (C)　　2. (E)　　3. (C)　　4. (A)　　5. (E)　　6. (C)

7. (B、D)　　　8. (C)　　9. (B)　　10. (D)　　11. (B)

12. (C) → began　　13. (C) → saying　　14. (A) → but

二、

1. (**D**)　　2. (**A**)　　　3. (**E**)　　4. (**D**)　　　5. (**B**) → so

6. (**C**)　　7. (**A**)　　　8. (**C**)　　9. (**B**)

10. (**B**) → in order that　　11. (**C**)　　12. (**A、C、D**)

13. (**D**)　　14. (**A、B、C、D**)　　15. (**B**)　　16. (**C**)

17. (**A**)　　18. (**E**)　　19. (**A**)　　20. (**B**)　　21. (**B**)

22. (**C**)　　23. (**A**)　　24. whether (*or* if)　　25. (**A**)

26. that　　27. (**B**) → yet

【解析】

一、

1. A *as well as* B「A 和 B 一樣」，強調 A，故動詞要與 A 一致。

3. 祈使句之後接 and，有條件句的作用，故原句＝ If you respect yourself, (then) people will respect you.

4. *not ~ but ⋯* 不是～而是⋯

9. 此處 while（然而）做連接詞，相當於 but。

10. 要了解別人的語言，就是要了解他的文化，因為語言是由文化衍生出來，並且反映其文化。

13. and 連接動名詞 doing 和 saying，做 avoid 的受詞。
    avoid V-ing 避免～

14. 運動或比賽的目的，不是去傷害對手，而是藉較高的技巧（足球比賽時用兩隻腳而下西洋棋時用比較敏捷的頭腦）來打敗他。

二、

1. (A) 如果　(B) 雖然（後面須接名詞）　(C) 除非　(D) 雖然

2. *except that*「只可惜」，後接名詞子句。*go with ~* 和～相配

4. *not ~ until ⋯* 直到⋯才～

7. 「在面試時，他對她的分析和語言能力印象非常深刻，所以派她做主編。」本題是 *so ~ that ⋯* 的句型。*editor-in-chief* 主編

9. as〔*so*〕*far as ~ be concerned*　就（某人）而言

10. in order to + 原形動詞；in order that + 子句。

11. A *is to* B *what* C *is to* D.　A 之於 B 猶 C 之於 D。
    = A *is to* B *as* C *is to* D. = *As* C *is to* D, *so* A *is to* B.
    〔so 之後的主詞和動詞可倒裝〕

13. 禮貌之於交易猶如油料之於機器。
    courtesy〔'kɜtəsɪ〕*n.* 禮貌

15. 沒有一項預算案會成功，除非能慎重地執行。
    budget〔'bʌdʒɪt〕*n.* 預算案

17. 他愛他的堂兄弟們，雖然他們既不和藹又不慷慨。
    neither ~ nor…　既不 ~ 又不…

18. *make up one's mind*　下定決心
    as soon as ~「一 ~ 就…」，其前後兩個子句通常都用過去簡
    單式。

25. (A) 雖然　(B) 因為　(C) 而且　(D) 從 ~ 以來一直

27. 句子中已有從屬連接詞（Al）though，不可以再有對等連接詞
    but，但卻可以和 yet 連用。

精選模擬考題

(　) 1. He worked hard _____ he might succeed in the entrance examination.

(A) lest　　　　　(B) so that

(C) unless　　　　(D) though

(　) 2. Ask her _____ it is true or not.

(A) which　　　　(B) that

(C) what　　　　 (D) whether

(　) 3. Work harder, _____ you will not succeed in the exam.

(A) and　(B) so　(C) or　(D) lest

(　) 4. _____ we can expect no help from others, let's try to do our best.

(A) Since　　　　(B) For

(C) Lest　　　　 (D) That

(　) 5. _____ years went on, he grew smarter.

(A) When　　　　(B) During

(C) As　　　　　(D) Though

(　) 6. I was just reading a detective story _____ she entered my room.

(A) since　　　　(B) that

(C) unless　　　　(D) when

(　　) 7. I cannot accept the fact _____ he is dead.
　　　　(A) if　　(B) that　　(C) why　　(D) which

(　　) 8. It will be long _____ he comes back.
　　　　(A) when　　　　　(B) before
　　　　(C) that　　　　　 (D) by

(　　) 9. You may sit _____ you like.
　　　　(A) for　　　　　　(B) but
　　　　(C) though　　　　 (D) where

(　　) 10. We could not walk fast _____ the road was muddy.
　　　　(A) on account of　　(B) being that
　　　　(C) because of　　　 (D) because

(　　) 11. It never rains _____ it pours.
　　　　(A) when　　　　　 (B) but
　　　　(C) so　　　　　　 (D) or

(　　) 12. It's foolish to take a taxi _____ you can easily
　　　　walk to the station.
　　　　(A) before　　　　　(B) that
　　　　(C) unless　　　　　(D) when

(　　) 13. It matters little who finds the truth, _____ the truth
　　　　is found.
　　　　(A) because　　　　　(B) so long as
　　　　(C) till　　　　　　 (D) when

( ) 14. It was not long _____ my friend's prediction was fulfilled.

    (A) before   (B) during

    (C) except   (D) for

( ) 15. We do not necessarily grow wiser _____ we grow older.

    (A) as   (B) than   (C) that   (D) which

( ) 16. I felt as _____ the end of the world had come.

    (A) at   (B) in   (C) of   (D) though

( ) 17. She held her breath _____ fear she should be found.

    (A) for   (B) beyond

    (C) at   (D) from

( ) 18. I don't doubt _____ you will win.

    (A) while   (B) can

    (C) that   (D) when

( ) 19. You will fail _____ you work hard.

    (A) if   (B) unless

    (C) otherwise   (D) since

( ) 20. _____ you eat too much of that cheese, you may feel ill.

    (A) Though   (B) So

    (C) Until   (D) If

(　) 21. People do not know the value of health _____ they lose it.

    (A) until　(B) when　(C) while　(D) if

(　) 22. He often worked late _____ he could earn more money.

    (A) so far　　　　　　(B) so long

    (C) so that　　　　　　(D) lest

(　) 23. Make haste in order _____ you may catch the train.

    (A) to　　(B) for　　(C) that　　(D) than

(　) 24. I hid the book _____ he should see it.

    (A) and　(B) where　(C) lest　(D) so

(　) 25. Say that again _____ I'll knock you down.

    (A) and　(B) for　(C) so　(D) but

(　) 26. _____ there is a will, there is a way.

    (A) Unless　　　　　　(B) Until

    (C) Where　　　　　　(D) For

(　) 27. Come early, _____ you won't get anything to eat.

    (A) or　　(B) for　　(C) unless　(D) so

(　) 28. He said _____ nothing would make him change his mind.

    (A) which　　　　　　(B) why

    (C) that　　　　　　(D) nor

( ) 29. Nobody knows _____ she should do such a stupid thing.
(A) how (B) why (C) which (D) than

( ) 30. He has broken the law; _____ he must be punished.
(A) for   (B) since
(C) therefore   (D) but

( ) 31. No sooner had the bell rung _____ he rushed downstairs.
(A) than (B) since (C) that (D) while

( ) 32. I shall not leave _____ he comes back.
(A) since   (B) until
(C) except   (D) while

( ) 33. _____ we were very tired after the journey, we were in good spirits.
(A) Because   (B) Since
(C) Though   (D) For

( ) 34. _____ men sow, so will they also reap.
(A) Before   (B) Until
(C) Unless   (D) As

( ) 35. I doubt _____ he will succeed.
(A) until (B) if (C) unless (D) when

(　　) 36. He shall not be paid _____ the work is properly done.

     (A) except   (B) but

     (C) unless   (D) without

(　　) 37. Make hay _____ the sun shines.

     (A) therefore   (B) since

     (C) before   (D) while

(　　) 38. I don't know _____ he is coming today, but I'll wait for him.

     (A) if   (B) unless

     (C) because   (D) where

(　　) 39. Come at once; _____ you will be too late.

     (A) and (B) when (C) while (D) otherwise

(　　) 40. He is welcomed _____ he goes.

     (A) otherwise   (B) because

     (C) wherever   (D) however

(　　) 41. The day will come _____ my words will come true.

     (A) if (B) when (C) while (D) unless

(　　) 42. He fell with such a gush of blood _____ his fellows thought he would die on the spot.

     (A) as well as   (B) lest

     (C) that   (D) because

(C) 43. _____ I know, he is a very honest man.
    (A) So long as   (B) As well as
    (C) So far as   (D) Provided that

(B) 44. Don't count your chickens _____ they are hatched.
    (A) when   (B) before
    (C) that   (D) as

(C) 45. Scarcely had I returned home _____ it began to rain.
    (A) for   (B) as   (C) when   (D) after

【精選模擬考題解答】

1.(**B**)	2.(**D**)	3.(**C**)	4.(**A**)	5.(**C**)	6.(**D**)
7.(**B**)	8.(**B**)	9.(**D**)	10.(**D**)	11.(**B**)	12.(**D**)
13.(**B**)	14.(**A**)	15.(**A**)	16.(**D**)	17.(**A**)	18.(**C**)
19.(**B**)	20.(**D**)	21.(**A**)	22.(**C**)	23.(**C**)	24.(**C**)
25.(**A**)	26.(**C**)	27.(**A**)	28.(**C**)	29.(**B**)	30.(**C**)
31.(**A**)	32.(**B**)	33.(**C**)	34.(**D**)	35.(**B**)	36.(**C**)
37.(**D**)	38.(**A**)	39.(**D**)	40.(**C**)	41.(**B**)	42.(**C**)
43.(**C**)	44.(**B**)	45.(**C**)			

【解析】

1. *entrance examination* 入學考試

3. 原句＝If you don't work harder, (then) you will not succeed in the exam.

4. since 作「既然」解。   *do one's best* 盡力

5. 隨年歲的增長，他越來越聰明。
    as years go on 隨年歲的增長   smart〔smɑrt〕*adj.* 聰明的

6. detective〔dɪˈtɛktɪv〕*n.* 偵探　*adj.* 偵探的

7. that 引導名詞子句，做 the fact 的同位語。

10. muddy〔ˈmʌdɪ〕*adj.* 泥濘的

13. 只要能找到眞理，誰發現的並不重要。

14. prediction〔prɪˈdɪkʃən〕*n.* 預言　　fulfill〔fulˈfɪl〕*v.* 實現

16. 我覺得世界末日好像已經來臨。
　　as though = as if　好像

17. *hold one's breath*　屏息
　　for fear (*that*) ~ = *lest* (*that*) ~　以免~

18. doubt 在否定句中接 *that* 引導之子句做受詞，在肯定句中則接
　　if 引導的子句做受詞。

21. 直到失去健康，人們才知道健康的價值。
　　not ~ until⋯　直到⋯才~

23. *make haste*　急忙；趕快

26. 有志者，事竟成。

31. 鈴聲一響，他就衝下樓去。
　　no sooner ~ than⋯ = *hardly*〔*scarcely*〕*~ when*⋯　一⋯就~

34. 「種瓜得瓜，種豆得豆。」通常寫成 As you sow, so shall you reap.

37. 未雨綢繆。

42. 他跌倒時，血流如注，他的夥伴們以爲他會當場死亡。
　　on the spot　當場

44. 不要打如意算盤。

8. 介系詞

1. 介系詞的受詞

介系詞通常放在名詞、代名詞之前，形成副詞片語或形容詞片語，但也有以動名詞、不定詞、片語、子句做為受詞者。

【例】 He will be home *by five*. 【名詞】
（他最遲五點以前會回來。）

Here is a letter *for him*. （這裡有一封他的信。）【代名詞】

Until then I knew nothing about it. 【名詞】
（在那時之前，我對這件事一無所知。）

He went away *without saying a word*. 【動名詞】
（他一句話也沒說就走開了。）

The sun was *about to set*. （太陽快下山了。）【不定詞】

A black cat came out *from under the desk*. 【片語】
（一隻黑貓從桌底下走出來。）

He's worrying *about which way he should go*. 【子句】
（他正在為該走哪條路煩惱。）

2. 介系詞用法的分類

> 1. 表時間的介系詞

(1)
- **at**：用於指時間的一點。
- **in**：用於指比較長的時間。
- **on**：用於指特定的日子、時候等。

【例】 I will come to see you *at* 10 a.m. *on* Sunday.
（星期日早上十點我會來看你。）

I was born *on* the 17th of October *in* 1968.

（我出生於 1968 年 10 月 17 日。）

He takes a walk *in* the morning. （他在早上散步。）

We arrived here *on* the morning of August 1st.

（我們於 8 月 1 日早上到達這裡。）

(2) **from**：表示**某事開始的時間**，與那件事歷時多久無關。

since：表示**時間的繼續**，通常與現在完成式連用。

He works *from* 9 *to* 5 every day.

（他每天從九點工作到五點。）

He *has been* working *since* morning.

（他從早上一直工作到現在。）

(3) **to**：表示**時間的終點**。

till 或 **until**：表持續到某時為止，須與表持續性動作的動詞

（如 wait, stay, go on）連用。

by：表示**最遲在…之前**，須與表非持續性動作的動詞

（即瞬間動詞，如 start, reach, finish）連用。

【例】 Even *to* this day he has been ignorant of the fact.

（甚至到今天，他還不知道實情。）

I will *wait* here *till* six o'clock. （我將在這裡等到六點。）

I will *start by* six o'clock. （我最遲將在六點以前出發。）

(4) **in**：用於未來式，表「**再過（若干時間）**」；用於過去式，表

「**花費（若干時間）**」。

after：表示**過了若干時間之後**。

within：表示**在若干時間以內**。

【例】 They *finished* the game *in* three hours.

（他們花了三小時完成比賽。）

She *will be* back *in* a week.

（再過一星期她就回來了。）

She came back *after* a week.

（過了一星期之後，她就回來了。）

I'll be home *within* a week.

（我將在一星期以內回家。）

(5) ⎰ **for**：表示**持續一段時間**，與表持續性動作的動詞連用。

during：表在…**期間**，與表持續性動作的動詞連用。

through：表整個…**期間**，或從開始到結束，也可用

all through 或 throughout。

【例】 I walk (*for*) two hours every day.

（我每天走兩個小時的路。）

He was happy *during* his lifetime.（他一生都很快樂。）

The rain lasted (*all*) *through* the night.

（雨持續下了一整個晚上。）

---

2. 表示場所的介系詞

(1) ⎰ **on**：用於街道名稱。

at：用於小地點，如郵局、車站，或門牌號碼。

in：用於較寬廣的地方。

（當兩個地名連用時，大的地名用 in，小的地名用 at。）

【例】 Mr. Smith lives *on* Park Street.

（史密斯先生住在公園街。）

We met him *at* the station.（我們到車站接他。）

I arrived *at* New York *in* America.

（我到達美國的紐約。）

(2) 　　on：表示**和表面接觸**的意思。

　　above：表示「在…上方」，並隔有間隔。

　　over：表示在某物的上方，有「**越過、橫過、覆於～之上**」

　　　　　　的意思

　　up：表示「**從下往上**」，與 down 的動作相反。

【例】 There is a little house *on* the hill.

　　　　（山丘上有一間小屋。）

　　　　The moon rose *above* the hill. （月亮升上山頂。）

　　　　There is a bridge *over* the river.

　　　　（河上有一座橋。）

　　　　They ran *up* the hill. （他們跑上了山丘。）

(3) 　　**under**：在…的下面，與 over 意義相反。

　　　below：與 above 的意義相反，表示「在…下方」，並有間隔。

【例】 There is a boat *under* the bridge.

　　　　（橋下有一艘船。）

　　　　My house stands a mile *below* the bridge.

　　　　（我的房子座落在橋下一哩的地方。）

(4) 　　**between**：在二者之間；「夾在當中」的意思。

　　　among：在三者或三者以上之間；「夾雜著」的意思。

【例】 Taichung is *between* Taipei and Tainan.

　　　　（台中在台北和台南之間。）

　　　　She was sitting *among* the boys.

　　　　（她正坐在一群男孩中間。）

(5) ⎰ **along**：「沿著」。
　　⎱ **across**：「橫過」，表示動態；「在…的那一邊」，表示位置。
　　　 through：「從這邊穿到那邊」，表示貫通。

【例】 I walked *along* the street. (我沿著那條街走。)
　　　 I walked *across* the road. (我走過馬路。)
　　　 I live *across* the river. (我住在河的對岸。)
　　　 There is a shortcut *through* the field.
　　　 (有條捷徑穿過田野。)

(6) ⎰ **to**：表示運動的目的地、到達點。
　　⎱ **towards**：只表示運動方向，與是否到達無關。
　　　 for：與 start, leave 等具出發意味的動詞連用，表示其目的地。

【例】 We walk *to* school every day. (我們每天走路上學。)
　　　 The ship sailed *toward(s)* the west. (那艘船航向西方。)
　　　 We left *for* Rome in July. (我們七月時動身前往羅馬。)

---

3. 其他用法的介系詞

(1) ⎰ **from**：表示外傷、疏忽等外在的原因。
　　⎱ **of**：表示情緒上或生病、飢餓、衰老、死亡等內在的原因。

【例】 He became ill *from* eating too much.
　　　 (他因吃太多而生病了。)
　　　 Many people die *of* cancer. (許多人死於癌症。)

(2) ⎰ **of**：表示在成品中可見到原材料的性質；物理變化。
　　⎱ **from**：表示在成品中已看不出材料原來的性質；化學變化。
　　　 into：表變化的結果，由材料變為成品。

【例】 Her dress is made *of* silk. (她的衣服是絲織的。)
　　　 This juice is made *from* apples.
　　　 (這種果汁是用蘋果製成的。)
　　　 Flour is made *into* bread. (麵粉做成麵包。)

(3) ┌ **except, but**：「除了…之外」，表示否定的意思。
　　│ **besides**：「除了…之外，還…」，表示另外附加的意思。
　　└ **without**：「沒有…；無…」。

【例】 I know nothing *except* 〔*but*〕 this.

　　　　（除此之外，我什麼都不知道。）

　　　　I know something *besides* this.

　　　　（除此之外，我還多少知道一些。）

　　　　Without you, I should be helpless.

　　　　（若沒有你，我就無依無靠了。）

(4) ┌ **by**：「以…計」，表示標準（度量、單位等）。
　　│ **at**：表示比率、單位價格、速度。
　　└ **for**：表示總價錢。

【例】 Eggs are sold *by* the dozen.（蛋按打出售。）

　　　　Eggs are sold *at* 50 dollars a dozen.

　　　　（蛋以每打五十元的價格出售。）

　　　　The house was sold *for* $ 100,000.

　　　　（這房子以十萬元售出。）

(5) ┌ **by, by means of**：表示方法。
　　│ **with**：表示工具。
　　└ **through**：「經由」，表示間接的手段、方法。

【例】 You can succeed only *by* working hard.

　　　　（只有努力工作，你才能成功。）

　　　　He made a wooden house *with* a knife.

　　　　（他用一把刀子，製成一間木屋。）

　　　　I knew it *through* Jack.（我經由傑克而知道那件事。）

3. 介系詞的慣用語

1. 介系詞片語

as far as 遠至；就…的程度	on account of 因為…
as to 至於；關於	owing to 由於
as for 至於	thanks to 幸虧；由於
instead of 而不是	because of 因為；由於
in spite of 儘管	except for 除了…之外；只是
according to 根據	but for 如果沒有；要不是

【例】 He gave me advice *instead of* money.

（他給我忠告，而不是錢。）

Thanks to her help, I could finish it in time.

（由於她的幫忙，我才能及時完成。）

2. 動詞 + 介系詞

ask after 問候（= *inquire after*）	call on〔at〕拜訪
depend on 依賴（= *rely on*）	get over 克服
make up for 彌補；補償	get through 完成
look after 照料（= *watch over*）	
stand for 代表	consist of 由～組成

【例】 "B.B.C." *stands for* British Broadcasting Corporation.

（BBC 代表英國廣播公司。）

Please *look after* my baggage.

（請幫我看一下行李。）

We must *make up for* the lost time.

（我們必須彌補失去的時間。）

Water *consists of* hydrogen and oxygen.

（水是由氫和氧所組成。）

歷屆聯考試題

一、介系詞用法的分類：

（一）表時間

（　　）1. We usually stay at home _____ Christmas.
　　　　(A) in　　　(B) at　　　(C) to　　(D) while

（　　）2. Please wait a while; I will come _____ a minute.
　　　　(A) of　　　(B) on　　　(C) in

（　　）3. My father will be back _____ four.
　　　　(A) since　(B) for　　(C) till　(D) by　(E) in

（　　）4. _____ a clear night we can look up at the sky and see into space.
　　　　(A) On　　　(B) Over　　(C) Through
　　　　(D) At　　　(E) For

_____ 5. John will go to college _____ high school.

（二）表地方

（　　）1. _____ some maps, and _____ many newspapers, the island of Taiwan is still called Formosa.
　　　　(A) In, on　　　　　(B) On, in　　　　　(C) By, on
　　　　(D) On, on　　　　　(E) For, on

（　　）2. I met a friend _____ the way to school.
　　　　(A) on　　　(B) into　　(C) of　　(D) for　(E) up

( ) 3. When dinner was served, the host sat his guests _____ the table.

    (A) by   (B) at   (C) on   (D) in

( ) 4. My uncle left _____ Africa last week.

（三）表原因理由及目的

( ) 1. 改錯：He rented the house <u>because</u> the <u>convenience</u> of
                                (A)   (B)

    <u>its</u> location.
    (C)

( ) 2. At the meeting, Mary gave rise _____ her feelings.

    (A) to   (B) of   (C) by   (D) on

( ) 3. Please don't make faces _____ me.

    (A) at   (B) on   (C) with (D) for

( ) 4. Why was she angry _____ herself?

    (A) for   (B) to   (C) with (D) about

( ) 5. He has the qualifications _____ being a teacher.

    (A) to   (B) for   (C) on

( ) 6. My wife is looking _____ the dog, but she can't find it.

    (A) for   (B) up   (C) with (D) from (E) as

____ 7. Although British woolens are known throughout the world, the British are even better known _____ their cotton goods.

_____ 8. Fresh air is essential _____ good health.

_____ 9. The letters "R.O.C." stand _____ the Republic of China.

_____ 10. He prayed to God _____ help.

（四）表其他

(　　) 1. Hard work will result _____ success.
      (A) in   (B) to   (C) from (D) for

(　　) 2. He bought the house _____ a low price.
      (A) with   (B) in   (C) on   (D) at

(　　) 3. I think I have to thank her _____ person for the wonderful birthday gift she gave me.
      (A) with   (B) by   (C) in   (D) of

(　　) 4. A friend _____ need is a friend indeed.
      (A) for   (B) with (C) by   (D) in

(　　) 5. Mary's ability is always superior _____ Debbie's.
      (A) in   (B) of   (C) than (D) over (E) to

(　　) 6. A traffic accident prevented him _____ coming.
      (A) to   (B) from (C) in   (D) at

(　　) 7. The big fire _____ his parents.
      (A) deprived him of   (B) deprived him
      (C) derived of   (D) derived from
      (E) derived him of

(   ) 8. What's wrong _____ your eyes? Have you been crying?

       (A) from   (B) with   (C) up   (D) into   (E) after

(   ) 9. The success of the picnic will depend _____ the weather.

       (A) for   (B) on   (C) of

____ 10. We Chinese live _____ rice.

____ 11. Please pay attention _____ your homework.

____ 12. He would like to take a trip to the U.S. _____ airplane.

____ 13. What's wrong _____ your car?

____ 14. He is a very good friend _____ mine.

____ 15. I do not agree _____ you on this point.

____ 16. The factory produces the most products _____ the lowest cost.

二、其他重要介系詞的用法

(   ) 1. The judge took the boy's age _____ account.

       (A) into   (B) onto   (C) on   (D) to

(   ) 2. Don't do things _____ your will.

       (A) to   (B) against   (C) by   (D) with

(　) 3. Though he is young, he can see ＿＿＿＿ that difficult
      problem.
      (A) in　　(B) into　(C) to　　(D) for

(　) 4. If she had taken the train, she would have been involved
      (A)   (B)
      to the accident. (改錯)
      (C)

(　) 5. We are traveling ＿＿＿＿ a speed of 90 kilometers an
      hour.
      (A) at　　(B) of　　(C) on　　(D) in

(　) 6. We should have the courage to speak the truth ＿＿＿＿
      any circumstances.
      (A) on　　(B) by　　(C) under (D) at

(　) 7. He said nothing, and went out.
      = He went out ＿＿＿＿ saying a word.
      (A) with　(B) in　　(C) without

(　) 8. This teacher writes ＿＿＿＿ his left hand.
      (A) with　(B) for　　(C) in

(　) 9. It is easy to find fault ＿＿＿＿ others.
      (A) from　(B) with　(C) for

(　) 10. Prepositions deal mainly ＿＿＿＿ spatial relations
       between objects.
       (A) by　　(B) with　(C) to　　(D) for

( ) 11. I have no hobbies _____ playing tennis.

    (A) without (B) beside (C) expect (D) except

( ) 12. I cannot make _____ what he is saying.

    (A) from   (B) of   (C) in   (D) out

( ) 13. We are waiting _____ John to arrive.

    (A) for   (B) on   (C) at

( ) 14. A colonel is superior _____ a major.

    (A) than   (B) above (C) on   (D) to

( ) 15. Let's take a look _____ the house in which she lived.

    (A) against (B) with   (C) at

( ) 16. Have you left any _____ my sister?

    (A) at   (B) against (C) for

( ) 17. _____ a rule, he comes to office at 8:30.

    (A) In   (B) By   (C) As   (D) For

( ) 18. My father will be back _____ four.

    (A) since (B) for   (C) till   (D) by   (E) in

( ) 19. Many students specialize _____ computer science.

    (A) for   (B) at   (C) over (D) on   (E) in

( ) 20. Our principal is a little man <u>with</u> thick glasses.

    (A) putting on   (B) wearing（選同義詞）

    (C) dressing   (D) taking

    (E) fitting

(   ) 21. John is sweet _____ the girl next door.

      (A) on   (B) off   (C) for   (D) of

(   ) 22. Within hours, help was _____ the way.

      (A) in   (B) into   (C) at   (D) on

(   ) 23. John was never fully aware _____ the extent of his failures.

      (A) of   (B) off   (C) from   (D) at

(   ) 24. The police informed the prisoner _____ his legal rights.

      (A) with   (B) for   (C) of   (D) against

(   ) 25 We must keep them _____ knowing our plans.

      (A) of   (B) for   (C) from   (D) in

_____ 26. I didn't know _____ this yesterday.

_____ 27. Habitual tardiness at work is irritating to the one _____ charge.

_____ 28. If you are hard to get _____ with, you are likely to find that you have difficulty in making friends.

_____ 29. The meeting must be put _____ because the airplane could not arrive on time.

_____ 30. My friend told me that the country is rich _____ natural resources.

_____ 31. We had some difficulty carrying _____ the plan.

_____ 32. What is the matter _____ you?

_____ 33. Most people may not be familiar _____ the
communists.

_____ 34. Through all his efforts, he finally gave _____ his bad
habits.

_____ 35. He tends to think of everything _____ terms of money.

_____ 36. 許多人認為他是一位學者。
Many people mistook him _____ a scholar.

_____ 37. Owing to lack of funds, we will have to throw _____
the new project.

_____ 38. Some of the modern lighthouses are equipped _____
automatic lights.

_____ 39. Sickness prevented my friend _____ coming to my
birthday party.

_____ 40. We divided the cake _____ three parts.

_____ 41. She is interested _____ painting.

_____ 42. He likes to enter _____ conversation with strangers.

_____ 43. Accidents arise _____ carelessness.

_____ 44. It is good _____ you to come down to see me off.

_____ 45. From earliest times, men have made great discoveries _____ chance.

_____ 46. The rules of polite conduct may be different _____ country to country.

_____ 47. My brother is very good _____ math.

_____ 48. A teacher imparts knowledge _____ his students.

_____ 49. The form of magazines differs _____ that of newspapers.

_____ 50. Today, jet airplanes fly _____ the oceans very fast.

【歷屆聯考試題解答】

一、

(一)　1.(**B**)　　2.(**C**)　　3.(**D**)　　4.(**A**)　　5. after

(二)　1.(**B**)　　2.(**A**)　　3.(**B**)　　4. for

(三)　1.(**A**) → because of　　2.(**A**)　　3.(**A**)　　4.(**C**)
　　　5.(**B**)　　6.(**A**)　　7. for　　8. to (*or* for)
　　　9. for　　10. for

(四)　1.(**A**)　　2.(**D**)　　3.(**C**)　　4.(**D**)　　5.(**E**)
　　　6.(**B**)　　7.(**A**)　　8.(**B**)　　9.(**B**)　　10. on
　　　11. to　　12. by　　13. with　　14. of　　15. with
　　　16. at

二、　1.(**A**)　2.(**B**)　3.(**B**)　　4.(**C**) → in　5.(**A**)　6.(**C**)
　　　7.(**C**)　8.(**A**)　9.(**B**)　10.(**B**)　　11.(**D**)

12. (**D**)   13. (**A**)   14. (**D**)   15. (**C**)   16. (**C**)   17. (**C**)

18. (**D**)   19. (**E**)   20. (**B**)   21. (**A**)   22. (**D**)   23. (**A**)

24. (**C**)   25. (**C**)   26. about   27. in   28. along   29. off

30. in   31. out   32. with   33. with   34. up   35. in

36. for   37. out   38. with   39. from   40. into/in   41. in

42. into/in   43. from   44. of   45. by   46. from

47. at/in   48. to   49. from   50. across/over

【解析】

一、

（一） 1. *at Christmas* 在聖誕節那天

2. *in a minute* 馬上   3.「*by* + 時間」表「最遲在～之前」。

（二） 3. *sit* + 人 + *at the table* 使某人就座

serve〔sɜv〕*v.* 上（菜）   host〔host〕*n.* 主人

4. *leave for* 動身前往

（三） 1. *because of* + 名詞 因為～

2. *give rise to* 發表（意見）

3. *make faces at* + 人 對某人扮鬼臉

4. *be angry with* + 人 對某人生氣

〈比較〉 *be angry at* + 事 對某事生氣

5. *have the qualifications for* ～ 有擔任～的資格

qualification〔͵kwɑləfəˈkeʃən〕*n.* 資格

6. *look for* 尋找

7. 雖然英國的毛織品聞名全球，但英國的棉製品卻更有名。

cotton goods 棉製品

be known for + 名詞（物產；特徵） 以～聞名

8. *be essential to* ～ 對～而言是必要的

9. *stand for* 代表   10. *pray for* 祈禱

（四）　1. *result in* 導致　　*result from* 起因於

2. *at a low price* 以很低的價格

3. *in person* 親自

4. 「患難見眞情。」　　*in need* 在患難中

6. *prevent* + 人 + *from* + *V-ing* 阻止某人做~；
使某人不能~

7. *deprive* + 人 + *of* + 物 奪走某人的某物
deprive〔dɪ'praɪv〕*v.* 剝奪

8. *What's wrong with*~? ~怎麼了？

10. *live on* 以~爲主食；靠~維生

11. *pay attention to* 注意　attention〔ə'tɛnʃən〕*n.* 注意

14. 表從屬、所有的關係時，介系詞用 of。此句爲雙重所
有格用法。句型是：a (this, that…) + 名詞 + of + 所有
代名詞 (mine, yours…)。

15. *agree with* + 人「同意某人」；*agree to* + 事「贊同某
事」。

二、　1. *take* ~ *into account* 將~列入考慮

2. *against one's will* 違背某人的意願

4. *be involved in* ~ 牽涉到~

5. *at a speed of* ~ 以~的速度

6. *under any circumstances* 在任何情況下

9. *find fault with* 對~吹毛求疵；挑剔~

10. 介系詞主要是處理受詞之間的空間關係。
deal with 處理
preposition〔ˌprɛpə'zɪʃən〕*n.* 介系詞
spatial〔'speʃəl〕*adj.* 空間的

12. *make out* 了解

14. 上校比少校大。
colonel (ˈkɜnḷ) *n.* (陸、空軍) 上校
major (ˈmedʒɚ) *n.* (陸、空軍) 少校
be superior to 高於；大於

15. *take a look at* 看 (= *look at*)

17. *as a rule* 通常 (= *usually*)

19. *specialize in~* 專攻~

20. (A) put on 戴上　　(B) wear 戴著

21. *be sweet on* + 人　愛上某人

22. 「幾小時內，救援就會到。」　　*on the way* 在途中

23. *be aware of* 覺察到　　extent (ɪkˈstɛnt) *n.* 程度

24. *inform sb. of sth.* 通知某人某事
legal (ˈligḷ) *adj.* 法律上的

25. *keep~from…* 使~不能…

27. 習慣性的拖延工作，令負責的人生氣。
habitual (həˈbɪtʃuəl) *adj.* 習慣的
tardiness (ˈtɑrdɪnɪs) *n.* 拖延
irritating (ˈɪrə,tetɪŋ) *adj.* 令人生氣的
in charge 負責的

28. 如果你很難相處，你可能覺得交朋友很困難。
get along with 相處　　*be likely to* 可能

29. *put off* 延期　　*on time* 準時

30. *rich in~* 有豐富的~　　*natural resources* 天然資源

31. *carry out* 實現　　*have difficulty* + *V-ing* 做~有困難

32. 原句 = What is *wrong* with you? (你怎麼了？)

33. *be familiar with* 熟悉

Communist (ˈkɑmjuˌnɪst) *n.* 共產主義者

34. *give up* 放棄；戒除

35. *in terms of~* 以~觀點

36. *mistake* A *for* B 把 A 誤認爲是 B

37. *throw out* 放棄

38. 有些現代燈塔裝有自動照明燈。

be equipped with 裝配有

40. *divided~into*… 將~分成…

41. *be interested in* 對~感興趣

42. 他喜歡和陌生人交談。　*enter into* 加入

43. *arise from* 起因於　carelessness (ˈkɛrlɪsnɪs) *n.* 粗心

45. 從最早期以來，人們就會偶然地創造偉大的發明。

by chance 偶然地

46. 「禮儀會因地而異。」　conduct (ˈkɑndʌkt) *n.* 行爲

47. *be good at~* 擅長~

48. *impart~to* + 人 「傳授~給某人」

49. A *differ from* B　A 和 B 不同

50. *fly across* 「飛越」，across 爲介系詞。

(A) across 表「橫越」，爲動詞。

心得筆記欄

PART-2

比較・否定・關係詞

 命題焦點：

▶ 1. 「比較」是聯考的焦點，要注意原級、
　比較級、最高級的用法及其慣用語。

▶ 2. 常考部分否定、雙重否定及few, little,
　hardly的用法。

▶ 3. 關係詞的重點在格的用法，即先行詞與
　關係子句動詞的一致。

1. 形容詞・副詞的比較

1. 形容詞・副詞比較級和最高級的構成

1. 規則變化

(1) 單音節及部分二音節的字，在字尾加-er 及-est。

short	shorter	shortest	
large	larger	largest	【字尾 e 不發音時】
dry	dri*er*	dri*est*	【子音＋y，須將 y 變成 i】
gray	gray*er*	gray*est*	【母音＋y 則不變】
hot	hot*ter*	hot*test*	【短母音＋子音時，須重複字尾】

☞ 二音節字結尾為-**er**, -**ow**, -**le**, -**y**，則加-er 及-est 形成比較級和最高級，這類的字有 clever, narrow, idle, noble, simple, gentle, happy, pretty。

(2) 大部分二音節的字，及三音節以上的字，通常在原級前面加 more, most。

famous	*more* famous	*most* famous
useful	*more* useful	*most* useful
easily	*more* easily	*most* easily

☞ trustworthy（值得信任的）雖為三音節，但卻加-er, -est：
trustworthy　trustworthier　trustworthiest

☞ 原為加-er, -est 的二音節字，**增加否定的字首（un-）後**，雖變成三個音節，其比較級和最高級**依然在字尾加-er, -est**。

easy	easier	easiest
*un*easy	*un*easier	*un*easiest

2. 不規則變化

good / well	*better*	*best*	bad / ill	*worse*	*worst*
many / much	*more*	*most*	little	*less*	*least*

far
- *farther*　*farthest*　（指距離）
- *further*　*furthest*　（指程度）

old
- older　oldest　（老；舊）
- *elder*　*eldest*　（長幼的順序）

late
- later　latest　（時間）
- *latter*　*last*　（順序）

2. 原級的用法

1. 同等比較：A…as ＋ 原級（＋ 名詞）＋ as B

【例】 She runs *as fast as* Paul.（她跑得和保羅一樣快。）

My room is *not as* 〔*so*〕 *large as* yours.

（我的房間不像你的那麼大。）

☞ so～as 不可用於肯定句。

2. 原級的慣用法

⑴ **as～as ＋ S. ＋ can = as～as possible** 「儘可能」

【例】 Do it *as* quickly *as you can*.（儘可能做快點。）

Do it *as* quickly *as possible*.

<例外> Do it *as* best you *can*.（盡力去做。）

不用 as～as 的形式。

(2) **as~as any**：是一種最高級的表達方式。

【例】 He works *as* hard *as any other* student in his class.

（他比班上其他學生更用功。）

(3) **not so much** A **as** B 「與其說是 A，不如說是 B」

【例】 He is *not so much* honest *as* clever.

（與其說他誠實，不如說他聰明。）

3. 比較級的用法

(1) A ＋ 比較級 ＋ **than** ＋ B 「A 比 B～」

【例】 John is *taller than* I. (約翰比我高。）

Tom's salary is *lower than* that (= *the salary*)
of his wife.

（湯姆的薪水比他太太的低。）

(2) **more** ＋ 原級(A) ＋ **than** ＋ 原級(B) 「與其說是 B，不如說是 A」

【例】 He is *more* mad *than* stupid.

（與其說他笨，不如說他瘋了。）

☞ 同一人或物，比較其兩種性質或狀態時，不管是單音節
或多音節，一律用 more～than 表示。

【例】 She is *more wise than diligent*.

（與其說她勤勉，不如說她聰明。）

(3) *the* ＋ 比較級 ＋ **of the two** 「兩者中較～」

【例】 Dick is *the taller of the two*.

（狄克是兩者中較高的一位。）

＜注意＞ 此處的比較級前面，一定要用定冠詞 the。

⑷ **the ＋ 比較級～，the ＋ 比較級…「越～，就越…」**

【例】 *The older* we grow, *the poorer* our memory will become.（我們年齡越大，記憶力就會越差。）

☞ 這類句型，前半部為從屬子句，後半部為主要子句，主要子句可倒裝（即 V. ＋ S.）。

【例】 *The higher* up we go, *the colder* **becomes the air**. （我們爬得越高，空氣就變得越冷。）

⑸ **比較級 ＋ and ＋ 比較級…「越來越～」**

【例】 She is growing *fatter and fatter*. （她變得越來越胖了。）

The story has got *more and more exciting*. （這故事變得越來越刺激了。）

⑹ **the ＋ 比較級 ＋（理由）「因～而更加～」**

【例】 I like her *all the more* for her freckles. （我因她的雀斑而更喜歡她。）

He is *none the happier* for his wealth. （他並不因財富而更快樂。）

If you start at once, you'll get there *the sooner*. （如果你立刻動身，你將更快到達那裡。）

⑺ **不及 — 劣等比較**

① **less ＋ 原級 ＋ than**（＝ not so ＋ 原級 ＋ as）

【例】 This watch is *less* expensive *than* that one.

＝ This watch is *not so* expensive *as* that one. （這支錶沒有比那支貴。）

② {
no more than = only 「只」
not more than = at most 「最多」
}
{
no *less* than = as many as 或 as much as 「多達」
not *less* than = at least 「至少」
}

【例】 He walked *no more than* ten miles. (他只走了十哩。)

He has *no less than* five children.
(他有五個孩子之多。)

He was in hospital *not more than* a week.
(他住院最多不超過一個禮拜。)

He has *not less than* ten dollars. (他至少有十元。)

③ {
no more…than = not…any more than 「和~一樣不…」
no less…than = as…as 「和~一樣…」
}

【例】 A whale is *no more* a fish *than* a horse is.
(鯨魚和馬一樣不是魚。)

He is *no less* busy *than* a bee. (他像蜜蜂一樣忙。)

(8) 含比較級的慣用法

【例】 the *upper* 〔*lower*〕 classes　上層〔下層〕階級

the *younger* generation　年輕的一代

sooner or *later*　遲早

a *higher* education　高等教育

more or *less*　多多少少

4. 最高級的用法

| 1. the ＋ 最高級 ＋ of [in] |

【例】 Iron is *the most useful of* all metals.
(鐵是所有金屬中最有用的。)

She's *the most diligent* girl *in* our class.
(她是本班最勤勉的女孩。)

⑴ 最高級副詞之前，the 可以省略。

【例】 Jack studies (*the*) *hardest* in our class.

（傑克是本班最用功的。）

⑵ 最高級形容詞做為補語時，the 可以省略。

【例】 Tom is (*the*) *youngest* of all.

（湯姆是所有人當中最年輕的。）

⑶ 同一人或同一物相比較時，最高級不加 the。

【例】 The lake is *deepest* at this point.

（這個地點是此湖最深之處。）

She's *happiest* when she's cooking.

（她在煮飯時最快樂。）

2. 最高級的否定含 even 的意思

【例】 *The best* student in the class was unable to solve the problem. (= *Even the best* student…)

（甚至連班上最好的學生，也解不出這個問題。）

(*Even*) *The strongest* do not always live longest.

（〔即使〕最壯的人，也未必活得最久。）

3. 原級和比較級可用來表示最高級

Jim is *the tallest* student in his class.

（吉姆是班上最高的學生。）

Jim is *taller than any other* student in his class.

No other student in his class is *taller than* Jim.

No other student in his class is *as* 〔*so*〕 *tall as* Jim.

> Time is *the most precious* thing of all.
> （時間是萬物之中最寶貴的。）
> Time is *more precious than any other* thing.
> Nothing is *more precious than* time.
> Nothing is *as* 〔*so*〕 *precious as* time.

5. 注意事項

1. A 倍數 as～as B 「A 是 B 的～倍」

【例】 Our club has *twice as* many members *as* yours.

= Our club has *twice the number of* your members.

（我們社團的成員是你們的兩倍。）

This desk is *half as* wide *as* that one.

= This desk is *half the width of* that one.

= *That* desk is *twice the width of* this one.

（這張書桌是那張的一半寬。）

2. 不用比較級形容詞的比較

senior 年長的，junior 年少的，superior 較好的，
inferior 較差的，anterior 較早的，prior 較早的，
posterior 時間較後的

【例】 He is two months *senior to* me. （他比我大兩個月。）

= He is *senior to* me by two months.

= He is *my senior* by two months. 【senior 做名詞用】

歷屆聯考試題

一、原級的用法

(　) 1. A cow is _____ as a horse.
    (A) strong as an animal   (B) as a strong animal
    (C) as strong an animal   (D) as animal
    (E) as an animal strong

(　) 2. People have to keep the environment as clean and
    healthful _____.
    (A) as possible   (B) as they are possible
    (C) as can possible   (D) as can

(　) 3. The pedestrian has _____ rules to follow as the driver
    of a vehicle.
    (A) as many   (B) so much
    (C) more   (D) such a

(　) 4. 這種衣料和那種衣料同樣地厚。
    This material is _____ that.
    (A) the same thick as   (B) the same thickness as
    (C) as thickness as   (D) as same thick as
    (E) same thicker than

(　) 5. A computer which could function like a human brain
    would have to be _____ the earth's surface.
    (A) as large as   (B) large like
    (C) with the largeness of   (D) large of

二、比較級的用法

(　　) 1. As Edison grew _____, he never lost his interest in science.
   (A) elder　　　(B) more old　　　(C) oldest
   (D) older　　　(E) the older

(　　) 2. John came _____ than all the others.
   (A) later　　　(B) latest　　　(C) latter
   (D) last　　　(E) the last

(　　) 3. The study of mathematics today is even more
   　　　　　　　　　　　　　　　　　(A)　(B)
   complicated as it was ten years ago. (改錯)
   　(C)　　　　　(D)

(　　) 4. The more you learn, the more _____ you can get a job.
   (A) easily　　　(B) easy　　　(C) ease
   (D) easeful　　　(E) easiness

(　　) 5. 她是兩姊妹中較高的一個。
   (A) She is the taller than the two sisters.
   (B) She is the taller of the two sisters.
   (C) She is taller than the two sisters.
   (D) She is taller of the two sisters.

(　　) 6. He is the taller _____ the two boys.
   (A) than　　　(B) in
   (C) of　　　(D) between

(　) 7. He has three times _____ books as I have.
 　　(A) as many 　　　　　(B) more
 　　(C) many 　　　　　　(D) as much

(　) 8. Our hypothesis that the more the water is polluted,
 　　_____ it will injure the growth of plants is supported.
 　　(A) the more seriously
 　　(B) the more serious
 　　(C) the better seriously
 　　(D) the better serious

(　) 9. If we owe more than we own, the result is _____.
 　　(A) restaurant 　　　　(B) income
 　　(C) possession 　　　　(D) variety
 　　(E) bankruptcy

(　) 10. Every day our world becomes _____.
 　　(A) smaller and smaller
 　　(B) small and small
 　　(C) small and smaller
 　　(D) little and little

(　) 11. We must mine and use coal more efficiently _____
 　　in the past.
 　　(A) than 　　(B) thus 　　(C) therefore 　　(D) then

(　) 12. Above all, each part costs so little that it was cheaper
 　　to buy a new one _____ to repair a worn one.
 　　(A) to 　　(B) when 　　(C) than 　　(D) as

( ) 13. We are no less diligent than American students.

    (A) 我們比美國學生更勤勉。

    (B) 我們和美國學生同樣地勤勉。

    (C) 美國學生比我們勤勉。

    (D) 我們不比美國學生勤勉。

    (E) 我們不如美國學生用功。

( ) 14. (A) Alice is the most attractive of all girls.

    (B) Alice is attractive than all girls.

    (C) No other girl is more attractive than Alice.

    (D) No other girl is so attractive as Alice.

( ) 15. She is my _____ ten years.

    (A) senior to   (B) junior

    (C) senior by   (D) major   (E) inferior

( ) 16. Tom is tall and bulky so that he needs _____ any other student.

    (A) twice   (B) room

    (C) as much   (D) as

( ) 17. 他的書比我的多兩倍。(選錯的)

    (A) I have half as many books as he has.

    (B) He has many books as twice as I have.

    (C) I have half the number of his books.

    (D) He has twice as many books as I have.

( ) 18. "Are you older than Tom?"

    "Yes, I am older than _____."

    (A) he   (B) his   (C) him   (D) himself

(　) 19. Some students are not so much concerned with mastering English as with getting a good grade.
  (A) 有些學生學英文，關心的是得高分，而不求精通。
  (B) 有些學生學英文，只關心得到好的成績。
  (C) 有些學生精通英語，而不關心成績的好壞。
  (D) 有些學生精通英語，因之獲得好成績。
  (E) 有些學生因欲獲得高分而精通了英語。

____ 20. The merchant grew more _____ more tired through want of sleep.

____ 21. The older he becomes, _____ more experience he has.

____ 22. 梅花滿天下，越冷越開花。
The plum-blossoms bloom all over the world; the _____ the weather, the _____ beautifully they bloom.

____ 23. Chicago is larger than any city in Illinois. (改錯)
　　　　(A)　　　(B)　　　(C)　　　　(D)

____ 24. The more one knows about the shortage of energy, the
　　　　　　　　　　(A)　　(B)　　　　　　　　　　　　　　　　　
more you understand the importance of saving energy.
(C)　　　(D)
(改錯)

____ 25. Tom is taller than any else student in his class. (改錯)

____ 26. My elder brother is senior than I by five years. (改錯)

_____ 27. The <u>metal covering</u> was <u>more stronger</u> <u>than</u> the wooden
     (A)   (B)   (C)

  <u>one</u>.（改錯）
  (D)

三、最高級的用法

(   ) 1. You are _____ students in the school.

   (A) the diligentest (B) more diligent

   (C) diligenter   (D) the most diligent

(   ) 2. He is _____ student in our class.

   (A) tallest   (B) the tallest

   (C) the taller (D) taller

(   ) 3. _____ our baseball team, Jim is the best player.

   (A) Through (B) Between

   (C) On   (D) In

(   ) 4. This is _____ plan I have ever made.

   (A) bad   (B) worse

   (C) the worst (D) the badest

_____ 5. He was about the happiest man I _____ knew.

_____ 6. Diamonds, <u>an</u> hardest substance in nature, are valuable
  crystals of carbon.（改錯）

 7. 她是最年輕的。（中翻英）

_____

【歷屆聯考試題解答】

一、　1. (**C**)　　2. (**A**)　　3. (**A**)　　4. (**B**)　　5. (**A**)

二、　1. (**D**)　　2. (**A**)　　3. (**D**) → than　　　4. (**A**)　　5. (**B**)

　　　6. (**C**)　　7. (**A**)　　8. (**A**)　　9. (**E**)　　10. (**A**)　　11. (**A**)

　　　12. (**C**)　　13. (**B**)　　14. (**B**)　　15. (**C**)　　16. (**A**)　　17. (**B**)

　　　18. (**A**)　　19. (**A**)　　20. and　　21. the　　22. colder, more

　　　23. (**C**) → any other24. (**D**) → one understands

　　　25. other　26. to me　27. (**B**) → much stronger/stronger

三、　1. (**D**)　　2. (**B**)　　3. (**C**)　　4. (**C**)　　5. ever

　　　6. the　　　7. She is the youngest of all.

【解析】

一、　1. *be* + *the same* + 名詞 + *as* ~「和~一樣的」

　　　3. pedestrian〔pəˈdɛstrɪən〕*n.* 行人
　　　　 vehicle〔ˈviɪkl̩〕*n.* 車輛

二、　1. grow older 指「年齡增長」，grow elder 指「輩分增高」。

　　　3. 比較級的連接詞用 than，故 (D) as 要改成 than，修飾
　　　　 比較級可以用 much, even, still, 或 far。

　　　5. *the* + 比較級 + *of the two* + 名詞　「二者中較~的」

　　　7. 他的書有我的三倍多。

　　　8. 我們的假設得到證實：水污染愈厲害，對植物成長的
　　　　 傷害就愈嚴重。
　　　　 「*the* + 比較級，*the* +比較級」表「愈~，就愈…」。
　　　　 又修飾動詞 injure 須用副詞，故選 (A)。
　　　　 hypothesis〔haɪˈpɑθəsɪs〕*n.* 假設

11. mine〔maɪn〕*v.* 採礦　　coal〔kol〕*n.* 煤炭

13. **no less ~ than…**　和…一樣~

15. 原句 = She is senior to me **by** ten years.（她大我十歲。）

16. bulky〔'bʌlkɪ〕*adj.* 龐大笨重的
　　twice as much (many) ~ as…　…的兩倍~

20. 由於缺乏睡眠，這商人變得越來越疲倦。
　　more and more　越來越　　want〔wɑnt〕*n.* 缺乏

22. plum-blossom〔'plʌm,blɑsəm〕*n.* 梅花

23. Chicago（芝加哥）在 Illinois（伊利諾州）境內，
　　比較時要將自己除外，故 any（任何一個）要改成
　　any other（任何其它的）。

24. 人們越知道能源的短缺，就越了解節約能源的重要。
　　此處前半句與後半句主詞要一致，故選 (D)。

27. 金屬封套比木製的要堅固得多。
　　stronger 本身已是比較級，之前不再加 more，故
　　more 要改成 much。

三、　6. 最高級形容詞之前，要用定冠詞 the。
　　crystal〔'krɪstl̩〕*n.* 水晶　　carbon〔'kɑrbən〕*n.* 碳

精選模擬考題

(　) 1. Some computers can work 500,000 times faster _____ a man.
　　 (A) better　(B) to　　　(C) then　　(D) than

(　) 2. Speaking is _____ difficult than writing.
　　 (A) less　(B) worse　(C) little　(D) least

(　) 3. He is junior _____ by two years.
　　　 (A) than you　　　　　(B) to she
　　　 (C) to me　　　　　　(D) than me

(　) 4. She is no _____ beautiful than her sister.
　　　 (A) little　(B) less　(C) least　(D) much

(　) 5. The city grew _____.
　　　 (A) big and big
　　　 (B) more and more
　　　 (C) more and more bigger
　　　 (D) more and more big

(　) 6. He is _____ of the two boys.
　　　 (A) more diligent　　　(B) the more diligent
　　　 (C) the most diligent　(D) the diligenter

(　) 7. Her doll is _____ prettier than mine.
　　　 (A) more　(B) much　(C) very　(D) most

(   ) 8. He was _____ runner of all.

       (A) faster   (B) the faster

       (C) fastest   (D) the fastest

(   ) 9. I like the child _____better for his honesty.

       (A) so   (B) as well

       (C) all the   (D) as much

(   ) 10. The sun sets _____ in summer than in winter.

       (A) slower   (B) more slowly

       (C) latter   (D) later

(   ) 11. The style is unattractive, but the substance is _____ valuable than it appears.

       (A) more   (B) much   (C) very   (D) even

(   ) 12. The scientist was the first to discover that a convex lens — that is, a glass with a rounded surface — will make things appear_____.

       (A) smaller   (B) larger

       (C) distorted   (D) more large

(   ) 13. At what point is the lake _____?

       (A) deepest   (B) the deepest

       (C) deeper   (D) the deeper

(   ) 14. She has three times _____ books as I have.

       (A) more   (B) as

       (C) as many   (D) so many

(　) 15. You have only one brother, but I have ＿＿＿ nine
　　　 brothers and sisters.
　　　 (A) no less than　　　(B) no more than
　　　 (C) not less than　　 (D) not more than

(　) 16. The ＿＿＿ we go up, the cooler it becomes.
　　　 (A) high　　　　　　(B) higher
　　　 (C) more high　　　 (D) very higher

(　) 17. "Am I troubling you?" No, not in the ＿＿＿.
　　　 (A) less　　　　　　(B) least
　　　 (C) later　　　　　 (D) latter

(　) 18. Of the two boys, he is ＿＿＿.
　　　 (A) younger　　　　 (B) the younger
　　　 (C) youngest　　　　(D) the youngest

(　) 19. He is ＿＿＿.
　　　 (A) more clever than wiser
　　　 (B) cleverer than wiser
　　　 (C) more clever than wise
　　　 (D) clever than wise

(　) 20. His brother is ＿＿＿ as old as he is.
　　　 (A) two　　(B) double　　(C) twice　　(D) dozen

(　) 21. London is ＿＿＿ city in Europe.
　　　 (A) the largest　　　(B) largest
　　　 (C) the larger　　　 (D) larger

( ) 22. Smith is _____.
    (A) more rich than generous
    (B) less rich to generous
    (C) much rich than generous
    (D) very rich to generous

( ) 23. We have _____ students than your school does.
    (A) less   (B) much less
    (C) fewer   (D) more fewer

( ) 24. This cloth is _____ that.
    (A) superior than   (B) better to
    (C) superior of   (D) superior to

( ) 25. New York is larger than _____ city in the United States.
    (A) all   (B) any   (C) any other   (D) some

( ) 26. She is _____ taller than her younger sister.
    (A) very   (B) much   (C) little   (D) many

( ) 27. The boy is _____ the girls.
    (A) taller than   (B) the tallest of
    (C) tallest than   (D) the taller than

( ) 28. My coat is much more expensive than _____.
    (A) you   (B) your   (C) he   (D) his

( ) 29. He is taller than I _____ two inches.
    (A) for   (B) at   (C) on   (D) by

【精選模擬考題解答】

1.（**D**）	2.（**A**）	3.（**C**）	4.（**B**）	5.（**B**）	6.（**B**）
7.（**B**）	8.（**D**）	9.（**C**）	10.（**D**）	11.（**A**）	12.（**B**）
13.（**A**）	14.（**C**）	15.（**A**）	16.（**B**）	17.（**B**）	18.（**B**）
19.（**C**）	20.（**C**）	21.（**A**）	22.（**A**）	23.（**C**）	24.（**D**）
25.（**C**）	26.（**B**）	27.（**A**）	28.（**D**）	29.（**D**）	

【解析】

5. *grow bigger and bigger* 變得越來越大

9. *all the better for~* 因~而更加…

11. 這樣式不吸引人，但是質料比表面看起來還要有價值。

12. 這位科學家是第一個發現凸透鏡 — 也就是有圓表面的玻璃 — 會使東西看起來比較大的人。

　　convex〔ˋkɑnvɛks〕*adj.* 凸起的

　　凸透鏡會使東西看起來較大，故選 larger 而非 smaller。

15. 你只有一個哥哥，而我的兄弟姊妹卻多達九個。

　　(A) *no less than* 多達

　　(B) no more than　只有

　　(C) not less than　至少

　　(D) not more than　至多

17. *not in the least* = *not at all* 一點也不

20. 表比較時，「兩倍的」，可用 twice。

23. fewer 後接可數名詞，less 接不可數名詞，故選 (C)。

28. 「我的外套比他的（外套）貴得多。」同類才能相比。

　　(D) he = his coat。

2. 否 定

> 含有否定字詞或否定意義的句子，稱爲否定構句，
> 分爲部分否定、全部否定、準否定，及雙重否定。

1. 部分否定及全部否定

all, both, every, always, quite 等，與否定詞 (not 或 no) 連用時，意思爲「並非全都～」、「不一定～」，稱爲「部分否定」。相反地，對全部事物加以否定者，稱爲「全部否定」。

> a. I do*n't* know *all* of these words. 【部分否定】
> (這些字我並非全都認得。)
>
> b. I do*n't* know *any* of these words. ⎫
> I know *none* of these words.   ⎬ 【全部否定】
> (這些字我全都不認得。)

> a. You can*not* do *everything*. (你並非每件事都會做。)
> b. You can*not* do *anything*. ⎫ (你什麼也不會做。)
> You can do *nothing*.   ⎭ 【全部否定】

> a. I do*n't* buy *both*. (我並非兩者都買。)【部分否定】
> b. I do*n't* buy *either*. ⎫
> I buy *neither*.   ⎭ (我兩個都不買。)【全部否定】

2. 準否定

用 little, few, hardly, scarcely, rarely, seldom 等近於否定的字，意思爲「幾乎不；很少」，以形成否定構句，稱爲「準否定」。但是 a few, a little (一些)，則不是準否定。

Few students can speak Russian.

（很少有學生會說俄語。）

<例外> There are *a few* passengers in the bus.

（公車上有一些乘客。）

He slept *little* last night. （他昨晚睡得很少。）

<例外> Please wait *a little*. （請等一下。）

【例】 I can *hardly* believe the news.

（我幾乎無法相信這消息。）

He *seldom* makes a mistake. （他很少犯錯。）

☞ little 當副詞，置於 know, think, dream, imagine 等
動詞前，意思為「完全不～」(= not at all)。

【例】 He *little thought* what would happen.

（他一點也沒想到會發生什麼事。）

Little did I *dream* that he was here.

（我完全沒想到他會在這裡。）

3. 雙重否定

一句話中用了兩個否定字，即「雙重否定」。這時因負負得正之理，
而表示肯定的意思。

(1) **There is no～that…not…**「沒有～不…」

【例】 *There is no* enemy on earth *that* he could *not*
conquer. （世上沒有他征服不了的敵人。）

(2) **no〔not〕～but…**「沒有～不…」

【例】 There is *no* rule *but* has exceptions.

= There is *no* rule *that* has *no* exceptions.

（凡是規則都有例外。）

⑶ **never~but…**「每~必…」

【例】 I *never* see you *but* I think of your father.
（我每次見到你，必定想起你父親。）

⑷ **not〔never〕~without**「每~必…」

【例】 I *never* see you *without* thinking of your father.
（我每次見到你，必定想起你父親。）

They *never* meet *without* quarreling.
（他們每次見面必定吵架。）

4. 否定的慣用語

⑴ **cannot~too…**「再也不爲過」

【例】 You *cannot* be *too* careful about your health.
（你再怎麼注意健康也不爲過。）

⑵ $\left\{ \begin{array}{l} \textbf{far from} \sim \\ \textbf{anything but} \sim \end{array} \right\}$ 「一點也不」(= not at all)

【例】 He is *far from* (being) happy.（他一點也不快樂。）

The bridge is *anything but* safe.
（這座橋一點也不安全。）

☞ **nothing but**「只；不過」(= only)

【例】 It is *nothing but* a joke.（這只是個玩笑罷了。）

⑶ **the last** + 名詞 「最不可能的；最不願意的」(= the least likely)

【例】 He is *the last man* to do such a thing.
（他是最不可能做這件事的人。）

He is *the last person* you should offend.
（他是你最不應該冒犯的人。）

5. 否定構句應注意事項

⑴ 否定詞放在句首，主詞與動詞必須倒裝。

【例】 *Never* again *did he enter* the house.

（他再也不曾踏進這間房子。）

Little did I expect he would win the first prize.

（我一點也沒想到他會得第一名。）

⑵ 修辭疑問句：形式為疑問句，但含有否定的意思。

【例】 *Who knows* what has become of him?

(= *No one knows* what has become of him.)

（誰知道他怎麼了？）

What is the use of my going to see her?

(= *It is no use* my going to see her.)

（我去看她有什麼用呢？）

＜比較＞ *Who would not* weep at the sad news?

(= *Everyone would* weep…)

（聽到這悲傷的消息，誰會不哭呢？）

⑶ **be no** ＋ 名詞（補語），或是放在形容詞前面，意思為「絕非～」，
這時的 no 比單純否定語氣更強。

【例】 He is *no* fool. （他絕非傻瓜。）【注意：沒有冠詞或定冠詞】

He is *no* stranger to me. （對我而言，他絕非陌生人。）

(= *I know him well.*)

He has spent *no* small sum of money.

（他絕非只花掉一小筆錢。）

歷屆聯考試題

( ) 1. Her bedroom was so small that she could _____ move in it.
  (A) nearly   (B) recently
  (C) mainly   (D) hardly

( ) 2. There is no one _____ knows this song.
  (A) which   (B) by whom
  (C) but   (D) having
  (E) like

( ) 3. Not only _____, but he saw her.
  (A) did he come   (B) he came
  (C) came he   (D) he comes
  (E) he did come

( ) 4. 他們兩人都不知道這件事。
  (A) Not all of them knew this.
  (B) Neither of them knew this.
  (C) Either of them knew this.
  (D) None of them knew this.

( ) 5. They have no prejudice against foreigners at all.
  (A) 他們仇視外國人。
  (B) 他們向外國人宣戰。
  (C) 他們與外國人有瓜葛。
  (D) 他們對外國人毫無偏見。

6. 那個老人既不知如何賺錢，也不知如何花錢。(中翻英)

_____

【歷屆聯考試題解答】

1. (**D**)　　2. (**C**)　　3. (**A**)　　4. (**B**)　　5. (**D**)

6. The old man knows neither how to make money nor
   how to spend it.

【解析】

2. 沒有人不知道這首歌。
   no [*not*] ~ *but*⋯　沒有 ~ 不⋯

3. *Not only* + *did* + S. + V., *but* (*also*) + S. + 過去式動詞 + ~.
   「S. (過去) 不僅 ~ 而且⋯。」

4. neither 表「兩者都不 ~」。

精選模擬考題

( ) 1. We _____ recognized each other, because we hadn't met since we were quite young.
    (A) really   (B) haven't
    (C) hardly   (D) actually

( ) 2. I can't give you any because there's _____ left.
    (A) some   (B) no   (C) none   (D) any

( ) 3. He could _____ work after his long illness.
    (A) hard   (B) hardly
    (C) hard to   (D) hardly to

( ) 4. That is all I have to say. I have _____ more to say.
    (A) something   (B) everything
    (C) much   (D) nothing

( ) 5. Not _____ can be a poet.
    (A) all people   (B) anyone
    (C) everyone   (D) anybody

( ) 6. I offered two proposals, but _____ was accepted.
    (A) both   (B) each
    (C) neither   (D) one

( ) 7. _____ but fools would believe such nonsense.
    (A) All   (B) Anybody
    (C) Everybody   (D) None

( ) 8. We could hardly see _____ around here after dark.

    (A) anybody   (B) nobody

    (C) somebody   (D) everybody

( ) 9. You can't have _____ of these books—not this one, nor that one.

    (A) either (B) both   (C) all   (D) any

( ) 10. She spoke so quietly that we could _____ hear her.

    (A) almost   (B) rarely

    (C) hardly   (D) little

( ) 11. He is far from a liar.

    = He is _____ a liar.

    (A) anything but   (B) something but

    (C) so   (D) nothing but

( ) 12. He slept _____ last night.

    (A) little (B) few (C) hardly (D) rarely

( ) 13. I don't know any of these words.

    = I know _____ of these words.

    (A) no (B) none (C) one (D) some

( ) 14. _____ students can speak Russian.

    (A) Few (B) Little (C) Seldom (D) Scarcely

( ) 15. I can _____ believe the news.

    (A) less (B) few (C) hardly (D) rarely

( ) 16. He _____ makes a mistake.

    (A) seldom   (B) hard   (C) few   (D) little

( ) 17. There is no rule _____ has exceptions.

    (A) but   (B) can   (C) that   (D) what

( ) 18. I never see you _____ thinking of your father.

    (A) but   (B) without   (C) and   (D) with

( ) 19. They never meet _____ quarreling.

    (A) but   (B) without   (C) and   (D) with

( ) 20. There was only snow.

    = There was _____ snow.

    (A) some   (B) something

    (C) anything but   (D) nothing but

( ) 21. _____ enter the house.

    (A) Never did he again

    (B) Never again he

    (C) Never again did he

    (D) Never he did again

( ) 22. I know him well.

    = He is _____ stranger to me.

    (A) not   (B) so   (C) a   (D) no

( ) 23. I could _____ understand what he said.

    (A) hard   (B) hardly   (C) few   (D) less

【精選模擬考題解答】

1. (**C**)　　2. (**C**)　　3. (**B**)　　4. (**D**)　　5. (**C**)　　6. (**C**)

7. (**D**)　　8. (**A**)　　9. (**A**)　　10. (**C**)　　11. (**A**)　　12. (**A**)

13. (**B**)　　14. (**A**)　　15. (**C**)　　16. (**A**)　　17. (**A**)　　18. (**B**)

19. (**B**)　　20. (**D**)　　21. (**C**)　　22. (**D**)　　23. (**B**)

【解析】

1. 「我們幾乎認不出彼此，因爲我們從很年輕的時候到現在，都沒見過面。」　　hardly ('hɑrdlɪ) *adv.* 幾乎不
    recognize ('rɛkəg,naɪz) *v.* 認出

4. 我沒有別話的要說。

5. 並不是每個人都能成爲詩人。
    not everyone (不是每一個人)，是部份否定的說法。

6. 我提出兩個建議，但都沒被接受。
    由 but 判斷，應該選擇否定的 neither (兩者都不)。
    proposal (prə'pozḷ) *n.* 提議

7. 「只有傻瓜才會相信這麼荒唐的事。」在此 none but，等於 only。　　nonsense ('nɑnsɛns) *n.* 胡說八道；荒唐的事

8. 因爲動詞有否定副詞 hardly (幾乎不) 修飾，故選 (A) anybody，其他的選項只能出現在肯定句。
    after dark 天黑之後

9. 「你不能擁有這兩本書中的任何一本──這本不行，那本也不行。」　　*not ~ either* 兩者皆不 (= *neither*)

11. *far from* 絕不；一點也不 (= *not at all* = *anything but*)
    liar ('laɪɚ) *n.* 說謊的人

13. *not ~ any*「一點也不」(= *none*)，爲完全否定的用法。

14. few 修飾可數名詞，little 修飾不可數名詞。

3. 關 係 詞

1. 關係代名詞

1. 關係代名詞的用法

⑴ **who, whose, whom** 用以指人。

【例】 *The girl **who*** is wearing a red dress is Helen.

（穿紅衣服的女孩是海倫。）

Tom loves *a girl **whose*** father is a farmer.

（湯姆喜歡上一個父親是農夫的女孩。）

The people (***whom***) you met at the party are college professors.

（你在宴會上遇見的人，是大學教授。）

⑵ **which, of which**〔**whose**〕用以指動物或事物。

【例】 *The rice **which*** grows here tastes good.

（這裡種的米很好吃。）

What is *the building **whose*** roof (= the roof *of which*) is seen from here?

（從這裡看得到屋頂的，是什麼建築物？）

The house (***which***) I have bought stands on a hill.

（我買的房子座落在山丘上。）

⑶ **that** 用以指人、動物或事物，無所有格。

【例】 *The letter **that*** came this morning is from my mother.

（今天早上寄來的信，是我母親寄的。）

Tennis is *the sport* (***that***) I like best.

（網球是我最喜愛的運動。）

2. 關係代名詞與介系詞

⑴ 關係代名詞與介系詞的位置

關係代名詞做介系詞的受詞時，介系詞置於 whom 和 which 之前後皆可，但介系詞不可放在 that 前面。

【例】 This is the girl *of whom* I spoke.

= This is the girl (*whom*) I spoke *of*.

= This is the girl (*that*) I spoke *of*.

（這就是我提過的那個女孩。）

The hotel *at which* we stayed is cheap.

= The hotel (*which*) we stayed *at* is cheap.

= The hotel (*that*) we stayed *at* is cheap.

（我們住的旅館很便宜。）

⑵ **during**, **beyond**, **except** 通常置於關係代名詞前面。

【例】 The years *during which he was away* were long years to her. （他離開的期間，對她而言是一段漫長的歲月。）

3. 限定用法與補述用法

限定用法：用形容詞子句限定先行詞，關係代名詞前不需逗號。

補述用法：關係代名詞之前需逗號，用以補充說明先行詞的意思。

a. He had *two sons* *who* became teachers. 【限定用法】

b. He had *two sons*, *who* became teachers. 【補述用法】

☞ a 句表示他除了有兩個當老師的兒子，還有其他孩子。

b 句表示他只有兩個兒子。

c. There are *some discs* *which* you should listen to.

（有些你該聽聽的 CD。）

d. Nancy brought *some discs*, *which* we enjoyed listening to. （南西帶來一些 CD，我們都很喜歡聽。）

⑴ 補述用法做爲插入句，對主題加以補充說明。

【例】 *Mr. Johnson*, **who** showed us around the city, was a tour guide.
（強森先生是個導遊，是他帶我們參觀這個城市的。）

⑵ 補述用法的關係代名詞，常常可以用「連接詞（and, but, for…）
＋ 代名詞」來代換。

【例】 I met *an old man*, **who** (= *and he*) asked me the way to the station.
（我碰見一位老人，他問我到車站怎麼走。）

I will lend you *this English book*, **which** (= *and it*) is very interesting.
（我會借你這本英文書，它非常有趣。）

⑶ 補述用法可以用片語或子句做爲先行詞，其關係代名詞通常是
which 和 as。

【例】 *I lost my way*, **which** (= and this) delayed me considerably. （我迷路了，這使我遲到很久。）

He told me *to do it in a day*, **which** I found impossible.
（他要我一天內做完，我覺得那是不可能的。）

---

4. that 的用法

⑴ 只作限定用法，即 that 前不可有逗點，先行詞可以是人、動物，
或事物。但 that 不可以當 whose，且其前不可以有介系詞。

【例】 I want a man *that* (= *who*) understands English.
（我需要一位懂英文的人。）

I wish to read a book *that* (= *which*) is both easy and interesting. （我想讀一本淺易又有趣的書。）

⑵ the man
$$\begin{cases} \textit{that} \text{ you spoke } \textit{of} \cdots\cdots \text{（正）} \\ \textit{of that} \text{ you spoke} \cdots\cdots \text{（誤）} \end{cases}$$

下述情形通常只能用 that。

① 當先行詞附有最高級形容詞的時候。

【例】 He is *the greatest* man *that* ever lived.

（他是有史以來最偉大的人物。）

② 先行詞之前有 the only, the same, the very, the first, the last，或 all, only, any, no, every 時。

【例】 This is *the same* watch *that* I lost yesterday.

（這就是我昨天掉的錶。）

All that glitters is not gold.

（閃爍者未必是金；金玉其外，敗絮其中。）

③ 為加強句中某部分的語氣，而採用"It is…that"的結構時。

【例】 *It's* a nightingale *that* is singing over there.

（在那邊唱歌的是隻夜鶯。）

④ 先行詞是「人＋動物或事物」時。

【例】 Look at *the boy and the dog that* are running down the hill.

（看看那正跑下山的男孩和小狗。）

⑤ 先行詞是疑問代名詞，為避免重複時。

【例】 *Who that* is honest can do such a thing?

（哪個誠實的人會做這種事呢？）

---

5. what 的用法

⑴ what 是兼做先行詞的關係代名詞，等於 the thing(s) which 或 all that。

【例】 Do *what* (= *the thing which*) I tell you.
（做我告訴你的事。）

What I like best for breakfast is cornflakes.
（我最喜歡吃的早餐是玉蜀黍片。）

He spent *what* (= *all that*) he had earned.
（他花光所賺的錢。）

⑵ what 的慣用語

① { **what is called**
　 what we〔you〕call } 「所謂的」

【例】 We are living in *what is called* the Atomic Age.
（我們生活在所謂的原子時代裡。）

② { **what is more** 「而且」
　 what is better〔worse〕「更好〔糟〕的是」

【例】 He is hard-working (and) *what is more*, honest and punctual.
（他工作努力，而且既誠實又準時。）

③ { **what with** … **and** (what with) … 「半因…半因」── 表原因
　 what by … **and** (what by) … 「半藉…半藉」── 表手段

【例】 *What with* overwork *and* undernourishment, he fell ill. （半因工作過度，半因營養不良，他病倒了。）
What by threats *and* entreaties, he finally accomplished his purpose.
（半靠威脅，半靠懇求，他終於達到目的。）

④ { **what one is** 「某人現有的樣子；今日的成就」
{ **what one was** 「某人過去那個樣子」

【例】 My parents have made me *what I am*.

（我能有今日是雙親所賜。）

He is not *what he was*.

（他已非昔日的他了。）

---

6. whoever, whomever, whatever, whichever 的用法

(1) 複合關係代名詞做名詞用。

【例】 I'll employ *whoever* (= *anyone who*) works hard.

（我會雇用任何努力工作的人。）

I'll employ *whomever* (= *anyone whom*) you recommend.

（我會雇用你推薦的任何人。）

Take *whichever* (= *any one that*) you want.

（你想要的就拿去。）

Do *whatever* (= *anything that*) you like.

（做你喜歡做的事。）

(2) 複合關係代名詞做形容詞用。

【例】 You may choose *whichever* book you like.

（你可以挑選你喜歡的任何一本書。）

I'll give you *whatever* help I can.

（我會給你我可以提供的任何幫助。）

7. as, but, than 的用法

(1) 先行詞為 such, the same 時，用 as。

【例】 You should read only *such* books *as* you can
understand easily.
（你應該只讀那些可以容易了解的書。）

It was *such* a fine day *as* we rarely see in England.
（這麼好的天氣，我們在英國倒很少見。）

This is *the same* watch *as* I lost.
（這錶跟我掉的那只一樣。）

☞ the same～as 是指同種類，the same～that 指同一物。

【例】 This is *the same* watch *that* I lost.
（這錶正是我掉的那只。）

(2) as 可用以代替整個句子。

【例】 *Jim wasn't at home*, *as* is often the case with him.
（吉姆不在家，他常常如此。）

He was an Australian, *as* I could tell by his accent.
（他是澳洲人，這點我可以由他的口音斷定。）

(3) but 含否定意義（＝ who～not ; that～not）

【例】 There is *no child but* likes toys（= *who does not like*
toys）.（沒有小孩子會不喜歡玩具的。）

Nobody comes to his house *but* is（= *who is not*）
welcome.（沒有人到他家裡會不受歡迎。）

(4) 比較級形容詞＋先行詞時，要用 than。

【例】 He spends *more money than* I earn.
（他花的錢比我賺的還多。）

She asks for *more than* is necessary.
（她要求的比實際所需的還多。）

2. 關係副詞的用法

關係副詞有 when, where, how, why 用於表示時間、地點、方法、理由等名詞之後。

1. 限定用法：用以修飾先行詞

【例】 I don't know *the time when* the meeting will
be held. (我不知道開會的時間。)

The town where he lives is about six miles away.
(他住的城鎮約有六哩遠。)

This is *the reason why* I came early.
(這就是我為什麼早來的原因。)

2. 補述用法：關係副詞前面要用逗點

【例】 We got to the park, *where* we rested for an hour.
(我們到達公園，在那裡休息了一小時。)

Wait till noon, *when* she'll be back.
(等到中午，那時她就回來了。)

3. 關係副詞之先行詞的省略

【例】 This is *where* (= *the place* where) he lives.
(這是他住的地方。)

Sunday is *when* (= *the day* when) I am least busy.
(星期天是我最不忙的時候。)

That's *why* (= *the reason* why) he was absent.
(那就是他為什麼缺席的原因。)

☞ 除此之外，也可以用 the way 或 how 表示方法。

【例】 This is *how* he did it. (這就是他做這件事的方法。)
= This is *the way* he did it.
= This is *the way in which* he did it.

---

4. 複合關係副詞 whenever, wherever, however 的用法

(1) whenever, wherever 可用以加強語氣。

【例】 ***Whenever*** my uncle visits our house, he brings us presents.

（每次舅舅來我家拜訪，總會帶禮物給我們。）

You'll be welcome ***wherever*** you go.

（你到哪裡都受歡迎。）

(2) whenever, wherever, however 可表示讓步。

【例】 ***Whenever*** (= *No matter when*) you (may) come, you'll find me at home.

（不論你什麼時候來，我都會在家。）

Wherever (= *No matter where*) he is, he must be found. （不論他在哪裡，一定會被發現。）

However (= *No matter how*) carefully I (may) write, I sometimes make mistakes.

（不論我如何細心地寫，有時還是會寫錯。）

歷屆聯考試題

一、關係代名詞的用法

(　　) 1. You may give the prize to the one _____ you think best.
  (A) whom (B) who (C) what (D) which

(　　) 2. This is the boy _____ I have been waiting.
  (A) and him   (B) and whom
  (C) and who   (D) whom
  (E) for whom

(　　) 3. I have a book _____ very interesting.
  (A) it is   (B) it's
  (C) which is   (D) and which is

(　　) 4. After interviewing a number of applicants for a job, a personnel manager will recall only those _____ have made a strong impression.
  (A) that (B) which (C) who (D) whom

(　　) 5. Mary is his only daughter, to _____ he gave most of his property.
  (A) who (B) whom (C) which

(　　) 6. He is the only one of the students who _____ English with fluency.
  (A) speaks (B) speak (C) speaking

(　　) 7. A camera is a lightproof box _____ light is admitted through a small hole.

      (A) for which   (B) into which

      (C) from what   (D) to whom

(　　) 8. I have a girlfriend _____ name is Mary.

      (A) her   (B) who's   (C) which

      (D) whose   (E) who

(　　) 9. We often come across people _____ whom we disagree.

      (A) to   (B) in

      (C) with   (D) in regard for

(　　) 10. John didn't tell me _____ Mr. Wilson had said to him.

      (A) why   (B) which   (C) what   (D) that

_____11. A man without friends is miserable.

      = A man _____ has no friends is miserable.

_____12. The bamboo _____ grows taller bends lower.

(　　) 13. Farmers <u>trap</u> and kill <u>such</u> animals as <u>is</u> <u>harmful</u> <u>to</u>
             (A)   (B)   (C) (D) (E)

      their crops. (改錯)

二、限定用法及補述用法

(　　) 1. I met Mary, _____ told me the news.

      (A) that   (B) who   (C) which

(　) 2. The man _____ I met in the street just now is my teacher.

    (A) whom　(B) who　(C) which

(　) 3. Is that the man _____ you are waiting?

    (A) whom　(B) who　(C) whose　(D) for whom

(　) 4. My father, _____ you met, is a merchant.

    (A) who　(B) which　(C) whom　(D) whose

(　) 5. Marco Polo, _____ traveled to the Orient with his father and uncle, wrote a book about his travels.

    (A) which　(B) who　(C) whom　(D) that

三、that 的用法

(　) 1. "I like your hat." "But it is the same _____ the one you are wearing now."

    (A) what　(B) which　(C) that　(D) as

(　) 2. There are programs on television that _____ how to do things.

    (A) explain　(B) explains

    (C) explaining　(D) explained

四、複合關係代名詞

(　) 1. I will write to you _____ I have leisure.

    (A) wherever　(B) whatever

    (C) whenever　(D) however

    (E) whoever

(   ) 2. You may give your pen to _____ wants it.
      (A) whatever   (B) whoever   (C) whichever
      (D) whenever   (E) whomever

(   ) 3. He didn't mean _____ he said.
      (A) what   (B) that   (C) which   (D) it

(   ) 4. I will do _____ I can for you.
      (A) which   (B) that   (C) what   (D) where

(   ) 5. 我愛一切美的事物。
      I love _____.
      (A) is beautiful   (B) all is beautiful
      (C) what is beautiful   (D) that is beautiful
      (E) what beautiful is

(   ) 6. The prize will be given to _____ answers the
      questions correctly.
      (A) who   (B) whom   (C) whoever   (D) that

7. 當我疲倦時，我就在桌上打個盹。〔中翻英〕

_____

五、as, but, than 的用法

(   ) 1. There is no mother but _____ her children.
      (A) loved   (B) loves   (C) loving
      (D) lovely   (E) love

(　　) 2. There is no one _____ knows this song.

　　(A) which 　　(B) by whom 　　(C) but

　　(D) having 　　(E) likes

_____ 3. Read only such books _____ you can understand.

六、關係副詞的用法

(　　) 1. I hope you will find this valley a beautiful place

_____ you may spend your weekend.

　　(A) which 　　(B) that 　　　　(C) when

　　(D) where 　　(E) what

(　　) 2. She came on the day _____ her grandmother died.

　　(A) which 　　(B) where 　　　　(C) when

(　　) 3. A garage is a place _____ cars are stored or repaired.

　　(A) where 　　(B) which 　(C) what 　(D) ✕

(　　) 4. I don't remember _____ he lives.

　　(A) the number 　　　　(B) the address

　　(C) the street 　　　　　(D) the house

　　(E) where 　〔註：在此 where 是疑問副詞而不是關係副詞。〕

(　　) 5. This is the house _____ which I was born.

　　(A) in 　　(B) for 　　　(C) at 　　　(D) on

(　　) 6. Send your application to the appropriate department

manager in the company _____ you'd like to work.

　　(A) where 　　(B) which 　　(C) that 　　(D) who

【歷屆聯考試題解答】

一、　1. (**A**)　2. (**E**)　3. (**C**)　4. (**C**)　5. (**B**)　6. (**A**)
　　　7. (**B**)　8. (**D**)　9. (**C**)　10. (**C**)　11. who/that
　　　12. that/which　　13. (**C**) → are

二、　1. (**B**)　2. (**A**)　3. (**D**)　4. (**C**)　5. (**B**)

三、　1. (**D**)　2. (**A**)

四、　1. (**C**)　2. (**B**)　3. (**A**)　4. (**C**)　5. (**C**)　6. (**C**)
　　　7. Whenever I get tired, I take a nap at the table.

五、　1. (**B**)　2. (**C**)　3. as

六、　1. (**D**)　2. (**C**)　3. (**A**)　4. (**E**)　5. (**A**)　6. (**A**)

【解析】

一、　1. 關係代名詞做 think 的受詞，故選 (A) whom。

　　　2. *wait for*「等待」，原句亦可寫成：This is the boy whom I have been waiting for.

　　　4. 「在面試了許多應徵者之後，人事主任只記得那些印象深刻的。」　applicant ('æpləkənt) *n.* 應徵者
　　　a personnel manger　人事主任
　　　recall (rɪ'kɔl) *v.* 憶起

　　　5. 關係代名詞做 to 的受詞，故選 (B) whom。
　　　property ('prɑpətɪ) *n.* 財產

　　　6. 「the only one of＋複數名詞」做先行詞，其後子句用單數動詞。　fluently ('fluəntlɪ) *adv.* 流利地

　　　7. 照相機是個防光的盒子，光線只能經由一個小孔進入盒內。
　　　lightproof ('laɪt'pruf) *adj.* 防光的

9. 「***disagree with*** + 人」表「不同意某人」，而介係詞
with 可移至到關代的前面，故選 (C)。
come across 偶然想到

11. miserable〔'mɪzərəbḷ〕*adj.* 悲慘的；可憐的

12. 竹子長得愈高，彎得愈低。
bamboo〔bæm'bu〕*n.* 竹子　　bend〔bɛnd〕*v.* 彎曲

13. 農夫們誘捕並殺死那些對農作物有害的動物。
動詞必須與先行詞一致，先行詞為 animals，故用複數
動詞 are。本題先行詞有 such 修飾，故用準關係代名
詞 as。　　trap〔træp〕*v.* 誘捕
harmful〔'hɑrmfəl〕*adj.* 有害的

二、　4. 本題中 whom you met 是插入語，補充說明 father。
關係代名詞做 meet 的受詞，故選 (C) whom。

5. 馬可波羅曾和他的父親及舅舅到東方旅遊，並寫了
一本遊記。

三、　2. 本句的先行詞為 programs，故其後子句用複數動詞，
選 (A) explain。

四、　1. leisure〔'liʒɚ〕*n.* 空閒

五、　1.「沒有不愛孩子的母親。」　***no~but***… 沒有～不…
but 是準關係代名詞，本身含有否定的意思，作用相
當於 that…not。

六、　1. 後面子句已經是完整的子句，故在此須填關係副詞，又
先行詞是 place，表地點，關係副詞用 where。
valley〔'vælɪ〕*n.* 山谷

3. garage〔gə'rɑdʒ〕*n.* 車庫；修車廠

精選模擬考題

( ) 1. He is the man _____ I believe can help you.
(A) who
(B) whom
(C) whoever
(D) whomever

( ) 2. I will employ the man _____ they say is a fluent speaker of English.
(A) what
(B) which
(C) whom
(D) who

( ) 3. I have two sons both of _____ are married.
(A) who
(B) whose
(C) whom
(D) whosever

( ) 4. She has a new car of _____ she is very proud.
(A) that
(B) which
(C) whom
(D) it

( ) 5. You must not use words _____ meaning you don't understand well.
(A) that
(B) which
(C) whose
(D) what

( ) 6. There is no mother _____ loves her own children.
(A) who
(B) that
(C) but
(D) whom

( ) 7. _____ he may say, I don't believe him.
      (A) What   (B) However
      (C) Whatever   (D) How

( ) 8. You may welcome _____.
      (A) whoever comes
      (B) whoever like you
      (C) whomever loves you
      (D) whomever will come

( ) 9. He was becoming fat, _____ bothered him very much.
      (A) which   (B) that
      (C) what   (D) how

( ) 10. I was told to go there not by taxi but on foot, _____ advice I followed.
      (A) that   (B) which
      (C) whose   (D) what

( ) 11. The village is now very different from _____ it was ten years ago.
      (A) what   (B) as
      (C) that   (D) which

( ) 12. He was one of the first to recognize _____ has been called the Industrial Revolution.
      (A) who   (B) which
      (C) that   (D) what

( ) 13. I had been waiting for a bus for an hour, _____
I met John.

(A) which   (B) when

(C) that   (D) how

( ) 14. You may give the book to _____ wants it.

(A) who   (B) whoever

(C) whomever   (D) whosever

( ) 15. At last he found the very man _____ he wanted.

(A) which   (B) whom

(C) that   (D) as

( ) 16. This book is for students _____ native language is
not English.

(A) of whom   (B) of which

(C) which   (D) whose

( ) 17. The train ran over a man and his horse _____ were
just crossing the track.

(A) who   (B) which

(C) whom   (D) that

( ) 18. Jack came yesterday, _____ was a pleasant surprise
to us.

(A) who   (B) that

(C) in which   (D) which

( ) 19. _____ he told me was a great surprise to me.

(A) Which   (B) Whom

(C) Who   (D) What

(　) 20. The man ＿＿＿＿ I spoke to yesterday is our English
teacher.
(A) who　　　　(B) whom
(C) whose　　　(D) what

(　) 21. You may go ＿＿＿＿ you like.
(A) wherever　　(B) how
(C) however　　(D) what

(　) 22. I want the same dictionary ＿＿＿＿ your sister has.
(A) what　(B) as　(C) like　(D) which

(　) 23. This is all ＿＿＿＿ I know about the matter.
(A) what　　　　(B) whom
(C) that　　　　(D) which

(　) 24. The girl, for ＿＿＿＿ he cared so much, died
so young.
(A) that　　　　(B) which
(C) who　　　　(D) whom

(　) 25. This is a proverb ＿＿＿＿ I do not understand the
meaning.
(A) which　　　(B) whose
(C) of which　　(D) that

(　) 26. One place ＿＿＿＿ I didn't look for it was the cupboard.
(A) for　　　　(B) in
(C) where　　　(D) what

( ) 27. The girl _____ he is speaking to is Tom's sister.
    (A) what   (B) who
    (C) which   (D) whom

( ) 28. The house _____ we live now was built three years ago.
    (A) why   (B) what
    (C) where   (D) when

( ) 29. Did you see my book _____ cover is red?
    (A) that   (B) whose
    (C) which   (D) of which

( ) 30. There can be no man _____ has some faults.
    (A) which   (B) whoever
    (C) that   (D) but

( ) 31. The gentleman is Tom's uncle, _____ they say is one of the greatest scientists in the world.
    (A) whom   (B) of whom
    (C) who   (D) whose

( ) 32. Do you know the lady _____ came to see me this morning?
    (A) which   (B) whom
    (C) who   (D) what

( ) 33. Do you remember _____ he said?
    (A) that   (B) which
    (C) of which   (D) what

( ) 34. This is the village _____ I was born.
    (A) where   (B) of which
    (C) which   (D) that

( ) 35. I will invite _____ wants to come to my birthday party.
    (A) whomever   (B) whosever
    (C) whoever   (D) who

( ) 36. Tell me the reason _____ you did so.
    (A) why   (B) what
    (C) how   (D) which

【精選模擬考題解答】

1. (**A**)	2. (**D**)	3. (**C**)	4. (**B**)	5. (**C**)	6. (**C**)
7. (**C**)	8. (**A**)	9. (**A**)	10. (**B**)	11. (**A**)	12. (**D**)
13. (**B**)	14. (**B**)	15. (**C**)	16. (**D**)	17. (**D**)	18. (**D**)
19. (**D**)	20. (**B**)	21. (**A**)	22. (**B**)	23. (**C**)	24. (**D**)
25. (**C**)	26. (**C**)	27. (**D**)	28. (**C**)	29. (**B**)	30. (**D**)
31. (**C**)	32. (**C**)	33. (**D**)	34. (**A**)	35. (**C**)	36. (**A**)

【解析】

1. I believe 是插入語，解題時可省略不看，故本題關代選當主格的 who。

2. they say 是插入語。 employ〔ɪmˋplɔɪ〕*v.* 雇用

7. 不論他說什麼，我都不相信。

9. 10. which 引導補述用法的形容詞子句，補充先行詞（逗號之前的整個句子）的意思。

11. 現在這村莊跟十年前非常不同。
    village (ˈvɪlɪdʒ) *n.* 村莊

12. 沒有先行詞，又必須做後面子句 called 的受詞，所以選 (D)
    what。　　*Industrial Revolution* 工業革命

13. 關係副詞 when 做補述用法時，通常前面會加逗點。

15. 先行詞有 very 修飾，故關係代名詞用 that。此處 very 作「就
    是；正是」解。

17. 先行詞同時有人(man)和非人(horse)，關係代名詞用 that。
    run over 輾過

18. 此處 which 為補述用法，代替逗點之前的整個句子。

22. the same~as 是指同種類的東西，the same~that 則指同一
    物，依句意，應該用 as。

24. 那個女孩 —— 他非常關心 —— 年紀輕輕就死了。

26. 表地方的關係副詞用 where。　　cupboard (ˈkʌbəd) *n.* 碗櫥

29. 這裡需要所有格修飾名詞，whose cover = the cover of
    which。

31. they say 是插入語，此處的關代做後面子句的主詞，故選 (C)
    who。

33. 本句中 what 是疑問代名詞，做 said 的受詞。what 引導的整
    個子句做 remember 的受詞。

35. 本題沒有先行詞，又後面子句中需要一個主詞，故選 (C)
    whoever。

36. 表原因，關係副詞用 why。

PART-3

時式・語態・假設法

▶1. 時式的考題集中在完成式。

▶2. 要注意哪些動詞一定要用被動語態，哪些不可用被動。

▶3. 與過去事實相反的假設，及if子句用現在式代替未來式的用法，是必考題。

1. 時 式 (1) —— 簡單式

1. 現在式的用法

(1) 表示**現在的動作或狀態**。

【例】 Here *comes* Tom. Here he *comes*. (他來了。)

☞ 因為語氣的關係，名詞做主詞時 → Here ＋ V. ＋ S. ，
代名詞做主詞時 → Here ＋ S. ＋ V.

【例】 I *understand* this rule now. (我現在了解這條規則。)
The book *belongs* to me. (這本書是我的。)
Our school *stands* on the hill. (我們學校在山丘上。)
I *want* something to drink. (我要點喝的東西。)

☞ 以上屬這類的動詞沒有進行式。

(2) 表示**現在的習慣或反覆的動作**。

【例】 My mother *gets* up earliest in my family.
(我母親是家裡起得最早的。)

She often *goes* shopping at the department store.
(她常在百貨公司購物。)

We *take* English five times a week.
(我們一週上五次英文。)

(3) **一般的眞理或格言**。

【例】 The sun *rises* in the east. (太陽從東方升起。)
Twice four *is* eight. (四的兩倍是八。)
God *helps* those who help themselves.
(天助自助者。)

(4) **代替未來式**：說話者敘述未來確定的事情，或表示出發、開始、
來往的動詞（如 go, come, start, leave, return, arrive, sail…），
可用現在式代替未來式。

【例】 It *is* Sunday tomorrow.（明天是星期日。）

We *leave* at nine *tomorrow morning*.
（我們明天早上九點出發。）

My aunt *comes* to see us *next Saturday*.
（下星期六我阿姨要來看我們。）

(5) 表時間或條件的**副詞子句**，以現在式代替未來式。

【例】 *When he comes*, let me know.
（他來的時候，請告訴我。）

Please wait here *till she is* ready.
（請在這裡等她準備好。）

If it is fine tomorrow, we will go on a picnic.
（如果明天天氣好，我們將去野餐。）

☞ 名詞子句仍以未來式表示未來的動作。

【例】 I don't know *if it will rain* next Saturday.
（我不知道下星期六是否會下雨。）

Tell me *when he will come*.（告訴我他什麼時候會來。）

(6) 「報上說」或「書上說」，用現在式的 "**says**"。

【例】 *The newspaper says* that the meeting will be held at
nine a.m.（報上說會議將在早上九點舉行。）

The book says that women can live longer than men.
（這本書上說女人比男人長壽。）

(7) It is + 一段時間 + since…，用 is 代替現在完成式。

【例】 *It is* (= *has been*) five years *since* I moved here.
（自從我搬到此地已五年了。）

2. 過去式的用法

(1) 表示**過去的動作或狀態**。

【例】 He *arrived* at a hotel and *took* a room on the fifth floor. (他到達旅館，並在五樓租了一個房間。)

I *bought* this coat while I *was* in England.
(這件外套是我在英國的時候買的。)

(2) 表示**過去的習慣及反覆的動作**。

常與時間副詞 every day, always, usually, seldom 等連用。

【例】 His family *always traveled* by car *before*.
(以前他的家人總是駕車旅遊。)

I *went* swimming *every day* during the summer.
(在夏天時，我每天都去游泳。)

☞ **used to** ＋ 原形動詞，表示過去的習慣動作，而現在已經沒有了。

【例】 We *used to spend* our vacations in the mountains.
(我們以前常在山區渡假。)

☞ **would** ＋ 原形動詞，也可以表示過去的習慣。

【例】 My mother *would go* downtown when she was not busy.
(我媽以前不忙的時候，常到市中心去。)

(3) 與 ever, never 連用，表示**過去的經驗**。

【例】 *Did* you *ever* meet him? (＝ *Have you ever met him*?)
(你曾遇見過他嗎？)

I *never dreamed* of seeing you again.
(我從沒想過會再見到你。)

⑷ **代替過去完成式。**

before, after, till, when, than 引導的子句中，已經表明了時間
的先後，可以用過去式代替過去完成式。

【例】 The task was more difficult *than* I *expected*
〔*had expected*〕. (這工作比我預期的還難。)

I reached the station *after* the train *started*
〔*had started*〕. (火車開動之後我才到達車站。)

3. 未來式的用法

1. 單純未來

單純表示未來的動作或狀態，自然的趨勢或必然之結果。

	第 一 人 稱	第 二 人 稱	第 三 人 稱
敘述句	I will 〔shall〕…	You will…	He will…
疑問句	Will 〔Shall〕I…?	Will 〔Shall〕you…?	Will he…?

☞ 和名詞則不可縮寫，如 John will 不可寫成 John'll。
否定時縮寫成 won't, shan't。

> I *will* be eighteen next year. (明年我就十八歲了。)
> *Will* 〔*Shall*〕 I be in time if I start now?
> (如果我現在開始還來得及嗎？)

> You *will* catch cold if you stand here long.
> (如果你在這裡久站，你將會感冒。)
> *Will* you be free this afternoon? (今天下午你有空嗎？)

> He *will* come of age next year. (他明年就成年了。)
> By the time you have washed and dressed, breakfast
> *will* be ready. (在你盥洗更衣完畢之際，早餐將已準備好了。)
> *Won't* they go on a picnic if it rains?
> (如果下雨他們將不去野餐嗎？)

2. 意志未來

	第一人稱	第二人稱	第三人稱
說話者（I）的意志	I will…	You shall…	He shall…
主詞自己的意志	I will…	Will you…?	He will…
徵求對方的意見	Shall I…?	You will…	Shall he…?

(1) 表示**說話者的意志**：句中主詞須依照說話者（I）的意志行事，表示說話者對主詞所做的允諾、命令或威脅。

【例】 I *will* do anything for you.
（我願意為你做任何事。）

You *shall* have this book. （你可以擁有這本書。）
（→ I *will* give you this book. ）

He shall never do that. （他永遠不能那麼做。）
（→ I *will* never let him do that. ）

(2) 表示**主詞**自己的意志：三種人稱都用 will，此時 will = *be determined to*（決意）; *be willing to*（願意）。

【例】 (a) I *will* give you my address.
（我願意給你我的地址。）

(b) If you *will* help me, I'll be much obliged.
（如果你願意幫助我，我會很感激的。）

(c) He says he *will* come.
（ = He says, "I *will* come." ）
（他說他要來。）

☞ 表條件的副詞子句（if, unless）為單純未來時，通常不用 will，如 I will tell him *if he comes*. 但是，要表示主詞的意志時，必須用 will，如例句 (b)。

(3) 疑問句用以徵求對方的意見。

【例】 ***Shall*** I help you? — Yes, please.

（要不要我幫忙？ — 好的，謝謝。）

Which ***will*** you take?（你要挑哪一個？）

Shall he come here?

(→ *Do you want him to* come here?)

（他可以來這裡嗎？）

---

3. 不用 **shall, will** 表示「簡單未來式」的方法

(1) **be going to** ＋原形動詞

【例】 ***Is*** Bess ***going to*** have a baby?

（貝絲將要生小孩了嗎？）

I ***am going to*** see the doctor tomorrow.

（我明天將去看醫生。）

What ***are*** you ***going to*** do with the money?

（你要如何處理這筆錢？）

☞ be going to 不能表示「天氣、年齡、時間」等自然的趨勢。

【例】 I ***shall*** be twenty next year.（我明年就二十歲了。）

Tomorrow ***will*** be the 20th of September.

（明天是九月二十日。）

☞ 句中若有表條件或時間的副詞子句時，也不可用 be going to。

【例】 *If I see him,* I ***will*** give him your message.

（倘若看到他，我會把你的話帶到。）

When he comes, I ***will*** tell you.

（他來的時候，我會告訴你。）

(2) $\left\{\begin{array}{l}\textbf{be about to} + \textbf{V.} \\ \textbf{be on the point of} + \text{V-ing}\end{array}\right\}$ 「就要；即將」

【例】 He *was about to* start.（他即將出發。）

We *were on the point of* leaving when he arrived.
（他到達時，我們正要離開。）

(3) 來去動詞（表往來、出發、到達）可用現在式或現在進行式表未來，通常和表示未來的時間副詞連用。

【例】 We *leave* Tainan *at six a.m.* and *arrive* in Taipei *at noon.*（我們將於上午六點離開台南，中午抵達台北。）

We *are having* guests *this evening.*
（我們今晚要請客。）

(4) **be to** + **V.**：① 預定的計劃，② 說話者的意志。

【例】 ① They *are to be* married next year.
（他們將於明年結婚。）

② You *are to bring* my baggage upstairs.
（你把我的行李拿到樓上去。）

歷屆聯考試題

一、現在式

(　　) 1. If it _____ tomorrow, we won't go to the Palace
Museum.
(A) rains　　(B) rained　　(C) will rain
(D) shall rain　　　　(E) had rained

(　　) 2. The diligent student _____ the library every week.
(A) goes to　　　　(B) was gone
(C) has to gone　　(D) will to go

(　　) 3. When you come at midnight, I _____.
(A) will sleep
(B) might sleep
(C) shall have been sleeping
(D) could be sleeping

(　　) 4. I'll give him my answer when he _____ here
tomorrow.
(A) will come　　(B) comes
(C) shall come　　(D) coming

(　　) 5. I shall have finished my dinner _____.
(A) when you arrive
(B) when you arrived
(C) when you had arrived
(D) when you have arrived
(E) when you were arrived

二、過去式

( ) 1. 昨天晚上，你曾看過了電視上轉播的籃球賽嗎？
  (A) Did you seen the basketball game on TV last night?
  (B) Have you seen the basketball game on TV last night?
  (C) Did you see the basketball game on TV last night?
  (D) Had you seen the basketball game on TV last night?

( ) 2. The bell _____ a few minutes ago.
  (A) ring (B) rang (C) ringed (D) has rung

( ) 3. John said that he _____ the kettle on.
  (A) would put   (B) will putted
  (C) was put   (D) to put

( ) 4. 這本書花了他七十元。
  (A) He cost seventy dollars for this book.
  (B) Seventy dollars cost him this book.
  (C) This book cost him seventy dollars.
  (D) This book cost seventy dollars for him.
  (E) This book spent him seventy dollars.

( ) 5. He asked when she _____ back.
  (A) is come (B) shall be (C) would be (D) comes

( ) 6. It _____ a little force to lift the heavy weight.
  (A) took   (B) has taken
  (C) taken   (D) take

(　) 7. Why _____ when you saw me?
　　　(A) weren't you stopping　　(B) haven't you stopped
　　　(C) didn't you stop　　　　(D) you don't stop
　　　(E) you haven't stopped

三、未來式

(　) 1. There _____ ten students at the picnic tomorrow.
　　　(A) is　　　(B) were　　　(C) will be
　　　(D) will have　　　(E) have

【歷屆聯考試題解答】

一、1.(**A**)　2.(**A**)　3.(**D**)　4.(**B**)　5.(**A**)
二、1.(**C**)　2.(**B**)　3.(**A**)　4.(**C**)　5.(**C**)　6.(**A**)　7.(**C**)
三、1.(**C**)

【解析】

一、1. *Palace Museum* 故宮博物院

　　3. 如果你半夜來，我可能正在睡覺。
　　　could 表推測，作「可能」解，此處 when = if。

　　4. 副詞子句中，動詞以現在式代替未來式。

　　5. 當你到達的時候，我應該已經吃完飯了。

二、1. 句中有明確的過去時間（last time），動詞用過去式。

　　4. cost（花費）須以「事」或「物」為主詞，且不可用被動
　　　語態。

　　5. 本句 when 引導名詞子句，做 asked 的受詞，子句中的
　　　動詞要與 asked 一致，故選過去式的 (C) would be。

　　6. 「舉起重物，要花一點力氣。」如果 (D) 改為 takes 也對。

精選模擬考題

(   ) 1. So far, we _____ nothing from him.
    (A) have been heard   (B) did not hear
    (C) have not heard   (D) have heard

(   ) 2. I _____ Taitung before.
    (A) will never visit   (B) have never visited
    (C) should never visited (D) never visit

(   ) 3. This dictionary _____ to her now.
    (A) belongs   (B) is belonging
    (C) is belonged   (D) has belonging

(   ) 4. When _____ from Germany?
    (A) you return   (B) you returned
    (C) have you returned   (D) did you return

(   ) 5. When Catherine _____ back from school, give her the
    message.
    (A) coming   (B) will come
    (C) is coming   (D) comes

(   ) 6. When I see Mr. Fox tonight, I _____ him of that.
    (A) reminded   (B) will remind
    (C) would remind   (D) have reminded

(   ) 7. Look! I bet that is your brother who _____ the street.
    (A) crosses   (B) is crossed
    (C) is crossing   (D) had crossed

(　　) 8. It will rain when the wind _____.
   (A) blows   (B) will blow
   (C) has been blown   (D) blowing

(　　) 9. I _____ it just now.
   (A) finish   (B) finished
   (C) will finished   (D) am finished

(　　) 10. Would you please give him this note the moment he
   _____?
   (A) arrives   (B) will arrive
   (C) will have arrived   (D) is going to arrive

(　　) 11. I _____ this pen a month ago.
   (A) had bought   (B) bought
   (C) have bought   (D) buy

(　　) 12. I _____ to Europe last year.
   (A) have gone   (B) went
   (C) have been   (D) would be

(　　) 13. You had better go back now before it _____ dark.
   (A) gets   (B) will get
   (C) will have   (D) got

(　　) 14. We'll go for a swim if it _____ fine tomorrow.
   (A) will be (B) is (C) was (D) were

(　　) 15. At present, Mr. Lee _____ another textbook.
   (A) writes   (B) wrote
   (C) is writing   (D) will write

(　　) 16. Copernicus discovered the earth _____ round.
    (A) is   (B) was
    (C) had been   (D) has been

(　　) 17. Since I _____ to you, I have had no trouble with
    my car.
    (A) last spoke   (B) was last spoken
    (C) had lost spoken   (D) been spoken last

(　　) 18. I do not know when my uncle _____ on me next.
    (A) calls   (B) will call
    (C) be calling   (D) be called

(　　) 19. I _____ that girl's name now.
    (A) remember   (B) am remembering
    (C) was remembered   (D) was remembering

(　　) 20. The instructor interrupted us as we _____ the
    last page.
    (A) finish   (B) were finishing
    (C) were finished   (D) have finished

(　　) 21. I wish you would tell me why you _____ her
    so much.
    (A) are liking   (B) like
    (C) will like   (D) had been liking

(　　) 22. The class will start when the last student _____.
    (A) arrives   (B) arrived
    (C) will arrive   (D) will have arrived

【精選模擬考題解答】

1. (**D**)	2. (**B**)	3. (**A**)	4. (**D**)	5. (**D**)	6. (**B**)
7. (**C**)	8. (**A**)	9. (**B**)	10. (**A**)	11. (**B**)	12. (**B**)
13. (**A**)	14. (**B**)	15. (**C**)	16. (**A**)	17. (**A**)	18. (**B**)
19. (**A**)	20. (**B**)	21. (**B**)	22. (**A**)		

【解析】

1. 到目前為止，我們沒有聽到他的消息。
   從以前發生到現在的事情，要用現在完成式。

3. belong「屬於」沒有進行式也沒有被動式，故選 (A) belongs。

4. when 引導的疑問句中，不可以用完成式，因為 when 指時間的一點，而完成式是「持續一段時間以後」的動作完成。

6. *remind* + 人 + *of* + 事「提醒某人某事」

9. *just now*「剛剛」，與過去式動詞連用。

10. 能請你在他到達時，給他這張便條嗎？
    表時間的副詞子句，用現在式代替未來式。

11. buy 是瞬間完成的動作，不可以用完成式，而且句中有 ago 時，動詞要用過去式。

14. 表條件的副詞子句，用現在式代替未來式。

15. *at present*「此刻；現在」與現在進行式連用。

16. 「哥白尼發現地球是圓的。」雖然 discovered 用過去式，但「地球是圓的」是不變的真理，故用現在式。

17. 自從上次和你談過以後，我的車就沒有問題了。

18. 本句 when 引導的是名詞子句，其未來的動作要用未來式。

19. 雖然本題有 now，但是 remember 沒有進行式，故用現在式。

20. 當我們正在完成最後一頁的時候，老師打斷了我們。
    instructor〔ɪnˈstrʌktɚ〕*n.* 教師
    interrupt〔͵ɪntəˈrʌpt〕*v.* 打斷

1. 時 式 (2) —— 進行式

1. 現在進行式的用法

1. 表示現在正在進行的動作

【例】 John *is watching* television now.
（約翰現在正在看電視。）

They *are working* on the farm.
（他們正在農場工作。）

2. 表示現在的習慣或反覆的行為

與 always, constantly, all the time, forever 等表連續的時間副詞連用，通常表示說話者認為不良習慣或表示不安、抱怨、讚賞等情緒。

【例】 She *is always smiling*.（她總是面帶微笑。）

He *is always complaining*.（他老是喜歡抱怨。）

He *is always finding* fault with me.
（他老是愛挑我的毛病。）

He *is bothering* me *every day*.（他天天都來煩我。）

<比較> He *bothers* me every day.【敘述事實】

3. 不完全不及物動詞的進行式表示「逐漸」「越來越…」的意思

【例】 Father *is getting* fat.（父親越來越胖了。）

The leaves *are turning* yellow.
（樹葉逐漸變黃了。）

Our house *is becoming* old.
（我們的屋子漸漸變舊了。）

4. 不用進行式的動詞

⑴ 表示狀態的動詞，沒有進行式。

be 是	need 需要	belong 屬於
represent 代表	lie 位於	want 缺乏
exist 存在	resemble 像	own 擁有
look 看起來	result 導致	depend on 依靠
have 有	seem 似乎	contain 包含
consist of 由~組成		

【例】 Nancy *is* happy. Betty *seems* happy, too.
（南西很快樂，貝蒂似乎也很快樂。）
She *resembles* her mother.（她長得像她媽媽。）
This box *contains* tins of fruit.
（這箱子裝有水果罐頭。）
Do you *have* any time for sport?（你有時間運動嗎？）

⑵ 表示心裡情感狀態的動詞，無進行式。

like 喜歡	know 知道	agree 同意
believe 相信	love 愛	hope 希望
notice 注意	forgive 原諒	hate 恨
wish 希望	forget 忘記	remember 記得
care 在意	mean 打算	desire 想要
respect 尊敬		

【例】 She *loves* swimming, but *hates* diving.
（她喜歡游泳，但討厭潛水。）
John *knows* my sister now.（約翰現在認識我妹妹了。）

<比較>
I *think* that you are right.（我想你是對的。）
I am *thinking of* going abroad.
（我正在考慮出國的事。）

(3) 感官動詞一般不用進行式。

see 看見	sound 聽	notice 注意到
hear 聽見	perceive 察覺到	taste 品嚐
feel 感到	smell 聞到	

【例】 Can you *see* that light over there?

（你看得到那邊的亮光嗎？）

I *feel* a sharp pain in my arm.

（我感到手臂一陣劇痛。）

☞ see 作其他意思解時（如遊覽、送行），可以有進行式。

【例】 They *are seeing* the sights of London.

（他們正在遊覽倫敦的名勝。）

I met a policeman when I *was seeing* her home.

（正當我送她回家的時候，我遇見一位警察。）

☞ **listen (to), watch, look (at)** 爲有意志的感官動詞，可以有進行式。

I *hear* her playing the piano.（我聽見她在彈鋼琴。）
I *am listening to* her playing the piano.
（我正在聽她彈鋼琴。）

What do you *see*?（你看到什麼？）
What *are* you *looking at*?（你正在看什麼？）

(4) 表一時性的動詞沒有進行式。

end 結束	admit 承認	refuse 拒絕	complete 完成
give 給	allow 允許	decide 決定	receive 收到
deny 否認	accept 接受	consent 同意	

【例】 He *admits* that he is wrong.（他承認他錯了。）

She *denies* that he is her boyfriend.

（她否認他是她的男朋友。）

2. 過去進行式的用法

1. 表示過去某一時候正在進行的動作

【例】 It *was raining* when we left home.

（我們離開家的時候，外面正在下雨。）

He *was writing* letters all afternoon.

（他整個下午都在寫信。）

☞ 通常連接詞 when 表短暫的、一定點的時間，其所引導的子句用過去簡單式。while 表繼續的一段時間，其所引導的子句用過去進行式。

> When the telephone *rang*, I was taking a shower.
> While I *was taking* a shower, the telephone rang.

2. 表過去反覆的動作

過去進行式與 always, continually, forever, all the time 等表連續的時間副詞連用，通常表示說話者認為不良的習慣。

【例】 They *were always missing* trains.

（他們老是趕不上火車。）

He *was constantly complaining* of something or other. （他常常抱怨這抱怨那的。）

In his youth, he *was always idling* away his time.

（他年輕的時候，總是遊手好閒。）

3. 未來進行式的用法

1. 表示未來某時將要進行的動作

【例】 We *will be traveling* on the train at this time tomorrow. （明天這時候，我們將正在搭乘火車旅遊。）

You *will be sleeping* when I come back.

（當我回來時，你將還在睡覺。）

If you go now, by the time you arrive there, he *will* still *be taking* an afternoon nap.

（如果你現在就去，當你到那裡的時候，他還在睡午覺呢！）

2. 表例行的或預定的未來行動

【例】 I'*ll be seeing* you next Saturday.

（我下星期六將會見到你。）

The Wangs *will be staying* with us again next year.

（明年王家將再來和我們小聚。）

We'*ll be gambling* in Las Vegas by this time next week. （下週的此刻我們將在拉斯維加斯豪賭。）

歷屆聯考試題

一、現在進行式

( ) 1. John is in his car. He is on his way to work. He
　　　　_____ to work.
　　　(A) was driving　　　(B) is driving
　　　(C) have driven　　　(D) drove
　　　(E) has driven

( ) 2. When are you _____ for Singapore?
　　　(A) leaving　　　(B) left　　　(C) being left

( ) 3. Listen! Someone _____ at the door!
　　　(A) knocked　　　(B) is knocking
　　　(C) has knocked　　　(D) will knock

_____ 4. The person who thinks he knows all the answers and
　　　is constantly forcing his ideas upon others and insist
　　　upon doing things in his own way is a pest. (改錯)

二、過去進行式

( ) 1. A letter _____ by him at nine o'clock yesterday.
　　　(A) wrote
　　　(B) were written
　　　(C) was being written
　　　(D) is being written

(   ) 2. Mother _____ when I got home.
      (A) is cooking   (B) was cooking
      (C) cooks   (D) has cooked
      (E) has been cooking

(   ) 3. When I _____ on the street, I met Mary.
      (A) walks   (B) had walked
      (C) walk   (D) was walking

【歷屆聯考試題解答】

一、 1. (**B**)   2. (**A**)   3. (**B**)   4. insist → insisting

二、 1. (**C**)   2. (**B**)   3. (**D**)

【解析】

一、 2. leave 屬於來去動詞，可以用進行式代替未來式，表示在最
       近的未來，即將發生。
       leave for 動身前往   Singapore 〔ˈsɪŋgəˌpor〕*n.* 新加坡

    3. 句中有 Listen!，Look! 時，要用現在進行式。
       knock at the door 敲門

    4. 認為自己知道所有的答案，不斷地將自己的意思強加在別
       人身上，並且堅持照自己的方式做事的人，是個討厭鬼。
       第二個 and 是連接 is forcing 和 (is) insisting 兩個動詞，
       故 insist 要改為 insisting。
       pest 〔pɛst〕*n.* 討厭的人或物

二、 1. 被動態的進行式：「be + being + 過去分詞」

    2. 「我到家的時候，母親正在煮飯。」主要子句用過去進行
       式，表示在過去某一時候正在進行的動作。

    3. 當我正在過馬路時，我遇見瑪麗。

精選模擬考題

( ) 1. At present, Mr. Wang _____ another novel.
    (A) writes   (B) wrote
    (C) is writing   (D) will write

( ) 2. The instructor interrupted us as we _____ the last page.
    (A) finish   (B) were finishing
    (C) were finished   (D) have finished

( ) 3. Mr. Smith _____ the Pacific by the time the news reaches him.
    (A) will cross   (B) shall cross
    (C) will be crossing   (D) will have been crossed

( ) 4. Look! I bet that is Jim who _____ the street.
    (A) crosses   (B) was crossed
    (C) is crossing   (D) has crossed

( ) 5. The taxi _____ very fast when it hit the bus.
    (A) had gone   (B) went
    (C) was gone   (D) was going

( ) 6. Bill _____ to the boss when I saw him.
    (A) talked   (B) was talked
    (C) was talking   (D) had talked

( ) 7. The storm began at half past ten while the class
_____ history.
(A) has studied   (B) was studying
(C) is studying   (D) had been studying

( ) 8. She _____ the piano when the guests arrived.
(A) played   (B) was playing
(C) had played   (D) have played

( ) 9. He _____ down on the bed.
(A) is still laying   (B) is still lying
(C) still laid   (D) is still lied

( ) 10. The boy _____ when his parents returned.
(A) sleeps   (B) slept
(C) is sleeping   (D) was sleeping

( ) 11. John _____ television now.
(A) is watching   (B) was watching
(C) watch   (D) see

( ) 12. He is always _____.
(A) complain   (B) complaining
(C) complained   (D) complains

( ) 13. He _____ for Japan the next day.
(A) leave   (B) leaved
(C) was leaving   (D) has left

(　) 14. Listen! Someone _____ the bell.

      (A) rings   (B) ringing

      (C) is ringing   (D) ring

(　) 15. I came across Jane while I _____ along the river.

      (A) have walked   (B) walk

      (C) am walking   (D) was walking

(　) 16. For the time being, Mr. Wang _____ another textbook.

      (A) writes   (B) wrote

      (C) is writing   (D) will write

【精選模擬考題解答】

1. (**C**)   2. (**B**)   3. (**C**)   4. (**C**)   5. (**D**)   6. (**C**)

7. (**B**)   8. (**B**)   9. (**B**)   10. (**D**)   11. (**A**)   12. (**B**)

13. (**C**)   14. (**C**)   15. (**D**)   16. (**C**)

【解析】

3. 史密斯先生接獲該消息時，將正在橫渡太平洋。

5. 計程車撞上巴士時，開得非常快。

   表過去某一時候正在進行的動作，用過去進行式。

7. 暴風雨在十點半的時候開始，當時學生們正在唸歷史。

9. lie〔laɪ〕*v.* 躺（過去式 *lay*；過去分詞 *lain*；現在分詞 *lying*）

   lay〔le〕*v.* 放置（過去式 *laid*；過去分詞 *laid*；現在分詞 *lying*）

12. 「他老是在抱怨。」　complain〔kəmˈplen〕*v.* 抱怨

15. *come across* 偶然遇到

16. *for the time being*「目前；暫時」與現在進行式連用。

1. 時 式 (3) —— 完成式

1. 現在完成式：have〔has〕+ p.p.

<u>1. 現在完成式的用法</u>

(1) 表現在剛剛完成之動作，常附有副詞，如：

now 現在	just 剛剛	already 已經
this week 本週	yet 尚（未）	lately 最近
recently 最近	this afternoon 今天下午	

【例】 I *have just written* a letter. （我剛剛寫好一封信。）

Have you *finished* your work *yet*?

（你的工作做完了沒？）

Yes, I *have already finished* it.

（是的，我已經做完了。）

Yes, I *already have*.

Has he *come yet*? （他來了沒？）

No, he *has* not *come yet*. （不，他還沒來。）

No, not *yet*. （不，還沒。）

(2) 表過去某時發生的動作，其結果影響到現在，或其狀態持續到現在。

【例】 I *have learned* the lesson by heart.

（我已把這一課背下來了。）

I *have caught* a cold. （我感冒了。）

He *has gone* to Australia. （他去澳洲了。）

⑶ 表過去某時到現在的經驗，常和 ever, never, in one's life
（在～一生中），once（一度），twice（兩次）等副詞連用。

【例】 I *have been* to Miami several times.

（我到過邁阿密好幾次。）

Have you *ever seen* a whale? — No, I *never* have.

（你看過鯨魚嗎？ — 不，我從未看過。）

☞ 口語中，可用過去式的「Did you ever ＋ 原形 V.?」及
「I never ＋ 過去式」表示經驗。

【例】 *Did* you *ever see* a giraffe?（你看過長頸鹿嗎？）

⑷ 表過去持續到現在的動作或狀態，常與 How long 或 for, since
所引導的副詞片語連用。

【例】 I *have known* him *for fifteen years*.

（我已經認識他十五年了。）

Mother *has been* sick *since last Monday*.

（媽媽自從上星期一就一直病到現在。）

How long have you *been waiting* here?

（你已經在這裡等多久了？）

---

2. 現在完成式用法上應注意事項

⑴ 不與表過去確定時間的副詞連用，如：yesterday, last month
〔year, Sunday〕,～ago, then, in 1986 等。

> He *has come* to Taipei *ten years ago*.（誤）
> He *came* to Taiwan *ten years ago*.（正）

⑵ 現在完成式不與疑問副詞 **when** 連用。

> *When have* you *seen* him?（誤）
> *When did* you *see* him?（正）— I *saw* him *yesterday*.

(3) 現在完成式不與 **just now** 連用，just now = a moment ago（剛剛；剛才）動詞要用過去式。

> He *has just returned* home. （誤）
> He *returned* home *just now*. （正）

(4)
> **have been**「曾經去過」表示經驗。
> **have gone**「已經去了…」表示動作的完成。

【例】 I *have been to* the station to see my uncle off.
（我到過車站給舅舅送行了。）

Have you *ever been to* 〔*in*〕 New York?
（你曾經去過〔住過〕紐約嗎？）

He *has gone* to France. （他已經去法國了。）

2. 過去完成式：had + p.p.

> 1. 過去完成式的用法

(1) 表示在過去某時之前**完成的動作、結果**。

【例】 I *had* just *written* a letter when he *came* back.
（當他回來時，我剛剛寫完一封信。）

He *had gone* fishing when I *visited* him.
（當我去拜訪他時，他已經去釣魚了。）

(2) 表示過去某時已有或未有的**經驗**。

【例】 I *recognized* him at once, as I *had seen* him before.
（因為以前曾見過他，我立刻認出他來。）

He *had* never *spoken* to a foreigner *before that time*.
（在那之前，他從未和外國人講過話。）

⑶ 表示在過去某時之前**繼續的動作**或**狀態**。

【例】 We **had been** there for ten years when the war *broke* out. (當戰爭爆發時，我們已在那裡住了十年。)

I **had known** her for six years when she *left* our town for Tainan.

（當她離開本鎮前往台南時，我已經認識她六年了。）

I **had been studying** for half an hour when my mother *called* me. (當媽媽叫我時，我已經讀了半小時的書。)

⑷ 表示過去未實現的希望或計劃，常用下列動詞：hope, expect, suppose, intend, mean, think, want。

【例】 I **had intended** to call on you yesterday.

(= I intended to call on you yesterday, *but I couldn't*.)

（我本來打算昨天去看你。）

⑸ 表過去兩個不同時間發生的動作、狀態，**先發生的用過去完成式，後發生的用過去簡單式。**

【例】 He *said* that he **had bought** a violin a few days before. （他說他幾天前買了一把小提琴。）

He *sent* me a picture that he **had taken**. （他寄給我一張他照的相片。）

We *moved* into the house which our father **had built**. （我們搬進爸爸蓋的房子。）

| 2. 使用過去完成式應注意事項 |

⑴ 敘述歷史事實時，不用過去完成式，只用過去式。

【例】 Our teacher told us Columbus $\begin{cases} had\ discovered\ (誤) \\ discovered\ (正) \end{cases}$ America in 1492.

（老師告訴我們哥倫布於 1492 年發現美洲。）

⑵ before, after 引導的副詞子句，因為已表示出時間先後，可用
過去式代替過去完成式。

【例】 After she (*had*) *left* the room, the thief came in.
（她離開房間後，小偷進來了。）

We (*had*) *arrived* home before it rained.
（下雨之前，我們已回到家了。）

3. 未來完成式：will〔shall〕+ have + p.p.

1. 未來完成式的用法

⑴ 表未來某時之前，或另一未來動作前，已完成之動作。

【例】 He *will have reached* New York *by five this evening*.
（今天傍晚五點前，他將已經到達紐約。）

He *will have reached* home *before the rain sets in*.
（在下雨之前，他將已經到家了。）

⑵ 敘述到未來某時已存在的經驗。

【例】 *If I visit London again, I'll have been* there three
times.（如果我再次參觀倫敦，我就去過那裡三次了。）

⑶ 敘述某事持續到未來某時為止，已經有若干時間了。

【例】 I *will have lived* in Taichung *for ten years next
January*.（到明年一月，我在台中就住滿十年了。）

In ten more minutes the baby *will have been sleeping*
a full hour.（再過十分鐘，小寶寶就睡了整整一個小時了。）

2. will have + p.p.表用以推測現在

【例】 Mother *will have received* my letter by now.
（媽媽現在可能已經收到我的信了。）

He *will have heard* that Elizabeth is going to get
married.（他可能已經聽說伊莉莎白將要結婚了。）

歷屆聯考試題

一、現在完成式

( )　1. So far, we _____ a reply.
　　(A) did have not　　　(B) had not
　　(C) have not had　　　(D) got not have

( )　2. All the other boys _____ for you since noon.
　　(A) waited　　　　　　(B) had waited
　　(C) had been waiting　(D) have been waiting

( )　3. I _____ her these two weeks.
　　(A) didn't see　　　　(B) saw
　　(C) haven't seen　　　(D) had seen

( )　4. Tickets to the basketball game _____ out since last Sunday.
　　(A) were sold　　　　(B) have been sold
　　(C) sold　　　　　　 (D) have sold

( )　5. He _____ nothing since yesterday morning.
　　(A) was eaten　　　　(B) ate
　　(C) has eaten　　　　(D) eats

( )　6. My father _____ to the United States many times.
　　(A) is going　　　　 (B) has gone
　　(C) has been　　　　 (D) was

(   ) 7. Education has _____ him into a different person.

    (A) transform   (B) transforming

    (C) transformed   (D) to be transform

(   ) 8. The electronic computer, the marvel of the machine age, has been in use only _____ 1946.

    (A) in   (B) at   (C) since   (D) for

(   ) 9. 你曾經去過香港嗎？

    Have you _____ _____ to Hongkong before?

(   ) 10. What _____ lately?

    (A) have you been doing

    (B) are you doing

    (C) do you do

    (D) are you going to do

二、過去完成式

(   ) 1. Before I could shake hands with him, he _____ the room.

    (A) leaved   (B) was leaving

    (C) would leave   (D) had left

(   ) 2. John _____ a lot about Jane before he met her.

    (A) was heard   (B) had heard

    (C) has heard   (D) has been hearing

    (E) had been heard

(　) 3. Our visit to Singapore last month was the first time we
　　　 _____ abroad.
　　　 (A) are travelling　　　 (B) travel
　　　 (C) had travelled　　　 (D) were to travel

(　) 4. He said he _____ me three years before.
　　　 (A) was met　　　 (B) had met
　　　 (C) has met　　　 (D) had been meeting

(　) 5. After he _____ his work, he went to bed.
　　　 (A) has finished　　　 (B) had finished
　　　 (C) had been finishing　 (D) had been finished

(　) 6. I knew right away there _____ been a mistake.
　　　 (A) would　　　 (B) had
　　　 (C) have　　　 (D) is

____ 7. He had no sooner reached there _____ it began to rain.

____ 8. I told <u>him</u> that I <u>finished</u> <u>the</u> work just <u>an</u> hour before.
　　　　　 (A)　　　　 (B)　 (C)　　　　 (D)　　 （改錯）

(　) 9. We went to the ball last night. Before that, we _____
　　　 to a party.
　　　 (A) go　　　 (B) gone
　　　 (C) have gone　　　 (D) had gone

____ 10. He had _____ (ride) all the way from Philadelphia.

三、未來完成式

( ) 1. Before you come back, the building _____.
    (A) will finish
    (B) shall be finish
    (C) will have been finished
    (D) shall has been finished

( ) 2. The train _____ when you reach the train station.
    (A) had left   (B) will have left
    (C) has left   (D) has been left
    (E) left

____ 3. By tomorrow night he _____ (finish) his work.

____ 4. Winds of hurricane force will have _____ (hit) the coast by dawn.

【歷屆聯考試題解答】

一、 1.(**C**)   2.(**D**)   3.(**C**)   4.(**B**)   5.(**C**)
    6.(**C**)   7.(**C**)   8.(**C**)   9. ever been   10.(**A**)

二、 1.(**D**)   2.(**B**)   3.(**C**)   4.(**B**)   5.(**B**)
    6.(**B**)   7. than/when   8.(**B**) → had finished
    9.(**D**)   10. ridden

三、 1.(**C**)   2.(**B**)   3. will have finished   4. hit

【解析】

一、 1. 到目前為止，我們還沒得到答覆。
　　　　過去發生的動作持續到現在，用現在完成式。

　　 3. these two weeks「這兩星期以來」與現在完成式連用。

　　 4. *sell out* 賣光

　　 7. 教育已經把他改造成另外一個人了。
　　　　transform A *into* B 把 A 變成 B

　　 8. 電腦 —— 機器時代的奇蹟 —— 從一九四六年一直使用到現在。

二、 1. *shake hands with*～　和～握手

　　 6. *right away* 立刻

　　 7. *no sooner* + 過去完成式 + *than* + 過去式「一～就…」

　　 9. 「昨天晚上我們參加一個舞會。在此之前，我們已參加了一個宴會。」　　ball〔bɔl〕*n.* 舞會

　　 10. *all the way* 老遠地
　　　　Philadelphia〔ˌfɪləˈdɛlfjə〕*n.* 費城

三、 1. 表示未來某時之前預定會完成的動作，要用未來完成式。
　　　　before you come back 是表時間的副詞子句，動詞用現在式代替未來式。

　　 4. 強烈的颶風在黎明之前將會侵襲海岸。
　　　　hurricane〔ˈhɜ˞ɪˌken〕*n.* 颶風

精選模擬考題

( ) 1. I _____ here since five o'clock.
   (A) am
   (B) have been
   (C) were
   (D) shall be

( ) 2. He _____ her a long time before he finally got married to her.
   (A) knows
   (B) was knowing
   (C) has known
   (D) had known

( ) 3. I _____ my keys. I cannot remember where I last saw them.
   (A) lose
   (B) loose
   (C) have lost
   (D) had lost

( ) 4. Up to now I _____ the plays of Shakespeare three times.
   (A) read
   (B) have been reading
   (C) have read
   (D) had read

( ) 5. I _____ reading the book.
   (A) just finish
   (B) have just finished
   (C) just finishing
   (D) was just finished

( ) 6. By next September she _____ the piano for three years.
   (A) will have been studying
   (B) will have study
   (C) has studied
   (D) had studied

(　　) 7. The house was smaller than he ＿＿＿＿＿ at first.

      (A) has thought   (B) had thought

      (C) was thinking   (D) thinks

(　　) 8. They ＿＿＿＿＿ for ten years.

      (A) marry   (B) married

      (C) have married   (D) have been married

(　　) 9. It's sure to rain. We ＿＿＿＿＿ a drop over a month.

      (A) have not   (B) had not

      (C) had not have   (D) have not had

(　　) 10. I was delighted to see several old friends whom I

      ＿＿＿＿＿ for five years.

      (A) don't see   (B) did not see

      (C) have not seen   (D) had not seen

(　　) 11. Two years ＿＿＿＿＿ since she came to live here.

      (A) have passed   (B) passed

      (C) were passed   (D) have past

(　　) 12. I ＿＿＿＿＿ reading for an hour when he came in.

      (A) was   (B) have been

      (C) had been   (D) will be

(　　) 13. We ＿＿＿＿＿ here since the beginning of the month.

      (A) are   (B) shall be

      (C) have been   (D) were being

(　) 14. He will return your book when he _____ it.

    (A) reads   (B) has read

    (C) read   (D) will read

(　) 15. I liked the book that I _____ from you.

    (A) borrow   (B) have borrowed

    (C) had borrowed   (D) will have borrowed

(　) 16. _____ you ever _____ a lion?

    (A) Do, see   (B) Did, seen

    (C) Have, seen   (D) Had, see

(　) 17. She _____ piano lessons since she was a child.

    (A) takes   (B) took

    (C) has taken   (D) is taken

(　) 18. Five and a half years _____ since we moved to this town.

    (A) passes   (B) passed

    (C) have passed   (D) is passed

(　) 19. I _____ English for more than three years.

    (A) was studied   (B) study

    (C) had studying   (D) have been studying

(　) 20. I _____ him since then.

    (A) know   (B) knew

    (C) have known   (D) had know

(　　) 21. I finished reading the book I ＿＿＿＿ from him.

      (A) borrow　　　　　(B) have borrowed

      (C) had borrowed　　(D) were borrowing

(　　) 22. He ＿＿＿＿ ill for a few days when his family called a doctor.

      (A) is　　　　　　　(B) was

      (C) has been　　　　(D) had been

(　　) 23. Please wait till I ＿＿＿＿ writing this last paragraph.

      (A) finished　　　　(B) have finished

      (C) had finished　　(D) will have finished

(　　) 24. He ＿＿＿＿ from influenza for a week.

      (A) suffer　　　　　(B) suffering

      (C) was suffered　　(D) has been suffering

(　　) 25. I ＿＿＿＿ here once or twice before.

      (A) am　　　　　　　(B) have been

      (C) went　　　　　　(D) have gone

(　　) 26. I lent him the book I ＿＿＿＿ the day before.

      (A) was buying　　　(B) have bought

      (C) had bought　　　(D) have been buying

(　　) 27. He said that the step I ＿＿＿＿ was a dangerous one.

      (A) take　　　　　　(B) taken

      (C) was taken　　　　(D) had taken

(   ) 28. We _____ much rain this year.

    (A) have   (B) had have

    (C) have had   (D) will having

(   ) 29. He _____ nothing before he saw me.

    (A) do   (B) has done

    (C) have done   (D) had done

(   ) 30. The road was muddy as it _____ the day before.

    (A) rained   (B) had rained

    (C) was raining   (D) has rained

(   ) 31. The other day I met a friend of mine whom I _____ for a long time.

    (A) did not see   (B) have not seen

    (C) had not seen   (D) do not see

(   ) 32. _____ him lately?

    (A) Do you see   (B) Are you seeing

    (C) Have you seen   (D) Had you see

(   ) 33. I _____ to Hawaii several times.

    (A) was   (B) have been

    (C) gone   (D) was gone

(   ) 34. My grandfather _____ these four years.

    (A) was dead   (B) died

    (C) has died   (D) has been dead

(　) 35. No sooner _____ gone to bed than a telegram was
brought in.
(A) has he　　　　　(B) did he
(C) had he　　　　　(D) he had

(　) 36. Almost everyone _____ for home by the time we
arrived.
(A) leaves　　　　　(B) left
(C) has left　　　　　(D) had left

(　) 37. So far, we _____ nothing from him.
(A) have been heard　(B) did not hear
(C) have not heard　　(D) have heard

(　) 38. Education has _____ him into a different person.
(A) transform　　　　(B) transforming
(C) transformed　　　(D) to be transform

【精選模擬考題解答】

1. (**B**)	2. (**D**)	3. (**C**)	4. (**C**)	5. (**B**)	6. (**A**)
7. (**B**)	8. (**D**)	9. (**D**)	10. (**D**)	11. (**A**)	12. (**C**)
13. (**C**)	14. (**B**)	15. (**C**)	16. (**C**)	17. (**C**)	18. (**C**)
19. (**D**)	20. (**C**)	21. (**C**)	22. (**D**)	23. (**B**)	24. (**D**)
25. (**B**)	26. (**C**)	27. (**D**)	28. (**C**)	29. (**D**)	30. (**B**)
31. (**C**)	32. (**C**)	33. (**B**)	34 (**D**)	35. (**C**)	36. (**D**)
37. (**D**)	38. (**C**)				

【解析】

1. since five o'clock「從五點鐘開始」，要用現在完成式。

2. 在過去某動作之前發生的持續性動作，要用過去完成式。

4. 至今，我已經讀過莎士比亞的劇作三次。

5. just（剛剛；剛才）與現在完成式連用。

6. 本題 (B) 錯，應改爲 will have studied；某動作會持續到未來某時，並暗示該動作在未來某時可能還在繼續進行時，用未來完成進行式，故選 (A)。

8. 副詞片語「for + 一段時間」，與現在完成式連用。本題選 (C) 或 (D) 都可以，因爲 marry 當主動或被動的意義相同。

9. 一定會下雨的，已經整整一個月沒下一滴雨了。
   be sure to + *V.* 一定會~

11. pass 的過去式和過去分詞是 passed；past（經過）是介系詞。

23. 請等到我把最後這一段寫完。
    paragraph〔'pærə,græf〕*n.*（文章的）段落

24. influenza〔,ɪnflʊ'ɛnzə〕*n.* 流行性感冒（= *flu*）

25. have been「曾經去過」，表示經驗。
    once or twice 一次或兩次

30. the day before「（過去某時的）前一天」，與過去完成式連用。

31. *the other day* 前幾天

2. 語 態

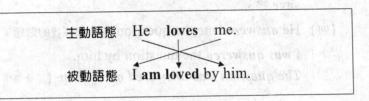

主動語態　He **loves** me.

被動語態　I **am loved** by him.

1. 敘述句被動語態的作法

1. 完全及物動詞 S + V + O 時

> My uncle *made* this chair yesterday.
> （我舅舅昨天做了這把椅子。）
> This chair *was made* by my uncle yesterday.

> Many farmers *use* this machine.
> （許多農夫使用這種機器。）
> This machine *is used* by many farmers.

2. S + V + IO（間接受詞）+ DO（直接受詞）時

因為有兩類受詞，故下列動詞可有兩種被動語態：give, leave, pay, show, teach, tell, lend, offer, award 等。

> The teacher *told* us a story.（老師講故事給我們聽。）
> We *were told* a story by the teacher.
> A story *was told* (to) us by the teacher.

☞ 下列動詞通常以**直接受詞**，做為被動語態的主詞：buy, bring, do, make, pass, sell, send, write, sing 等。

> Father *bought* me a watch.（爸爸買了一只錶給我。）
> A watch *was bought* for me by Father.
> *I was bought a watch by Father.*【不合習慣】

☞ 下列動詞通常以間接受詞，做爲被動語態的主詞：
answer, deny（否認），envy（嫉妒），refuse,
save 等。

【例】 He *answered* me the question.（他回答我的問題。）

⎰ I *was answered* the question by him.
⎱ *The question was answered me by him.*【不合習慣】

3. S＋V＋O＋C（受詞補語）

⎰ He *keeps* the room clean.（他保持房間的整潔。）
⎱ The room *is kept* clean by him.

⎰ We *saw* him *go out*.（我們看到他出去了。）
⎱ He *was seen* to go out.

⎰ They *made* him *come* home early.（他們讓他早回家。）
⎱ He *was made to come* home early.

☞ 感官動詞及使役動詞改爲被動時，**做補語的不定詞不可**
省略 to。

4. 應特別注意的被動語態

(1) 有助動詞的被動語態

⎰ Mary *will invite* him to the party.
⎱ （瑪麗將邀請他參加宴會。）
　 He *will be invited* to the party by Mary.

⎰ You *must do* this work.（你必須做這工作。）
⎱ This work *must be done* by you.

⎰ The storm *has blown* down the houses.
⎱ （暴風雨把房子吹垮了。）
　 The houses *have been blown* down by the storm.

(2) 有疑問詞的被動語態

> *What **did** he **say**?*（他說了什麼？）
> *What **was said** by him?*

> *When **does** Tom **open** the door?*
> （湯姆什麼時候打開門的？）
> *When **is** the door **opened** by Tom?*

> *Who **built** the house?*（這房子是誰蓋的？）
> *By whom **was** the house **built**?*

(3) 命令句形式的被動語態

> ***Do** it at once.*（馬上就做。）
> ***Let it be done** at once.*

(4) 有進行式的被動語態：be + being + 過去分詞

> The famous artist *is painting* her portrait.
> （這位有名的畫家正在畫她的畫像。）
> Her portrait *is being painted* by the famous artist.

> The students *were discussing* the problem.
> （學生們正在討論這個問題。）
> The problem *was being discussed* by the students.

(5) 有動詞片語的被動語態

> Everybody *laughed at* him.（人人都嘲笑他。）
> He *was laughed at* by everybody.

> They will *take care of* her.（他們會照顧她。）
> She will *be taken care of* by them.

> A foreigner *spoke to* me.（一個外國人對我說話。）
> I *was spoken to* by a foreigner.

(6) 有 They say that…的被動語態

> *They say that* he was a writer. (據說他是位作家。)
> *It is said that* he was a writer.
> (= *He* is said to *have been* a writer.)

> *They report that* the singer will come to Taiwan.
> (據報導這位歌星將來台灣。)
> *It is reported that* the singer will come to Taiwan.

2. by 的用法

| 1. 被動語態省略 by 的場合 |

(1) 主動語態的主詞為「一般人」時。

> We *can see* stars at night. (晚上看得到星星。)
> Stars *can be seen* at night.

> They [People] *speak* English and French in Canada.
> English and French *are spoken* in Canada.
> (在加拿大人們講英文和法文。)

(2) 主動語態的主詞太廣泛，不容易表達。

【例】 Many people *were killed* in the war.
(戰爭期間有許多人死亡。)

(3) 主動語態的主詞人盡皆知，不必再加以說明。

【例】 Mr. White *was elected* our mayor.
(懷特先生被選為本市市長。)

Was Chinese food served at that restaurant?
(那間餐廳供應中國菜嗎？)

2. 通常非行爲者，或無意志的被動語態，不用 by

> Snow *covered* the hills. (雪覆蓋在這座山上。)
> The hills *were covered with* snow.

> The news *surprised* me. (這消息使我吃驚。)
> I *was surprised at* the news.

> His new camera *pleased* the boy.
> (這台新相機使這男孩很高興。)
> The boy *was pleased with* his new camera.

3. 被動語態不用 by 的慣用法

【例】 The fact *is known to* everybody. (大家都知道這件事實。)

<比較> A tree *is known by* its fruit. (樹可以由其果實辨認出來。)

【例】 He *is interested in* music. (他對音樂有興趣。)

I *am satisfied with* your explanation.
(我對你的解釋感到滿意。)

I *was ashamed of* my ignorance.
(我爲自己的無知感到可恥。)

I *was born* in 1960. (我出生於一九六〇年。)

<比較> Cain *was borne* by Eve. (該隱爲夏娃所生。)

4. 被動語態的注意要點

(1) 被動語態可以表示動作，也可以表示狀態，究竟表示何種意義，
要視前後文關係來判斷。

> a. The door *was shut* at six o'clock. (六點關門。)【動作】
> b. The door *was shut* all day. (這門整天關著。)【狀態】

> a. My house *is painted* every three years. 【動作】
> (我的房子每三年油漆一次。)
> b. My house *is painted* white. (我的房子被漆成白色。)【狀態】

⑵ **get, become, grow** + **過去分詞**時，表示「轉變」。

【例】 Our house *gets painted* every three years.
（我們的房子每三年油漆一次。）

I *got acquainted* with him.（我認識了他。）
At last the truth *became known*.（最後終於真相大白。）
He *grew tired* of his quiet life.（他厭倦了平靜的生活。）

⑶ 有些進行式，形式上雖為主動，但包含被動的意思。

【例】 The article *is printing* (= *is being printed*).
（這篇文章正在列印中。）

What *is cooking* (= *is being cooked*) in the kitchen?
（廚房裡正在做什麼菜？）

⑷ 有些及物動詞做不及物動詞用時，形式為主動，但表被動意義，
如：sell, catch, lock, cut, read, wear, wash 等。

【例】 This book *sells* well.（這本書銷路很好。）
The book *reads* well.（這本書讀起來很有趣。）
This cloth will *wear* for years.
（這塊布料可以穿上好幾年。）

This suitcase won't *lock*.（這手提箱鎖不起來。）
This dress *washes* well.（這件衣服很好洗。）

⑸ **have, get** + **受詞** + **過去分詞**

【例】 He *had* his watch *fixed*.（他把錶拿去修理了。）
I *got* my photograph *taken*.（我去照相了。）

☞ have 在提及主詞本身的意志時，為使役動詞；無關主詞
的意志時，表示被動。

　He *had* his watch *fixed*.【使役】
　She *had* her purse *stolen*.（她的錢包被偷了。）【被動】

歷屆聯考試題

一、被動語態的用法

( ) 1. The internal operations of the machine _____ processing.
    (A) is calling
    (B) are calling
    (C) are called
    (D) is called

( ) 2. After the fight, a caretaker found that a young man _____ so he telephoned for an ambulance immediately.
    (A) who was injured
    (B) who had been injured
    (C) seriously injured
    (D) was seriously injured

( ) 3. Are we _____ watched?
    (A) being
    (B) be
    (C) have
    (D) having

( ) 4. Chinese and English are the two languages that _____ in all the high schools here in Taiwan.
    (A) are teaching
    (B) are taught
    (C) will teach
    (D) will be teaching

( ) 5. A modern oil refinery could not function if it _____ by humans.
    (A) was controlled
    (B) is controlled
    (C) were controlled
    (D) were controled
    (E) was controled

( ) 6. The fusion torch might save mankind from _____ in its own trash.
    (A) burying   (B) being bury
    (C) having buried   (D) being buried
    (E) having bury

( ) 7. He was made _____ it.
    (A) do   (B) to do   (C) did   (D) done

( ) 8. He was heard _____. (複選)
    (A) to sing   (B) sing
    (C) song   (D) singing

( ) 9. <u>During</u> a formal wedding party, the bride, who <u>is leaded</u>
      (A)   (B)
by the maid of honor, <u>wears</u> a bridal gown and make-up.
                (C)   (改錯)

( ) 10. Once clay _____, it can be converted by firing into a hard and enduring material.
    (A) shape   (B) has been shaped
    (C) has shaped   (D) has been shaping
    (E) shaped

____ 11. Oil is the basis of the petroleum industry, and is often <u>finding</u> with natural gas and with underground water.
                                           (改錯)

____ 12. A long time ago, farming <u>do</u> with the help of simple tools and animals. (改錯)

二、被動語態應注意要點

(　) 1. This house _____ to be haunted but nobody
believes it is now.
(A) was once believed
(B) once believed
(C) has once been believed
(D) had once been believe

(　) 2. Water _____ to put out a forest fire because water
is not available most of the time.
(A) can be used (B) is used
(C) can seldom be used (D) using

(　) 3. I found out that the letter _____ to the wrong address.
(A) had sent (B) was sending
(C) had been sent (D) sent
(E) has sent

(　) 4. Who wrote this book? = _____?
(A) By whom was this book written
(B) By whom this book is written
(C) Who is the author of this book
(D) Who is the owner of this book

(　) 5. I didn't enjoy the party because I _____.
(A) was boring (B) bore
(C) was bored (D) boring
(E) am boring

(   ) 6. This distinction between specialty shops and
department stores should _____.

(A) understands   (B) be understood

(C) being understood   (D) understand

三、不用 by 的被動語態

(   ) 1. I am not at all _____ about the news.

(A) excitement   (B) exciting

(C) excitedly   (D) excited

_____ 2. We were surprised _____ the news.

_____ 3. At last the watch was _____ (find).

_____ 4. The handle of the spoon had been _____ (grind) to
a fine point.

_____ 5. Mr. Kelchum had been _____ (bind) hand and foot
and thrown into a closet.

_____ 6. Peasants had been _____ (grind) under the heel
of the czar for centuries.

(   ) 7. We were greatly _____ by his speech.

(A) impressed   (B) impressing

(C) impressive   (D) impression

【歷屆聯考試題解答】

一、　1. (**C**)　　2. (**D**)　　3. (**A**)　　4. (**B**)　　5. (**C**)

　　　6. (**D**)　　7. (**B**)　　8. (**A、D**)　9. (**B**) → is led

　　　10. (**B**)　11. found　12. was done

二、　1. (**A**)　　2. (**C**)　　3. (**C**)　　4. (**A、C**)

　　　5. (**C**)　　6. (**B**)

三、　1. (**D**)　　2. at/by　　3. found　　4. ground

　　　5. bound　　6. ground　　7. (**A**)

【解析】

一、　1. 本句的真正主詞爲 operations，故用複數動詞＋過去分詞

　　　2. 在一場打鬥之後，管理員發現一名年輕男子傷得很重，
所以他立刻去打電話叫救護車。
caretaker〔'kɛr,tekɚ〕*n.* 管理員
ambulance〔'æmbjələns〕*n.* 救護車

　　　5. 假如由人類控制，現代化的煉油廠就無法產生作用。
本句爲與現在事實相反的假設語氣，故 be 動詞用 were，
又 control 的過去分詞爲 controlled。

　　　6. 「融解噴火器可能使人類免於被自己所製造的垃圾掩
埋掉。」　　 *save* A *from* B 　使 A 免於 B

　　　7. 使役〔感官〕動詞改爲被動時，做補語的不定詞不可省
略 to。

　　　8. 感官動詞改爲被動時，做補語的現在分詞不變；但不定
詞不可省略 to。

　　　10. 「一旦黏土已經成形，就可以經由火烤，而轉化成堅固、
持久的物質。」　　 *convert* A *into* B 　把 A 轉化成 B
enduring〔ɪn'djurɪŋ〕*adj.* 持久的

11. 石油是石化工業的基礎，它常和天然氣、地下水一起
被發現。
petroleum〔pə'trolɪəm〕*n.* 石油

二、 1. 這棟房子，曾被認為鬧鬼，但現在沒人如此認為了。
haunted〔'hɔntɪd〕*adj.* 鬧鬼的

2. 水很少被用來撲滅森林大火，因為大部分的時間都沒
有水。
put out 撲滅　　available〔ə'veləbḷ〕*adj.* 可獲得的

3. 本題名詞子句的主詞為 the letter，以物為主詞，一般
須用被動語態。

5. bored（感到無聊的）修飾人，boring（無聊的）修飾物。

6. 專賣店和百貨公司的差別，應該能被理解。
distinction〔dɪ'stɪŋkʃən〕*n.* 差別
specialty shop 專賣店

三、 1. 人＋ ***be excited about*** ＋物「某人對某物感到興奮」

2. ***be surprised at*** 對～感到驚訝

4. 湯匙的柄已經被磨成一個小點了。
grind〔graɪnd〕*v.* 研磨；磨碎
（過去式及過去分詞為 ***ground***）

5. 克爾漢先生手腳被綑綁，並丟到櫥櫃裡。
bind〔baɪnd〕*v.* 綑綁（過去式及過去分詞為 ***bound***〔baʊnd〕）

6. 幾世紀以來，農夫一直在專制君主的蹂躪下。
peasant〔'pɛznt〕*n.* 農夫（通常僅用於歐洲）
under the heel of ～ 在～的蹂躪下
czar〔zɑr〕*n.* 沙皇

7. ***be impressed by*** 對～印象深刻

精選模擬考題

(　) 1. My sister _____ her friend's cousin last month.
   (A) married to
   (B) married with
   (C) was married to
   (D) was married with

(　) 2. You will be taken good care _____.
   (A) by　　(B) of　　(C) beyond　　(D) from

(　) 3. I was made _____ for over an hour.
   (A) wait　(B) to wait　(C) waiting　(D) waited

(　) 4. Let this poem _____ by heart.
   (A) be learned
   (B) learn
   (C) have learned
   (D) learning

(　) 5. You _____ today.
   (A) finely dress
   (B) are finely dressed
   (C) are finely dressing
   (D) are finely dress

(　) 6. That book _____ well.
   (A) sells
   (B) is sold
   (C) selling
   (D) will selling

(　) 7. The children will _____ while she is away.
   (A) take care of
   (B) be taken care
   (C) be taken care of
   (D) be care of

(　) 8. We _____ when Joe came early.
　　　　(A) had surprised　　(B) were surprising
　　　　(C) surprised　　　　(D) were surprised

(　) 9. These machines ought _____ once a year.
　　　　(A) to be inspected　(B) to inspect
　　　　(C) be inspected　　　(D) inspect

(　) 10. Books in the Reference Library must not
　　　　_____ away.
　　　　(A) take　(B) taken　(C) to take　(D) be taken

(　) 11. Our principal is _____ the cause of education.
　　　　(A) devoting to　　　(B) devoted on
　　　　(C) devoted to　　　　(D) devoting on

(　) 12. You may be _____ $ 30 for not having equipped your
　　　　bicycle with a light.
　　　　(A) fine　(B) fined　(C) fining　(D) found

(　) 13. I believe the house was deliberately _____.
　　　　(A) set fire　　　　　(B) set to fire
　　　　(C) set on fire　　　　(D) set fire off

(　) 14. When he heard the bad news, he _____.
　　　　(A) was disappointed
　　　　(B) disappointed
　　　　(C) was disappointing
　　　　(D) was being disappointed

(　) 15. The doctor was _____ at once.
  (A) send   (B) sent by
  (C) sent for   (D) send for

(　) 16. He is so famous that he is _____ everybody.
  (A) known to   (B) known by
  (C) known with   (D) known

(　) 17. The teachers were _____ with the students' progress.
  (A) pleased   (B) pleasing
  (C) pleasant   (D) pleasure

(　) 18. The road _____ snow.
  (A) was covered by (B) was covered with
  (C) covered   (D) covered with

(　) 19. He cannot bear _____.
  (A) to being laughed (B) to be laughing
  (C) being laughed at (D) to being laughed at

(　) 20. He was made _____ it.
  (A) do (B) to do (C) doing (D) did

(　) 21. All of us _____ at the supper table last night.
  (A) were seated (B) be set
  (C) be sat   (D) was sitting

(　) 22. The child _____ last night.
  (A) drown   (B) was drowned
  (C) be drowned   (D) was drown

( ) 23. I am _____ to know of your success.
    (A) pleasant   (B) pleasing
    (C) pleased   (D) pleasure

( ) 24. It will _____ by me.
    (A) be done   (B) done
    (C) be do   (D) did

( ) 25. He _____ with his radio. It gives him a great deal of pleasure to listen to music.
    (A) pleases   (B) is pleased
    (C) pleasure   (D) is please

【精選模擬考題解答】

1.(**C**)   2.(**B**)   3.(**B**)   4.(**A**)   5.(**B**)   6.(**A**)
7.(**C**)   8.(**D**)   9.(**A**)   10.(**D**)   11.(**C**)   12.(**B**)
13.(**C**)   14.(**A**)   15.(**C**)   16.(**A**)   17.(**A**)   18.(**B**)
19.(**C**)   20.(**B**)   21.(**A**)   22.(**B**)   23.(**C**)   24.(**A**)
25.(**B**)

【解析】

1. 我妹妹上個月嫁給她朋友的表哥。
    marry = be married to

2. *take good care of* 好好照顧

5. 你今天打扮得很好看。

6. sell, lock, read 做不及物動詞，以主動的形式表被動意義。
    sell well 銷路很好

9. 「這些機器應該一年檢查一次。」　　*ought to* 應該

inspect〔ɪnˈspɛkt〕*v.* 檢查

11. 我們校長獻身教育的目標上。

cause〔kɔz〕*n.* 目標　　*be devoted to* 獻身；致力於

12. 你可能會因為腳踏車沒裝燈，而被罰三十元美金。

fine〔faɪn〕*v.* 處以罰鍰　　equip〔ɪˈkwɪp〕*v.* 裝備

13. 我相信房子是被故意縱火。

deliberately〔dɪˈlɪbərɪtlɪ〕*adv.* 故意地

set ~ on fire 放火燒 ~

14. disappointed（感到失望的）修飾人，disappointing（令人失望的）修飾物。

15. *send for* 延請（被動語態為 be sent for）　　*at once* 立刻

16. 「他很出名，大家都認識他。」　　*be known to* 為 ~ 所知

17. *be pleased with* 因 ~ 而高興

19. 原句 = He cannot bear to be laughed at. 「他不能忍受別人的嘲笑。」　　bear 可接 V-ing 或 to + V.。

21. *be seated* at the table = *sit* at the table 坐在餐桌旁

22. drown〔draʊn〕*v.* 使溺死；淹死

23. *know of* 得知（某事）

25. *a great*〔*good*〕*deal of* 許多的

3. 假設法

用以表示不可能實現的願望、想像、目的或與事實相反的假設，
依其與時間關係可分為與現在、過去、或未來事實相反的假設。

1. 與現在事實相反的假設

(1) **If～過去式～,…would (could, should, might) + 原形動詞**

> If I *had* money, I *could buy* the book.
> (*As I have no money*, I *cannot buy* the book.)【事實】
> (假如我有錢，我就能買那本書。)

> If I *knew* Italian, I *could* speak with him.
> (*As I don't know Italian*, I *cannot speak* with him.)
> (假如我懂義大利話，我就能和他交談。)【事實】

☞ 假設法中，be 動詞的過去式一律用 were。

【例】 If Peter *were* a fish, the cat *would eat* him.
　　　(假如彼得是魚，這隻貓就會把他吃了。)

(2) **I wish + 過去式動詞或 were**

> *I wish* I *were* as strong as you. (但願我和你一樣強壯。)
> (*I am sorry I am not* as strong as you.)

> *I wish* I *could* help you. (但願我能幫得了你。)
> (*I am sorry I cannot* help you.)

(3) **It is (high) time (that) + 過去式動詞 (或 should + 原形動詞)**

> *It is time* you *went* to bed. (你現在該上床睡覺了。)
> (= It is time for you to go to bed.)

【例】 *It is* (*high*) *time* you *should go* 〔*were going*〕.
　　　(你現在該走了。)

2. 與過去事實相反的假設

(1) **If~ 過去完成式~, …would (could, should, might) + have + p.p.**

> If we *had taken* the bus, we *would* 〔*should*〕 *have been* in time.
>
> (As we *did not* take the bus, we *were not* in time.)
>
> (假如我們搭了那輛公車，我們就〔應該〕來得及。)【事實】

> If I *had arrived* by noon, I *could have met* him.
>
> (As I *did not* arrive by noon, I *could not* meet him.)
>
> (假如我在中午以前抵達，我就能見到他。)

☞ 一般而言，假設法中主要子句與從屬子句的時式一致，但也有時式不一致的情形：

【例】 If it *had rained* last night, the ground *would be* wet *now*. (假如昨晚下過雨的話，現在地面就會是濕的。)

If I *had taken* your advice, I *would* 〔*should*〕 *be* happier *now*.

(假如我接受你的勸告，現在就會〔應該會〕更快樂。)

【if子句是與過去事實相反的假設，用過去完成式，主要子句是與現在事實相反的假設，用過去式。】

(2) **I wish + 過去完成式**

> *I wish* I *had learned* French. (但願我學過法文。)
>
> (I am sorry I *did not* learn French.)

> *I wish* I *had gone* there. (但願我去那裡了。)
>
> (I am sorry I *did not* go there.)

☞ that 子句裡的時式，不受主要子句中 wish 或 wished 的影響。

> I *wish* (that) I *had* a car. (現在我但願能有一輛車。)
>
> I *wished* (that) I *had* a car. (那時候我但願有一輛車。)

> I *wish* (that) I *had learned* how to drive.
> （現在我但願已經學會開車。）
>
> I *wished* (that) I *had learned* how to drive.
> （那時候我但願已經學會開車。）

3. 與未來事實相反的假設

$$\text{If} \sim \left\{ \begin{array}{l} \textbf{should} \\ \textbf{were to} \end{array} \right\} \sim, \cdots \left\{ \begin{array}{l} \textbf{would} \ (\textbf{will}) \\ \textbf{should} \ (\textbf{shall}) \\ \textbf{might} \ (\textbf{may}) \\ \textbf{could} \ (\textbf{can}) \end{array} \right\} + \text{原形動詞} \cdots\cdots$$

(1) **should** 作「萬一」解，表示可能性極小。

【例】 If it *should* rain tomorrow, we *would* (*will*) stay home. (萬一明天下雨，我們就留在家裡。)

What *will* (*would*) you tell him, if he *should* come?
（萬一他來了，你要告訴他什麼？）

☞ 只有在「should + 原形動詞」的形式中，主要子句才可使用祈使句。

【例】 If anyone *should* come to see me, *tell* him I am not at home. (萬一有人來看我，告訴他我不在家。)

(2) **were to** + 原形動詞，表示未來絕不可能。

【例】 If I *were to* go abroad, I *would* go to England.
（假如我要出國，我會去英國。）

If a comet *were to* hit the earth, what *would* become of us? (假如彗星撞擊地球，我們會變成什麼樣子？)

If the sun *were to* rise in the west, I *would* lend you the money.
（假如太陽打西邊出來，我就借錢給你。）

4. 其他假設法及注意事項

1. as if〔as though〕…「好像」

⑴ as if〔as though〕+ 過去式或 were，表示與現在事實相反的假設。

　【例】　He talks *as if* he *knew* everything.

　　　　　（他說話的樣子好像他樣樣都懂。）

　　　　　She looks *as if* she *were* ill.（她看起來好像生病了。）

　　　　　I felt *as if* I *were* flying in the air.

　　　　　（我感覺好像在空中飛。）

⑵ as if〔as though〕+ 過去完成式，表示與過去事實相反。

　【例】　She looks *as if* she *had been* ill.

　　　　　（她看起來好像生過病。）

　　　　　He looked *as if* he *had seen* a ghost.

　　　　　（他看起來好像見過鬼。）

　☞ as if, as though 所引導子句的時式不受主要子句影響。

　【例】　He $\left\{\begin{array}{l} \textit{talks} \\ \textit{talked} \end{array}\right\}$ *as if* he *had been* abroad.

　　　　　（他說話的樣子，好像他出過國。）

2. 假設語氣中 **If** 的省略

　　if 子句中有 were, had, should, would 時，if 可以省略，但主詞與動詞必須倒裝。

　【例】　*Should it* rain (= *If it should* rain), I *will* not come.

　　　　　（萬一下雨，我就不來。）

　　　　　Were I rich, I *would* buy an airplane.

　　　　　（假如我很富有，我就會買一架飛機。）

　　　　　Had I known it, I *would have been* more careful.

　　　　　（假如我早知道，我就會更小心。）

3. 表示假設的介詞片語

由主要子句的時式來判斷是與現在事實相反或與過去事實相反。

⑴ **but for**, **without**「若不是；如果沒有」

【例】 *But for* } your advice, they *would* fail.
Without

（如果沒有你的勸告，他們就會失敗。）

(= *If it were not for* your advice, …)

(= *Were it not for* your advice, …) 【省略 if】

But for } your help, I *should have died*.
Without

（如果沒有你的幫助，我應該早就死了。）

(= *If it had not been for* your help, …)

(= *Had it not been for* your help, …) 【省略 if】

⑵ **with**「如果（有）…的話」

【例】 *With* a milder climate, people *would* live longer.
（假如天氣更溫和的話，人們就能活得更久。）【與現在事實相反】

With (= *If he had had*) your help, he *would have succeeded*. 【與過去事實相反】

（假如有你的幫助，他早就成功了。）

4. 表示假設的不定詞、分詞

【例】 *To hear* him speak English, you *would* take him for an American. （聽他講英文，你會以為他是美國人。）

(= *If you heard* 〔*were to hear*〕 him speak English, …)

I *would* 〔*should*〕 be happy *to go* with you.

(= …*if I could go* with you.)

（假如能和你一起去，我會很高興的。）

Coming an hour earlier, you *might have met* him.

(= *If you had come* an hour earlier, …)

（如果你早一個小時來，可能就會遇見他。）

---

5. 含假設語氣的名詞片語

【例】 A *Chinese* *would not do* so.

(= If he were a Chinese, he would not do so.)

（若身爲中國人，就不會這樣做。）

A *true friend* *would not have betrayed* me.

(= If he had been a true friend, he would not…)

（若是眞正的朋友，就不會背棄我。）

☞ 連接詞也有假設語氣的用法。

【例】 We ran nearly all the way, *or* we *might have been* late for school.

（一路上我們幾乎全用跑的，否則上學可能就遲到了。）

5. 直說法條件句

直說法條件句，是以事實或普遍情況爲條件，說話者心中並未存與事實相反之意，因此不屬於假設語氣，動詞可適用於直說法的任何時式。

【例】 If you *have done* your work, you *may* go to the movies. （如果你做完了工作，就可以去看電影。）

If he *promised* to be here, he *will* certainly come.

（如果他答應過要來這裡，他就一定會來。）

If it *is* fine tomorrow, I *will* go.

（如果明天天氣好，我就會去。）

☞ 直說法條件句的主要子句也可用祈使句。

【例】 *Turn out* the lights *if* you leave.

（如果你離開，就把燈關掉。）

If the phone rings, *answer* it. （如果電話鈴響，就去接。）

歷屆聯考試題

一、與現在事實相反的假設

( ) 1. If I _____ you, I would go to the party with her.
　　　　(A) am　　　　　(B) were
　　　　(C) had been　　(D) be

( ) 2. If I had money, I _____ a large house.
　　　　(A) buy　　　　　(B) will buy
　　　　(C) would buy　　(D) would bought

( ) 3. It is high time that you _____ to her.
　　　　(A) proposed　　　(B) were propose
　　　　(C) proposing　　　(D) have proposed

( ) 4. I wish I _____ play a musical instrument.
　　　　(A) can　　　　(B) could　　　(C) must
　　　　(D) would　　　(E) do

_____ 5. What would you <u>do</u> if you <u>would</u> fail? (改錯)

二、與過去事實相反的假設

( ) 1. If he <u>had followed</u> your advice, he <u>would have</u> <u>past</u> the
　　　　　　　　(A)　　　　　　　　　　　　　　(B)　　　　(C)
　　examination. (改錯)

(　　) 2. What _____ had I not had those two persons?
    (A) will my life be   (B) my life would be
    (C) would my life have been
    (D) will my life have been

(　　) 3. If he had not helped me, I might have failed.
    = But that he _____ me, I might have failed.
    (A) did not help   (B) had not helped
    (C) had helped   (D) helped

(　　) 4. If I _____ enough money then, I would have bought that fancy bike.
    (A) have   (B) had
    (C) have had   (D) had had

(　　) 5. If I had learned to swim last summer, I _____ able to swim now.
    (A) will have been   (B) had been
    (C) would be   (D) will be

三、與未來相反的假設

(　　) 1. I would not change my mind if the sun _____ in the west tomorrow morning.
    (A) were to rise   (B) could rise
    (C) might rise   (D) will rise

四、假設法應注意事項

(　　) 1. _____ I not so busy, I would do it.
    (A) Had   (B) Be   (C) Were
    (D) Was   (E) Am

( ) 2. _____ it rained last night, the ground would be wet
now.
(A) Should (B) Would (C) When (D) Had

( ) 3. _____ for your help, I might have failed.
(A) Has it not been   (B) Had it not been
(C) Were it be   (D) Was it not

( ) 4. Had he gone there, he _____ her.
(A) had seen   (B) saw
(C) would have seen   (D) will have seen

( ) 5. Had you helped her, she _____.
(A) can succeed   (B) might succeed
(C) might have succeeded (D) would succeed

( ) 6. Had he not gone to the movie, he _____.
(A) would not have been hurt
(B) would not have hurted
(C) will not hurt
(D) might not hurt

( ) 7. _____ what was going to happen, I would never have
left her alone.
(A) If I known   (B) Should I know
(C) Had I known   (D) I'd known

( ) 8. I wish that I _____ about this yesterday.
(A) know   (B) knew
(C) have known   (D) had known

(　) 9. I wish _____.

     (A) she loves me

     (B) he will help me

     (C) I am a millionaire

     (D) I had 48 hours a day

     (E) they can arrive in time

(　) 10. _____, he might have died in the traffic accident.

     (A) If the ambulance didn't arrive in time

     (B) If someone had sent for an ambulance

     (C) If the doctor had arrived in time

     (D) Had the doctor not arrived in time

(　) 11. It looks _____ it might rain.

     (A) this　(B) as　　(C) as if　　(D) that

(　) 12. This machine can pull up trees as if they _____ weeds.

     (A) were　　　　(B) are

     (C) have been　　(D) had been

(　) 13. This young lady behaves as though she _____ an old woman.

     (A) is　(B) was　(C) were　(D) has been

(　) 14. _____, I should have failed.

     (A) But for he helped me

     (B) But that he had helped me

     (C) If he did not help me

     (D) But for his help

_____ 15. It was also necessary that this energy _____ controlled.

_____ 16. I would have helped you but I <u>had been</u> too busy.(改錯)

_____ 17. I wish I _____ (can, could) have an airplane.

_____ 18. The man talks as if he _____ a millionaire.

五、假設語氣的慣用語

(　　) 1. You may call this number _____ I am not at home.
  (A) in order that (B) so as to
  (C) in any case   (D) so that
  (E) if

(　　) 2. I would rather that you stayed at home.
  (A) 我必須停留在你家裡。
  (B) 我希望你停留在我家裡。
  (C) 我寧願你待在家裡。
  (D) 你可以待在我家裡。
  (E) 你希望我待在你家裡。

(　　) 3. Tom suggested _____ a cup of tea.
  (A) them having (B) them to have
  (C) they had   (D) they have

(　　) 4. I propose that he _____ chairman.
  (A) electing   (B) elected
  (C) elects   (D) be elected

(　) 5. I insist that he _____.
　　　(A)　goes　　　　(B)　go
　　　(C)　going　　　(D)　gone

六、直說法條件句

(　) 1. If he works hard, _____.
　　　(A)　he would succeed
　　　(B)　he might have succeeded
　　　(C)　he will succeed
　　　(D)　he will be succeeded

(　) 2. "I want to write her a letter, but I don't have any stamps."
　　　"I'll buy some for you if I _____ to the post office."
　　　(A)　will go　　(B)　shall go　　(C)　go

(　) 3. 假如下雨，比賽延期。
　　　If _____ rains, the game will be _____ off.

(　) 4. The train _____ when you reach the train station.
　　　(A)　had left　　(B)　will have left
　　　(C)　has left　　(D)　has been left
　　　(E)　left

(　) 5. If the room is dark, _____ on the light.
　　　(A)　to turn　　(B)　turning　　(C)　turn
　　　(D)　turns　　(E)　turned

【歷屆聯考試題解答】

一、 1.(**B**) 2.(**C**) 3.(**A**) 4.(**B**)
   5. would → should

二、 1.(**C**)→ passed 2.(**C**) 3.(**D**) 4.(**D**) 5.(**C**)

三、 1.(**A**)

四、 1.(**C**) 2.(**D**) 3.(**B**) 4.(**C**) 5.(**C**) 6.(**A**)
   7.(**C**) 8.(**D**) 9.(**D**) 10.(**D**) 11.(**C**) 12.(**A**)
   13.(**C**) 14.(**D**) 15. be 16. was 17. could 18. were

五、 1.(**E**) 2.(**C**) 3.(**D**) 4.(**D**) 5.(**B**)

六、 1.(**C**) 2.(**C**) 3. it, put 4.(**B**) 5.(**C**)

【解析】

一、 3. propose〔prə'poz〕*v.* 求婚

   4.「但願我會彈奏樂器。」 *musical instrument* 樂器

   5.「萬一失敗了,你怎麼辦?」「萬一」要用助動詞 should。

二、 2.「如果沒有那兩個人,我的生命會是什麼樣子呢?」本句
     為與過去事實相反的假設語氣,主要子句為 S. + would
     [could, should, might] + have + 過去分詞。本句是由…
     if I had not had those two persons? 省略 if 倒裝而來。

   3. *but that*「要不是」,後面接過去簡單式。

   4. 如果那時有足夠的錢,我會買那輛拉風的腳踏車。
     fancy〔'fænsɪ〕*adj.* 拉風的;新穎的

四、 1. 原句 = *If I were* not so busy,….本題為省略 If 之假設法。

   2. 原句 = *If it had* rained last night,….

   9. (A)(B)(C)(E)的答案均須改成與過去事實或現在事實相反
     的假設語氣。

10. 由 might have died 可知，本句為與過去事實相反的假設
語氣。　　***send for~***　派人去叫~
ambulance〔'æmbjələns〕*n.* 救護車

12. ***pull up*** 拔出　　weed〔wid〕*n.* 雜草

14. ***but for*** + 名詞 = ***but that*** + 子句　要不是
由 should have failed 可知，本句為與過去事實相反的
假設語氣，故 (B) 應改為 But that he helped me, (C) 應
改為 If he had not helped me。

15. 這能源也應該有必要被控制著。
本句是由…this energy should be controlled. 省略
should 而來。

18. millionaire〔,mɪljən'ɛr〕*n.* 百萬富翁

五、　2. S₁ + ***would rather*** (that) + S₂ + 過去式，表與現在或
未來事實相反的假設。

3. 湯姆建議他們應該來杯茶。
本句是由 Tom suggested ***that*** they ***should*** have…省
略 that 和 should 而來。

4. 我提議他應該被選為主席。
propose〔prə'poz〕*v.* 提議

5. 「我堅持他應該去。」　　insist〔ɪn'sɪst〕*v.* 堅持

六、　1. 如果他用功，他（將來）就會成功。
直說法的條件句中，if 子句和主要子句的時態適用於一
般直述句的時態。依句意，選 (C) 表示未來。

2. 表條件的副詞子句，須用現在式表示未來，不可用 will
表示未來，故選 (C)。

3. ***put off*** 延期

精選模擬考題

( ) 1. What would you do if you _____ a million dollars?
    (A) have   (B) had
    (C) had've had   (D) had have

( ) 2. If you could kindly assist me, I _____ be much
    obliged to you.
    (A) will   (B) can
    (C) could   (D) would

( ) 3. If I had known that, I _____.
    (A) wouldn't do so   (B) wouldn't have done so
    (C) won't do so   (D) won't done so

( ) 4. If I had had to do it, I _____ it at that time.
    (A) would have done (B) will do
    (C) will have done   (D) would do

( ) 5. If it _____ rain tomorrow, they will not go.
    (A) would   (B) should
    (C) is   (D) will

( ) 6. He would have come yesterday if he _____ nothing
    to do.
    (A) has   (B) had had
    (C) would have   (D) should have

(　　) 7. He talks as if he _____ everything about it.

      (A) knew   (B) know

      (C) is knowing   (D) known

(　　) 8. If I _____ your advice then, I should be happier now.

      (A) had taken   (B) took

      (C) should take   (D) would take

(　　) 9. If I _____ to tell you all I know, you would be amazed.

      (A) have   (B) ought

      (C) were   (D) must

(　　) 10. If he were honest, I _____ employ him.

      (A) will   (B) would

      (C) can   (D) may have

(　　) 11. If I _____ in your position, I would not do such a thing.

      (A) be   (B) am   (C) were   (D) are

(　　) 12. I _____ silent if I were you.

      (A) keep   (B) will keep

      (C) would keep   (D) was keeping

(　　) 13. The girl _____ if no one tries to help her.

      (A) drowns   (B) be drowned

      (C) should drown   (D) will drown

(　　) 14. I would have helped you if I _____ about your trouble.

      (A) heard   (B) have heard

      (C) had heard   (D) hear

( ) 15. If it had not been so cold, I _____ to see you yesterday.
    (A) would have come   (B) would come
    (C) had come   (D) came

( ) 16. I might be still out of a job if he _____ me three
    years ago.
    (A) did not employ
    (B) had not employed
    (C) have not employed
    (D) employ

( ) 17. I wish I _____ him yesterday.
    (A) met   (B) had met
    (C) would meet   (D) could meet

( ) 18. Isn't it high time you _____ to bed?
    (A) are going   (B) will go
    (C) have gone   (D) went

( ) 19. If I _____ your address, I would have written to you.
    (A) know   (B) were to know
    (C) had known   (D) would know

( ) 20. Oh, if only I _____ ten dollars then.
    (A) have   (B) had
    (C) should have   (D) had had

( ) 21. You will be much surprised if you _____ the fact.
    (A) know   (B) knew
    (C) will know   (D) would know

(　) 22. He would go mad if he _____ that.

(A) hears　　　　　(B) heard

(C) has heard　　　(D) would hear

(　) 23. _____ anything happen, please let us know immediately.

(A) If　(B) Should　(C) May　　(D) Since

(　) 24. _____ I known you were ill, I'd have called to see you.

(A) If　(B) As　　(C) Have　　(D) Had

(　) 25. She talks as if she _____ to many foreign countries.

(A) is　(B) were　(C) gone　　(D) had been

(　) 26. We must suggest that he _____ it by himself.

(A) do　(B) does　(C) is doing　(D) will do

(　) 27. Had you told him the truth, he _____ some suggestions.

(A) might make　　　(B) would made

(C) might have made　(D) had made

(　) 28. She loves the girl as much as if she _____ her own daughter.

(A) is　(B) were　(C) was　　(D) are

(　) 29. _____ I a millionaire, I should be able to make a tour around the world.

(A) Was　(B) Am　(C) Were　　(D) If

( ) 30. They wish you _____ there last week.
     (A) were   (B) had been
     (C) has been   (D) would have been

( ) 31. Bill would have taken more photographs if he _____ more film.
     (A) had had   (B) has had
     (C) should have   (D) would have

( ) 32. _____ he bought fifty eggs instead of two yesterday, there would have been no money left for the beef.
     (A) If   (B) Should   (C) Had   (D) Were

( ) 33. I wish I _____ your advice, but I didn't pay attention to you at that time.
     (A) had taken   (B) would take
     (C) took   (D) could take

( ) 34. _____ for your aid, I could not have succeeded.
     (A) But   (B) If
     (C) Should   (D) No

( ) 35. If the sun _____ to rise in the west, I would never break my word.
     (A) had   (B) would   (C) should   (D) were

( ) 36. If he _____ late, give him the message.
     (A) were coming   (B) would come
     (C) should come   (D) were come

(　) 37. If you had told me to do the report yesterday, I
　　　　_____ it by now.
　　　　(A) may finish　　　　　(B) should have finished
　　　　(C) finished　　　　　　(D) could finish

(　) 38. I wish I _____ my time when I was young.
　　　　(A) haven't wasted　　　(B) didn't waste
　　　　(C) wouldn't waste　　　(D) hadn't wasted

(　) 39. Had Tom told the truth, I _____ him.
　　　　(A) would have believed　(B) believed
　　　　(C) had believed　　　　(D) believe

(　) 40. She told me about the incident as if she _____ it with
　　　　her own eyes.
　　　　(A) saw　(B) sees　　(C) see　(D) had seen

(　) 41. If I had had that much money, I should _____ you.
　　　　(A) have been paid　　　(B) have pay
　　　　(C) been paid　　　　　　(D) have paid

【精選模擬考題解答】

1. (**B**)	2. (**D**)	3. (**B**)	4. (**A**)	5. (**B**)	6. (**B**)
7. (**A**)	8. (**A**)	9. (**C**)	10. (**B**)	11. (**C**)	12. (**C**)
13. (**D**)	14. (**C**)	15. (**A**)	16. (**B**)	17. (**B**)	18. (**D**)
19. (**C**)	20. (**D**)	21. (**A**)	22. (**B**)	23. (**B**)	24. (**D**)
25. (**D**)	26. (**A**)	27. (**C**)	28. (**B**)	29. (**C**)	30. (**B**)
31. (**A**)	32. (**C**)	33. (**A**)	34. (**A**)	35. (**D**)	36. (**C**)
37. (**B**)	38. (**D**)	39. (**A**)	40. (**D**)	41. (**D**)	

【解析】

2. 如果你肯好意幫助我，我會非常感激。
   be obliged to ~ 感激~

5. 「萬一明天下雨，他們就不去。」should 作「萬一」解。

8. 因條件句有 then（那時），所以用與**過去**事實相反的假設，而主要子句中有 now（現在），所以用與**現在**事實相反的假設。

9. 如果我告訴你我所知道的，你會嚇一大跳。

14. ***hear about ~*** 聽說~

16. 由 three years ago 可知，條件句爲與過去事實相反的假設，故用過去完成式。　***out of a job*** 失業

22. ***go mad*** 發狂；發瘋

23. 原句 = ***If*** anything ***should*** happen, ···.

24. 原句 = ***If*** I ***had*** known you were ill, ···.

26. 原句 = ···that he ***should*** do it by himself.

31. 如果那時候比爾有更多的底片，他會拍更多張照片。
    take photographs 拍照　　film〔fɪlm〕*n.* 底片

32. 「如果昨天他買了五十個蛋，而不是買兩個的話，就沒錢買牛肉了。」與過去事實相反的假設，應該用過去完成式，因省略 if，所以 had 移到最前面。

33. 由 at that time 得知，爲與過去事實相反的假設。
    pay attention to 注意

35. 如果太陽打西邊出來，我就不會違背諾言。
    were to + V. 表示未來絕不可能。
    break one's word 違背諾言（= ***break one's promise***）

39. 如果那時候湯姆告訴我實話，我就已經相信他了。
    tell the truth 說實話

40. incident〔'ɪnsədnt〕*n.* 事件

PART-4

動狀詞

▶1. 不定詞的重點在to的省略，it代替不定詞的用法，和so as to, enough to, too～to及prefer～to。

▶2. 常考分詞當補語的用法及分詞構句。

▶3. 要能分辨哪些動詞後面只能接動名詞，或只能接不定詞，並牢記be used to, look forward to之類，後面接動名詞而非原形不定詞的片語。

1. 不 定 詞

> 不定詞不受句中主詞人稱及數的影響，
> 分爲有 **to** 的不定詞與原形不定詞兩種。

1. 有 to 的不定詞用法

1. 不定詞可當名詞用，做主詞、受詞或補語

(1) 當主詞

【例】 *To err* is human, *to forgive* divine.
（犯錯是人，寬恕是神。）

To make a plan is easy, but *it* isn't easy *to carry* it out.
（訂計劃容易，但要實現很難。）

(2) 當受詞

【例】 I want *to stay* longer, but I don't like *to trouble* you.
（我想待久一點，但我不想打擾你。）

He found *it* difficult *to solve* the problem.
（他發現要解決這問題很難。）

(3) 當補語

【例】 The best way is *to do* one thing at a time.
（最好的方法是一次做一件事。）

They think him *to be* honest. （他們認爲他是誠實的。）

(4) 疑問詞 + 不定詞 = 名詞片語

【例】 I don't know *what to do*. （我不知道該怎麼辦。）

He couldn't decide *whether to go or not*.
（他無法決定去或不去。）

2. 不定詞可當形容詞用，以修飾名詞

【例】 He has a strong desire *to go* abroad.

（他出國的欲望很強。）

He isn't a man *to tell* a lie. （他不是會說謊的人。）

3. 不定詞可當副詞用，以修飾動詞、形容詞、副詞或整句

(1) 表目的

【例】 She went to the airport *to meet* her father.

（她去機場接她父親。）

(2) 表原因、理由

【例】 I am very glad *to see* you. （我很高興看到你。）

He must be a fool *to say* so.（一定是個傻瓜，才會這麼說。）

(3) 表結果

【例】 I went all the way to his house *only to find* him out.

（我大老遠跑去他家，卻發現他不在。）

(4) 表條件

【例】 *To hear* her talk on the phone, you would take her for a young girl.

（ = *If you heard* her talk on the phone, you… ）

（聽她電話裡的聲音，你會以為她是小女孩。）

(5) 修飾形容詞、副詞

【例】 The old man is *hard to please*. （這老人不易討好。）

（ = It's *hard to please* the old man. ）

Bad habits are *difficult to get rid of*.

（壞習慣難以戒除。）

（ = It is *difficult to get rid of* bad habits. ）

The tea is *too* hot for me ***to drink***.【不定詞修飾 too】

（這茶對我而言太熱不能喝。）

（ = The tea is so hot that I can't drink it. ）

This book is easy *enough* for a child ***to read***.

（這本書很簡單，可以給小孩讀。）【不定詞修飾 enough】

（ = This book is so easy that a child can read it. ）

⑹ 慣用法（用在 sure, likely, anxious, ready, willing, eager, apt 之後）

【例】 He is *sure **to show up*** on time.（他一定會準時出現。）

It is *likely **to rain*** this afternoon.（今天下午可能會下雨。）

⑺ 獨立用法

to tell the truth ⎫
to be frank with you ⎬ 老實說
to speak frankly ⎭

strange to say 說也奇怪

not to mention 更不用說

so to speak 好比是；可說是

to make a long story short 長話短說　　to sum up 總之

to make matters worse 更糟的是　　　　to begin with 首先

2. 原形不定詞的用法

1. 感官動詞之後用原形不定詞

感官動詞：see, hear, feel, watch, look at, listen to,
　　　　　overhear（偷聽），observe（察覺），
　　　　　perceive（發覺），notice（注意）

【例】 He *heard* his mother **call** him from the kitchen.

（他聽到母親在廚房裡叫他。）

I *saw* the girl **walk** into the shop.

（我看到那女孩走入店裡。）

＜比較＞ I saw the girl *walking* into the shop.

【強調動作的進行】

2. 使役動詞之後用原形不定詞

使役動詞：let, make, have, bid（命令）

【例】 My brother *let* me ***use*** his dictionary.

（我哥哥讓我用他的字典。）

　　　 The king *had* the artist ***paint*** his portrait.

（國王叫藝術家畫他的畫像。）

<比較> get 之後接有 to 的不定詞

He *got* me ***to mail*** the letter.

（他叫我寄這封信。）

3. 在被動語態中，感官或使役動詞後面的不定詞，不可省略 to

【例】 He was *seen **to enter*** the room.（他被看到走進房裡。）

　　　 We were *made **to study*** harder by our teacher.

（老師要我們更努力用功。）

4. **help** 之後接原形不定詞或有 to 的不定詞皆可

【例】 She *helps* her mother (***to***) ***do*** the dishes.

（她幫媽媽洗碗盤。）

3. 不定詞的完成式與否定形

1. 完成式不定詞：to + have + 過去分詞

⑴ 表示發生在主要動詞之前的動作：完成式不定詞在內容上，表示發
　生在主要動詞之前的時式，亦即主要動詞如果是現在式，不定詞則
　表示過去式或現在完成式，主要動詞若為過去式，則不定詞表示過
　去完成式。

【例】 He *seems **to have been*** rich.（他似乎曾經很富有。）

　　　 (= It *seems* that he *was* 〔*has been*〕 rich.)

He *seemed* **to have been** rich.

(= It *seemed* that he *had been* rich.)

I *am* sorry **to have kept** you waiting so long.

(= I *am* sorry that I *have kept* you waiting so long.)

（抱歉讓你久等。）

<比較>
{
He *seems* **to be** rich.
  (= It *seems* that he *is* rich.)
He *seemed* **to be** rich.
  (= It *seemed* that he *was* rich.)
}

(2) 表過去沒有實現的願望、期待或計劃。

wished, hoped, wanted, meant,
expected, planned, desired,   } + to have + 過去分詞
thought, would like

【例】 I *wished* **to have bought** a car, but I had no money.

（但願我已經買車，但我沒錢。）

---

2. 否定形不定詞：**not + to V.**

【例】 The boy pretended **not to see** the girl.

（這男孩假裝沒看見這女孩。）

I am very sorry **not to have answered** your letter
sooner. （抱歉沒儘快回信。）

4. 不定詞意義上的主詞

1. 雖未特別表示，但可了解前後關係時

【例】 I want **to help** my mother cook. （我要幫媽媽煮飯。）

It is dangerous **to swim** in the lake.

（在湖裡游泳很危險。）

---

2. 有表示意義上的主詞時

【例】 I want *you to prepare* your lessons every day.

（我要你每天溫習功課。）

He stood aside *for the old lady to pass*.

（他站到一旁給那老婦人過去。）

3. 請注意下列句型

(1) It is + 形容詞 + **for**…to～

這種句型所用的是表示**判斷某種行爲**的形容詞：important, necessary, easy, difficult, hard, impossible 等。

【例】 It is hard *for* us *to speak* correct English.

（對我們而言，說正確的英文是很難的。）

It was quite easy *for* him *to find* my office.

（對他而言，要找到我的辦公室相當容易。）

(2) It is + 形容詞 + **of**…to～

這種句型所用的是表示**人的特質**的形容詞：kind, good, nice, polite, rude（無禮的）, foolish, careless, wise, honest 等。

【例】 It is good *of* you *to lend* me your money.

（你眞好，借錢給我。）

It was careless *of* him *to leave* his bag in the train.

（他眞粗心，把袋子留在火車上。）

5. 注意下列有 **to** 的不定詞句型

1. S + V + to～

(1) 動詞爲不及物動詞時

此類動詞有 be, seem, appear, prove, turn out, happen, look, remain 等。

【例】 The clock *seems **to be*** wrong.（這鐘的時間似乎不對。）

　　　 The rumor *proved **to be*** false.（這傳言證實是假的。）

(2) 動詞爲及物動詞時

【例】 I didn't *mean **to hurt*** her feelings.

　　　（我不是有意傷害她的感情。）

　　　 Stop smoking if you *choose **to be*** healthy.

　　　（如果你選擇健康的話，就戒菸。）

---

2. S + V + O + to～

(1) 表示要求、期待、許可的動詞：ask, tell, want, order, warn, expect, advise, allow。

【例】 Mother *told* me *to turn* off the television.

　　　（媽媽叫我關掉電視機。）

　　　 The doctor *advised* her *to eat* green vegetables.

　　　（醫生勸她吃綠色蔬菜。）

(2) 動詞爲 find, think, believe 時，受詞要用不定詞。

【例】 I *found* the box *to be* full of apples.

　　　（我發現盒子裝滿蘋果。）

　　　 The parents *believed* their son *to be* honest.

　　　（這父母相信他們的兒子是誠實的。）

---

3. be + to V. 表示(1)預定 (2)義務 (3)命運 (4)可能 (5)意圖

(1) We *are **to have*** a party tomorrow.（我們明天將舉行宴會。）

　　　(= We *will* have a party tomorrow.)

(2) You *are **to stay*** here till we come back.

　　　(= You *must* stay here till we come back.)

　　　（你必須留在這兒，直到我們回來。）

⑶ He *was* never *to see* his hometown again.
（他再也看不到家鄉了。）

⑷ The star *is to be* seen early in the evening.
　（ = The star *can* be seen early in the evening. ）
（傍晚時看得到這顆星。）

⑸ If you *are to become* a great man, you should work hard.
　（ = If you *intend to* become a great man, you… ）
（如果你要成為一個偉人，你就應該要努力。）

4. in order to V., so as to V. 「以便～；為了～」

【例】 I went home *in order to* change my clothes.
　　（ = I went home *so that* I *might* change my clothes. ）
　　（我回家換衣服。）

　　She listened carefully *so as not to* miss a
　　single word.
　　（她仔細聽，以便一字也不漏。）

5. so…as to V. 「如此…以致於～」

【例】 He was *so* tired *as to* fall asleep as soon as he
　　went to bed.
　　（ = He was *so* tired *that he* fell asleep… ）
　　（他如此疲倦，以致於一上床就立刻睡著了。）

6. have only to～ 「只要；只好」

【例】 You *have only to* push the button to start the engine.
　　（你只要按下按鈕，就能發動引擎。）

---

7. 代不定詞：以 to 代替與前面相同的動詞，以避免重覆

【例】 She *went to the concert*, but I didn't want *to*.

（她去聽音樂會，但我不想去。）

The old woman doesn't *go out* as she used *to*.

（那老婦人不像往常一樣出去。）

---

8. 原形不定詞之慣用表達法

⑴ **had better** (= 'd better) 「最好」

【例】 You *had better* come at once. （你最好立刻來。）

We'*d better not remain* in school after five.

（五點以後我們最好不要留在學校裡。）

⑵ **cannot but V**. 「不得不～；忍不住～」

【例】 I *could not but laugh* at his funny joke.

(= I *could not help laughing* at his funny joke.)

（他的笑話很有趣，我忍不住笑了出來。）

⑶ **would rather V. than V**. 「寧願～而不願…」

【例】 I *would rather watch* television at home *than go*
to the movies.

（我寧願在家裡看電視，而不願去看電影。）

⑷ **do nothing but V**. 「只是～」

【例】 The baby *does nothing but cry* and *sleep*.

（嬰兒只是哭跟睡。）

⑸ **All *one* has to do is V**. 「某人所必須做的只是～」

【例】 *All I have to do is take* a rest.

（我所必須做的只是休息。）

歷屆聯考試題

一、有 to 的不定詞用法

(　　) 1. It is useless _____ to do this.
　　　(A) try　　(B) to try　　(C) tries　　(D) to trying

(　　) 2. She wanted _____ the flat decorated.
　　　(A) having　　　　(B) being
　　　(C) to have　　　　(D) to be

(　　) 3. Mary was about _____ up waiting when her friend arrived.
　　　(A) giving　　　　(B) given
　　　(C) to give　　　　(D) being given

(　　) 4. I gave him nothing _____.
　　　(A) drink　　　　(B) to drink
　　　(C) drinking　　　(D) drinks
　　　(E) drunk

(　　) 5. I don't like _____ in that way.
　　　(A) to treat　　　(B) to be treated
　　　(C) treated

(　　) 6. Would you like _____ for a walk?
　　　(A) to go　　　　(B) going
　　　(C) to going　　　(D) go
　　　(E) to be gone

(   ) 7. He ordered the work _____.

    (A) to started at once

    (B) at once start

    (C) to be started at once

    (D) start at once

(   ) 8. Almost all the computer learners know that the first step in preparing a program is _____ a flow chart.

    (A) drawn   (B) being drawn

    (C) drew   (D) to draw

(   ) 9. The words on the wall are _____ be recognized.

    (A) to vague too   (B) to vague to

    (C) too vague to   (D) too vague too

10. 活到老，學到老。

    One is never _____ old _____ learn.

11. He is, so to speak, a walking dictionary. (英翻中)

    _____

二、原形不定詞的用法

(   ) 1. She was seen _____ this room last night.

    (A) enter   (B) enter in

    (C) entered   (D) to enter

(   ) 2. We watched the child _____.

    (A) to play   (B) played

    (C) was playing   (D) play

(   ) 3. All these advertisements have the same purpose: to
　　　　 _____ people to buy something.
     (A) get   (B) make   (C) let   (D) have   (E) watch

(   ) 4. It is warm here. You had better _____ your coat.
     (A) to take off   (B) take off
     (C) taking off   (D) to take out
     (E) take out

(   ) 5. The baby did nothing but _____.
     (A) cries   (B) cried   (C) cryed   (D) cry

(   ) 6. 你只要在這支票上簽個字就好了。(選正確的)
     (A) All you have to do is sign the check.
     (B) The only thing you do is sign the check.
     (C) That will be fine to sign the check.
     (D) You only sign the check.
     (E) What you do is to sign your name on the check.

(   ) 7. "Let everything I touch <u>to turn</u> to gold," he asked.
                                            (改錯)

   8. 我寧願到山裡面，而不願到海濱去。
     I would _____ go to the mountains _____ to the seaside.

三、不定詞的完成式與否定形

(   ) 1. He seems _____ a long way in the sun.
     (A) to have walked   (B) to walk
     (C) walked   (D) walking

(　) 2. He told _____ home.

    (A) us not to go   (B) we go not

    (C) us not go   (D) us to not go

    (E) we not go to

(　) 3. 我承認我實在太笨了，竟不懂你所暗示的一切。

I admitted it was foolish of me _____ what you

hinted at.

    (A) have not to understood

    (B) have to not understood

    (C) to not have understood

    (D) not to have understood

    (E) to not have been understood

  4. I wished to have helped him. (英翻中)

_____

四、不定詞意義上的主詞

(　) 1. It is too difficult _____ her to decide where to go.

    (A) for   (B) to   (C) by

(　) 2. It is natural for them _____ money from banks

because now interest rates are higher than before.

    (A) no borrow   (B) not borrow

    (C) to not borrow   (D) not to borrow

  3. 你能幫助我，你實在是太好了。

It's kind _____ you to help me.

五、不定詞的省略

(　　) 1. "Should I drive you home?"

　　"I don't mind if you do. But you don't _____."

　　(A) have to do 　　　(B) have to take

　　(C) have 　　・　　(D) have to

(　　) 2. "Why did you open the door?"

　　"Because I was told _____."

　　(A) to open 　　　(B) open it

　　(C) and open 　　　(D) to

【歷屆聯考試題解答】

一、　1. (**B**)　　2. (**C**)　　3. (**C**)　　4. (**B**)　　5. (**B**)

　　6. (**A**)　　7. (**C**)　　8. (**D**)　　9. (**C**)　　10. too, to

　　11. 他好比是一部活字典。

二、　1. (**D**)　　2. (**D**)　　3. (**A**)　　4. (**B**)　　5. (**D**)

　　6. (**A**)　　7. turn/be turned　　8. rather, than

三、　1. (**A**)　　2. (**A**)　　3. (**D**)

　　4. 但願我幫了他的忙。（我原想幫忙他。）

四、　1. (**A**)　　2. (**D**)　　3. of

五、　1. (**D**)　　2. (**D**)

【解析】

一、　2. 她想請人裝潢公寓。

　　　have + 物 + 過去分詞　「使人做～」

　　　flat〔flæt〕*n.* 公寓　　*decorate*〔'dɛkə,ret〕*v.* 裝潢

3. *be about to* 正要　　*give up* 放棄

4. to drink 當形容詞片語，修飾 nothing。

6. 你想散個步嗎？
would like 想要，後面接不定詞。

8. *flow chart* 流程圖

9. vague〔veg〕*adj.* 模糊的　*too~to…* 太~以致於不能…

11. *so to speak* = *so to say*　可說是；好比是

二、 1. 被動態的感官動詞，其後接不定詞做補語，to 不可省略。

2. 感官動詞接受詞後，其接原形不定詞或現在分詞皆可。

3. get 不屬於感官動詞或使役動詞，其後接不定詞做爲受詞
補語。
advertisement〔͵ædvə'taɪzmənt〕*n.* 廣告

4. *had better not* + V. 最好不~

5. *do nothing but* + V. 什麼事都沒做，只~

6. *all one has to do is* + V. 某人所必須做的就是~

三、 1. 他似乎已經在陽光下走了一段很長的路。

2. 不定詞的否定，否定詞須放在 to 之前。

3. admit〔əd'mɪt〕*v.* 承認　*hint at* 暗示

四、 2. 「很自然的，他們不會向銀行借錢，因爲現在的利率比
以前高。」　*interest rate* 利率

五、 1. 原句 = But you don't have to *take me home.*

2. 原句 = Because I was told to *open it.*

精選模擬考題

(　) 1. ＿＿＿＿ to get up early to be on time ＿＿＿＿ the first train.
(A) You will be necessary, by
(B) It will be necessary for you, for
(C) It will be necessary to you, at
(D) It will be necessary for you, till

(　) 2. It is very kind ＿＿＿＿ you to say so.
(A) in　　(B) of　　(C) to　　(D) for

(　) 3. The class wanted him ＿＿＿＿ the presentation speech.
(A) makes　　　　　(B) make
(C) to make　　　　(D) to be make

(　) 4. I heard her ＿＿＿＿ a song.
(A) sing　(B) to sing　(C) sung　(D) sang

(　) 5. They made me ＿＿＿＿ it.
(A) to drink　　　　(B) drink
(C) drinking　　　　(D) drunk

(　) 6. I'll have him ＿＿＿＿ my photograph.
(A) take　(B) took　(C) taken　(D) taking

(　) 7. She did nothing but ＿＿＿＿.
(A) to smile　　　　(B) smiling
(C) smile　　　　　(D) smiles

(　　) 8. I cannot but _____ at hearing such a story.
    (A) to laugh   (B) laugh
    (C) laughing   (D) laughed

(　　) 9. He asked us _____ any noise.
    (A) don't make   (B) not to make
    (C) to not make   (D) make not

(　　) 10. She wished to buy it, though I advised her _____.
    (A) not   (B) not to
    (C) not to buy   (D) to not buy it

(　　) 11. "Why don't you spend more time studying?"
    "I don't want _____."
    (A) so   (B) to   (C) that   (D) X

(　　) 12. I heard him _____ English.
    (A) spoke   (B) speak   (C) speaks   (D) spoken

(　　) 13. He told his servant _____ those books away at once.
    (A) taking   (B) by taking
    (C) to take   (D) to took

(　　) 14. Please remember _____ this letter on your way home.
    (A) post   (B) posting
    (C) posted   (D) to post

(　　) 15. You'd better _____ there.
    (A) not to go   (B) not go
    (C) not going   (D) to not go

(　　) 16. Hard training _____ to win the game.

    (A) enabled him

    (B) made him

    (C) made him possible

    (D) made possible for him

(　　) 17. I would rather go to bed than _____ cards.

    (A) play   (B) playing

    (C) to play   (D) to be playing

(　　) 18. She got her son _____ the door.

    (A) fix   (B) to be fixed

    (C) fixed   (D) to fix

(　　) 19. My parents encouraged me to be a judge, but I didn't

    _____.

    (A) want

    (B) want one

    (C) want to become so

    (D) want to

(　　) 20. She did nothing but _____ all day.

    (A) cry   (B) to cry

    (C) crying   (D) cries

(　　) 21. They saw him _____ the room.

    (A) leave   (B) to leave

    (C) to be leave   (D) leaving to

(　) 22. I had the man _____ the house.
    (A) paint　　　　　　　(B) to paint
    (C) painted　　　　　　(D) painting

(　) 23. I got up early this morning _____ the first train.
    (A) so as to catch
    (B) so as catch
    (C) so as to catching
    (D) so as catching

(　) 24. _____ the room.
    (A) He made me to leave
    (B) I was made leave
    (C) I was made to leave
    (D) He made me to leaving

(　) 25. I am sorry _____ earlier.
    (A) to not come
    (B) not to come
    (C) not to have come
    (D) to not have come

(　) 26. I was so tired that I found _____ to go any farther.
    (A) impossibility　　　(B) impossible
    (C) it impossibility　　(D) it impossible

(　) 27. Can you get someone _____ it for me?
    (A) repair　　　　　　(B) to repair
    (C) repairing　　　　　(D) to repairing

(　) 28. He has never been heard ＿＿＿＿ ill of others.

      (A) speak　　　　　(B) to speak

      (C) speaking to　　　(D) spoken

(　) 29. I have a pen pal in Japan ＿＿＿＿ from time to time.

      (A) to correspond with

      (B) corresponding to

      (C) to correspond

      (D) correspond with

(　) 30. ＿＿＿＿ with you, I don't like her.

      (A) Been frank　　　(B) To be frank

      (C) Be frank　　　　(D) Be franking

(　) 31. It's quite late. We'd better ＿＿＿＿ home very soon.

      (A) going　　　　　(B) to be going

      (C) go　　　　　　　(D) to go

(　) 32. This book is too hard ＿＿＿＿.

      (A) for me to read it　(B) to me to read it

      (C) for me to read　　(D) of me to read it

【精選模擬考題解答】

  1. (**B**)　　2. (**B**)　　3. (**C**)　　4. (**A**)　　5. (**B**)　　6. (**A**)

  7. (**C**)　　8. (**B**)　　9. (**B**)　　10. (**B**)　11. (**B**)　12. (**B**)

13. (**C**)　14. (**D**)　15. (**B**)　16. (**A**)　17. (**A**)　18. (**D**)

19. (**D**)　20. (**A**)　21. (**A**)　22. (**A**)　23. (**A**)　24. (**C**)

25. (**C**)　26. (**D**)　27. (**B**)　28. (**B**)　29. (**A**)　30. (**B**)

31. (**C**)　32. (**C**)

【解析】

1. 對你而言，早點起床以便準時趕上第一班火車，是有必要的。
   it 是虛主詞，代替後面眞正的主詞 to get up…train。

3. 同學們要他發表開場演說。
   presentation〔ˌprɛznˈteʃən〕*n.* 介紹

6. 我會叫他幫我拍照。

10 雖然我勸她不要買，她還是想買那個東西。
   本題以 not to 代替 not to buy it。

14. *remember* + *to* + *V.* 記得去～
    <比較> *remember* + *V-ing* 記得曾做過～

16. *enable* + 人 + *to V.* = *make* + 人 + *V.* 使某人能～

19. encourage〔ɪnˈkɝɪdʒ〕*v.* 鼓勵
    judge〔dʒʌdʒ〕*n.* 法官

23. *so as to* + *V.* 以便～

25. 本句意思爲：I *should have come* earlier. （我應該早點到。）

28. 從沒聽過他說別人的壞話。
    speak ill of～ 說～的壞話

29. *pen pal* 筆友　　*correspond with*～ 與～通信
    from time to time 有時；偶爾

2. 分　詞

> 分詞是具有形容詞性質的動詞形態，
> 分為現在分詞與過去分詞兩種。

1. 修飾名詞、代名詞

1. 現在分詞修飾名詞、代名詞

⑴ **前位修飾**：分詞單獨修飾名詞時，原則上置於名詞之前。

【例】 I like the *rising* sun better than the *setting* sun.
（我喜歡旭日甚過夕陽。）

He has never seen such an *exciting* game.
（他從未看過這麼刺激的比賽。）

⑵ **後位修飾**：由若干個字所形成的分詞片語，或修飾 something,
anybody, nothing 這類不定代名詞，或指示代名詞 those 時，
分詞置於所修飾的字之後。

【例】 I got a letter from my *pen pal living* in England.
（我收到住在英國的筆友寄來的信。）

She lost a *purse containing* one hundred dollars.
（她遺失了一個裝有一百元的皮包。）

Let me tell you *something interesting*.
（讓我告訴你一件有趣的事。）

2. 過去分詞修飾名詞、代名詞

(1) 前位修飾

【例】 There were *fallen leaves* all over the garden.

（花園裡到處都是落葉。）

Spoken language is different from *written language*.

（語言與文字有別。）

(2) 後位修飾

【例】 He sent me *a letter written* in red ink.

（他寄給我一封用紅筆寫的信。— 他和我絕交了。）

The *languages spoken in Canada* are English and
French. （加拿大講英文和法文。）

Among *those invited* were some ladies.

（被邀請的人之中，有些是女士。）

☞ ⎧ a. 現在分詞表主動及進行的意思。
⎨ b. 及物動詞的過去分詞表被動。
⎩ c. 不及物動詞的過去分詞表主動的完成狀態。

【例】 (a) A *rolling* stone gathers no moss.

（滾石不生苔；轉業不聚財。）

(b) *Lost* time is lost forever.（失去的時間就是永遠失去了。）

(c) She wore a *faded* coat. （她穿了一件已經褪色的外套。）

2. 分詞做補語用

1. 現在分詞做主詞補語及受詞補語

(1) S + V + C（主詞補語）

【例】 *She* sat *listening* to the radio for hours.

（她坐著聽了好幾個小時的收音機。）

His eyes kept *following* the yellow butterfly.

（他的眼睛一直跟著那隻黃色的蝴蝶轉。）

⑵ **S + V + O + C**（受詞補語）

① I saw *an old woman **crossing*** the busy street.
（我看到一位老婦人正在穿越擁擠的街道。）

<比較> I saw an old woman *cross* the busy street.【表示狀態】

He could feel *his heart **beating*** fast.
（他可以感覺到自己的心跳得很快。）

② They kept *the fire **burning*** all night.
（他們讓火燃燒一整夜。）

She left *the baby **sleeping*** on the sofa.
（她把小寶寶留在沙發上睡覺。）

---

2. 過去分詞做主詞補語及受詞補語

⑴ **S + V + C**（主詞補語）

【例】 *All the villagers* seemed ***satisfied***.
（所有的村民似乎都很知足。）

He sat ***surrounded*** by his family.
（他坐著，四周圍著家人。）

The money lay ***hidden*** under the stone.（錢藏在石頭下。）

The weather remains ***unsettled***.（天氣依然不穩定。）

⑵ **S + V + O + C**（受詞補語）

【例】 I kept *the door **closed*** while I was sleeping.
（我睡覺時把門關上。）

Suddenly I heard *my name **called*** by the teacher.
（我突然聽到老師叫我的名字。）

He tried to make *himself **understood*** in English.
（他試圖用英文使人了解他的意思。）

(3) **S** + **have**〔**get**〕 + **O** + **C**（受詞補語）

【例】 I usually ***have** my hair **cut*** at the barber's.
（我通常在理髮廳理髮。）

She ***had** her new bicycle **stolen*** in front of the station.
（她的新單車在車站前被偷了。）

Where can I ***get** these shoes **mended***?
（我可以把這些鞋子拿到哪裡修理？）

He couldn't ***get** the car **started*** because it was very cold.（因為天氣很冷，所以他發不動車子。）

☞ 使役動詞 have, made 接過去分詞表被動，接原形表主動。感官動詞 see, hear 接過去分詞表被動，接原形、現在分詞表主動。

> I'll have *the door painted* by Tom.
> （我要叫湯姆油漆門。）
> I'll have *Tom paint* the door.

> I saw *a cat beaten* by him.（我看見他打貓。）
> I saw *him beat* a cat.

3. 分詞構句

分詞構句可置於 (a) 句首，(b) 句中，(c) 句尾，都要用逗點分開。

【例】 (a) *Not having received a reply*, I wrote to him again.
（因為沒收到回信，我又寫了一封信給他。）

(b) The book, *written in haste*, has many faults.
（這本書因為寫得很急，所以有許多錯誤。）

(c) I approached the sleeping baby, *walking on tiptoe*.（我踮起腳尖走近酣睡中的寶寶。）

⑴ **表時間**

　【例】 *Arriving* at the station, he found the train had gone.

　　　　（ = *When he arrived* at the station, he… ）

　　　　（當他到達車站時，發現火車已經開走了。）

　　　　Walking along the street, I met an old friend
　　　　of mine.

　　　　（ = *While I was walking* along the street, I… ）

　　　　（我沿著街道走的時候，碰見一位老友。）

⑵ **表附帶狀況**

　【例】 *Singing* merrily, she went out of her room.

　　　　（她愉快地唱著歌，走出房間。）

　　　　He put out his hand, *smiling* brightly.

　　　　（他伸出手，開朗地笑著。）

　　☞ 分詞構句可代替對等子句，用以補充說明。

　【例】 The express started at eight, *arriving* at Taipei at
　　　　eleven. (= The express started at eight, *and arrived*…)

　　　　（快車於八點出發，十一點到達台北。）

⑶ **表原因、理由**

　【例】 *Being* tired, the old man sat down to rest.

　　　　（ = *As he was* tired, the old man… ）

　　　　（因為累了，這老人坐下來休息。）

　　　　Having no money with me, I could not buy
　　　　the book.

　　　　（ = *Since I had* no money with me, I… ）

　　　　（因為身上沒錢，所以我無法買下那本書。）

⑷ **表條件**

【例】 ***Turning*** to the right, you will find the bank on your left. (= *If you turn* to the right, you…)

（向右轉，你就會發現銀行在你的左手邊。）

Driving very carefully, we may avoid accidents.

(= *If we drive* very carefully, we…)

（如果小心開車，就可以避免發生車禍。）

⑸ **表讓步**

【例】 ***Admitting*** what you say, I still think it difficult to put the plan into practice.

(= *Though I admit* what you say, I…)

（雖然我承認你說的話，但我還是認為要實現這個計劃很難。）

4. 分詞構句應注意的形式

⑴ **完成式**

【例】 ***Having done*** his homework, he *went* out to play.

(= *After he had done* his homework, he…)

（他在做完家庭作業之後，就出去玩了。）

Having lived abroad for a long time, I *have* few friends here.

(= *As I have lived* abroad for a long time, I…)

（因為在國外住了很久，所以我在這裡的朋友很少。）

⑵ **否定形**

【例】 ***Not knowing*** what to say, I remained silent.

(= *As I did not know* what to say, I…)

（因為不知道要說什麼，所以我保持沉默。）

Not having found the treasure, he *went* away disappointed.

（＝ *Since he had not found* the treasure, he… ）

（因為沒發現寶藏，他很失望地離去。）

(3) **獨立分詞構句**——前後主詞不相同的情況

【例】 *The weather **being*** fine, *we* played out of doors.

（＝ *As* the weather was fine, we… ）

（因為天氣好，所以我們在戶外玩。）

*The sun **having set***, *it* grew cold suddenly.

（＝ *When* the sun had set, it… ）

（當太陽下山時，天氣突然變冷了。）

He was watching television, *his wife **reading*** the newspaper beside him.

（＝ He was watching television *and* his wife was reading… ）

（他正在看電視，而他太太在他旁邊看報紙。）

(4) **being 的省略**：being ＋ 過去分詞或形容詞的分詞構句，通常省略 being。

【例】 ***Seen*** from a distance, the stone looks like a human face.

（＝ *When* 〔*If*〕 *it is seen* from a distance, the stone… ）

（從遠處看，這塊石頭看起來像一張人的臉。）

Unable to find the answer, the student remained silent.

（＝ *Since he was unable* to find the answer, the student… ）

（因為找不到答案，所以這名學生保持沉默。）

⑸ 分詞構句的慣用法

generally speaking 一般說來　　supposing (suppose) 如果

strictly speaking 嚴格地說　　providing (provided) 如果

roughly speaking 大致說來　　granting (granted) 即使

talking of 談到　　judging from~ 由~判斷

seeing (that) 既然　　considering (that) 就…來說

talking all things into consideration 從各方面來說

【例】 ***Generally speaking***, the students of this school are diligent. (一般說來，這學校的學生都很勤勉。)

Judging from his appearance, he must be very rich.
(由他的外表判斷，他一定非常富有。)

⑹ **有連接詞的分詞構句**：為了使分詞構句和主要子句的關係明確，分詞前保留連接詞。

【例】 ***While staying*** in London, I made friends with an English actress.
(當我待在倫敦時，我和一位英國女演員結交為朋友。)

5. 含分詞的慣用法

⑴ **with + O + 分詞 → 表示附帶狀態**

【例】 She smiled at me ***with her hand waving***.
(她向我招手微笑。)

He sat on the bench ***with his legs crossed***.
(他兩腿交叉坐在長椅上。)

She ran along the beach ***with her hair flying*** in the wind. (她沿著海灘跑，頭髮隨風飛揚。)

He listened to the music ***with his eyes closed***.
(他閉著眼睛聽音樂。)

歷屆聯考試題

一、修飾名詞、代名詞

(　　) 1. Some of these wild rices are similar to _____ rice but none are quite the same.
  (A) cultivate   (B) cultivating
  (C) be cultivated (D) cultivated

(　　) 2. Ten _____ by five is two.
  (A) divided   (B) by
  (C) divides   (D) define

(　　) 3. Scientists today are faced with the most _____ task of developing a vaccine against AIDS.
  (A) casual   (B) challenging
  (C) excited   (D) reverse

(　　) 4. John and his wife are no longer living together. They have a _____ marriage.
  (A) break   (B) broken
  (C) broke   (D) breaking

(　　) 5. The story of Marconi is an <u>excite</u> one. (改錯)

(　　) 6. I found <u>it</u> <u>interested</u> to speak English <u>with</u> <u>foreign</u>
    (A) (B)   (C) (D)
friends. (改錯)

二、做補語用

( ) 1. They plan to get _____ next month.
    (A) marry   (B) married
    (C) marriage   (D) marriages

( ) 2. The earth is a rotating sphere _____ through space.
    (A) move   (B) to move
    (C) moving   (D) moved

( ) 3. I become _____ after watching too much television.
    (A) bored   (B) boring
    (C) bore   (D) bores

( ) 4. Why don't you have your coat _____?
    (A) clean   (B) cleaned
    (C) cleans   (D) to clean

( ) 5. She found her money _____.
    (A) steal   (B) to steal
    (C) stealing   (D) stolen

( ) 6. Winds blow across the oceans, _____ the water into waves.
    (A) and pushing   (B) pushing   (C) push
    (D) to push   (E) and to push

( ) 7. Several boys are in the room <u>listen</u> to their teacher attentively. (改錯)

(　　) 8. We found <u>that</u> the house <u>stood</u> in the <u>distance</u> was
　　　　　　　　(A)　　　　　　(B)　　　　　　(C)

　　　<u>deserted</u>. (改錯)
　　　(D)

三、分詞構句

(　　) 1. It is customary to shake hands when _____.
　　　(A) introduce　　　(B) introduced
　　　(C) introducing　　(D) introduction

(　　) 2. We must render personal or military service to our
　　　country when _____ upon.
　　　(A) we have called
　　　(B) called
　　　(C) we called
　　　(D) calling

(　　) 3. _____ where I live, he often comes to see me.
　　　(A) Known　　　　(B) Knowing
　　　(C) To know　　　(D) Know
　　　(E) Have known

(　　) 4. The little boy finally entered, accompanied by his
　　　mother.
　　　(A) 這個小男孩最後走進來陪伴母親。
　　　(B) 這個小男孩最後陪母親走進來。
　　　(C) 這個小男孩最後由母親陪著走進來。
　　　(D) 母親養育的小男孩進來陪伴她。

(   ) 5. You must be careful when _____.

      (A) you driving   (B) are driving

      (C) driving   (D) you were driving

(   ) 6. <u>Sit</u> before us, he told us what he saw yesterday. (改錯)

(   ) 7. The <u>thick</u>, bad <u>smelling</u> liquid will <u>turn</u> green when
              (A)   (B)   (C)

      <u>expose</u> <u>to</u> light. (改錯)
      (D)   (E)

四、分詞構句應注意事項

(   ) 1. The pollution level _____ high today, people can
      not help breathing in car exhaust.

      (A) is   (B) has been

      (C) being   (D) has

(   ) 2. _____, we left off our work.

      (A) After setting the sun

      (B) Having set the sun

      (C) The sun having set

      (D) Being the sun set

      (E) Set the sun

(   ) 3. Abraham Lincoln, _____ as Honest Abe, was the
      sixteenth President of the United States.

      (A) known   (B) knows

      (C) knowing   (D) knew

(　) 4. The airport, _____ in Taoyuan, is officially named
Chiang Kai-Shek International Airport in
commemoration of the late President.
(A) locate　　　　(B) locating
(C) location　　　(D) located

(　) 5. Engines are machines _____ power or motion.
(A) produce　　　(B) that produce
(C) produced　　　(D) which producing

(　) 6. The poor <u>crippled</u> child <u>lay</u> <u>on</u> the ground became
　　　　　　　(A)　　　　　(B) (C)

my <u>daughter's</u> main <u>concern</u>. (改錯)
　　(D)　　　　　　(E)

(　) 7. <u>Seeing</u> by the policeman, the robber ran <u>toward</u> the
　　(A)　　　　　　　　　　　　　　　　(B)

<u>shopping mall</u> and <u>disappeared</u>. (改錯)
　　(C)　　　　　　(D)

(　) 8. _____, follow the directions on the bottle carefully.
(A) When taken drugs
(B) When in taking drugs
(C) When one takes drugs
(D) When he takes drugs
(E) When taking drugs

五、分詞的慣用語

(　) 1. _____ in simple English, this novel is easily understood.
  (A) Written
  (B) Writing
  (C) Wrote
  (D) To write

(　) 2. If _____, I will go to the party.
  (A) invite
  (B) inviting
  (C) to invite
  (D) invited

(　) 3. _____ carefully, this letter is very beautiful.
  (A) Type
  (B) Typing
  (C) Typed
  (D) To type

(　) 4. _____ my homework, I went home.
  (A) Having finished
  (B) Finished
  (C) Being finished
  (D) Finish

(　) 5. Turning to the left, _____.
  (A) the bus station will be found
  (B) the bus station will be found by you
  (C) you will find the bus station
  (D) you will be found the bus station

(　) 6. Walking into the park _____.
  (A) a beautiful scenery was seen
  (B) we saw beautiful scenery
  (C) a beautiful scenery had been seen
  (D) we has seen a beautiful scenery

(　) 7. While waiting for the doctor, _____.
　　　(A) there are many magazines that you can read
　　　(B) many magazines can be read by you
　　　(C) you can be read many magazines
　　　(D) you can read numerous magazines

【歷屆聯考試題解答】

一、 1.(**D**)　　2.(**A**)　　3.(**B**)　　4.(**B**)
　　 5. excite → exciting　6.(**B**) → interesting

二、 1.(**B**)　　2.(**C**)　　3.(**A**)　　4.(**B**)　　5.(**D**)
　　 6.(**B**)　　7. listen → listening　8.(**B**) → standing

三、 1.(**B**)　　2.(**B**)　　3.(**B**)　　4.(**C**)　　5.(**C**)
　　 6. Sit → Sitting/Seated/Sat　　7.(**D**) → exposed

四、 1.(**C**)　　2.(**C**)　　3.(**A**)　　4.(**D**)　　5.(**B**)
　　 6.(**B**) → lying　　7.(**A**) → Having been seen
　　 8.(**E**)

五、 1.(**A**)　　2.(**D**)　　3.(**C**)　　4.(**A**)　　5.(**C**)
　　 6.(**B**)　　7.(**D**)

【解析】

一、 1. *be similar to* 與…相似
　　　 cultivated (ˈkʌltəˌvetɪd) *adj.* 栽植的

　　 3. 「今日的科學家,面臨發展抵抗愛滋病的疫苗,這個最
　　　　具挑戰性的任務。」　　vaccine (ˈvæksɪn, -sɪn) *n.* 疫苗

二、 2. rotate (ˈrotet) *v.* 旋轉　　sphere (sfɪr) *n.* 球體

　　 6. 本句是由…, *and push* the water into waves. 簡化而來的
　　　　分詞構句。

三、 1. customary (ˈkʌstəmˌɛrɪ) *adj.* 習慣的
       shake hands 握手

   2. 本句由…***when we are called upon.***簡化而來。
      render (ˈrɛndə) *v.* 給與（協助等）　　***call upon*** 要求

   4. accompany (əˈkʌmpənɪ) *v.* 陪伴（某人）

四、 1. 本句由 ***Since the pollution level is*** high today,….
      簡化而來。
      breathe (brið) *v.* 吸入（空氣）
      exhaust (ɪgˈzɔst) *n.* 排氣

   4. 「位於桃園的機場被正式命名爲中正國際機場，以紀
      念先總統。」　　***in commemoration of*** 紀念

   6. 那個躺在地上的可憐跛腳孩子，成爲我女兒最關心
      的事。
      比較 lie 和 lay 的不同：

$$\begin{cases} \text{lie（躺）} - \textit{lay} - \text{lain} - \textit{lying} \\ \textit{lay}\text{（放置）} - \text{laid} - \text{laid} - \textit{laying} \end{cases}$$

五、 5. 向左轉，你就可以找到公車站。
      前面句子的主詞是 you，而非「公車站」，故 (A) (B) 不
      可選。

精選模擬考題

( ) 1. She wants to have a new dress _____.
    (A) made   (B) make
    (C) making   (D) to make

( ) 2. The window has been _____ all day long.
    (A) kept shutting
    (B) kept closed
    (C) keeping close
    (D) keeping closed

( ) 3. All the spectators grew _____ at the wonderful game.
    (A) excited   (B) exciting
    (C) to excite   (D) to exciting

( ) 4. He was sitting alone _____.
    (A) folded his arms
    (B) with his arms folding
    (C) his arms folded
    (D) with his arms folded

( ) 5. His work _____, he went to play tennis.
    (A) was done   (B) is done
    (C) been done   (D) done

( ) 6. Have you ever heard this opera _____ in Italian?
    (A) sing (B) sang (C) sung (D) have sung

(   ) 7. Looking into the room, _____.

       (A) I found it empty

       (B) there was no one there

       (C) no one was there

       (D) it was vacant

(   ) 8. There _____ no bus service, we had to walk all the way to the inn.

       (A) was   (B) being

       (C) having   (D) having been

(   ) 9. I am sorry to have kept you _____ so long.

       (A) wait   (B) waited

       (C) waiting   (D) have waited

(   ) 10. I saw something white _____ in the water.

       (A) movement   (B) mover

       (C) moves   (D) moving

(   ) 11. I got my baggage _____ by the porter.

       (A) carried   (B) carry

       (C) being carried   (D) carrying

(   ) 12. You had better have that decayed tooth _____ out.

       (A) pull   (B) being pulled

       (C) pulled   (D) pulling

(   ) 13. I left the door _____.
     (A) unlocked
     (B) having unlocked
     (C) being unlocked
     (D) having been unlocked

(   ) 14. When did you have your hair _____?
     (A) cuts
     (B) cut
     (C) being cut
     (D) having being cut

(   ) 15. I could not make myself _____ in English.
     (A) understood
     (B) understanding
     (C) having been understood
     (D) understand

(   ) 16. I must have this room _____ now.
     (A) sweep   (B) swept
     (C) sweeping   (D) having been swept

(   ) 17. I'll have my son _____ the luggage for you.
     (A) carries   (B) carry
     (C) carried   (D) to carry

(   ) 18. I'm afraid I must have the tooth _____ out.
     (A) pull   (B) pulling
     (C) pulled   (D) to pull

( ) 19. There was so much noise that the speaker couldn't make himself _____.
(A) to hear   (B) to be heard
(C) hearing   (D) heard

( ) 20. I was busy _____ my brother do kitchen work.
(A) helping   (B) to help
(C) helped   (D) in help

( ) 21. I found this book _____ from beginning to end.
(A) amused (B) enjoying
(C) interesting   (D) interested

( ) 22. When did you have your watch _____?
(A) mend   (B) to mend
(C) mended   (D) mending

( ) 23. I had him _____ it.
(A) translated   (B) translate
(C) to translate   (D) translating

( ) 24. I saw her _____ to remove a stain from the carpet.
(A) to try   (B) tries   (C) trying   (D) tried

( ) 25. _____ what to do, he asked for my advice.
(A) Not knowing   (B) Knowing not
(C) To know   (D) Knowing

( ) 26. I wanted the work _____ as soon as possible.
(A) done   (B) did   (C) doing   (D) do

(　) 27. Everything _____ satisfactorily arranged, they rose and started homeward.
    (A) having been   (B) had
    (C) was   (D) having

(　) 28. He had a fall and his leg was _____.
    (A) broken   (B) to break
    (C) break   (D) broke

(　) 29. The language _____ in the province is English.
    (A) speaking   (B) speaks
    (C) spoken   (D) spoke

(　) 30. I would like to have this house _____ white.
    (A) paint   (B) painted
    (C) to paint   (D) painting

(　) 31. I had my wallet _____.
    (A) be stolen   (B) stolen
    (C) get stolen   (D) had stolen

(　) 32. He had his shoes _____ on his way to the house.
    (A) clean   (B) to clean
    (C) cleaned   (D) cleaning

(　) 33. _____ from what you said, we have to help him.
    (A) Judge   (B) Judged
    (C) Judging   (D) To have judged

( ) 34. _____ finished my homework, I went out for a walk.
(A) Have (B) Having (C) Being (D) To have

( ) 35. Writing that is very _____ work.
(A) tired (B) tire (C) tiring (D) to tire

( ) 36. They listened to his talk with an _____ look.
(A) interest (B) interested
(C) interestive (D) interests

( ) 37. A _____ man will grab at any straw.
(A) being drowned (B) drowned
(C) drowning (D) drown

( ) 38. The film made us laugh, but it was not really _____ to watch.
(A) excited (B) exciting (C) to excite (D) excitable

( ) 39. She was a girl _____ Jane.
(A) names (B) naming (C) named (D) name

( ) 40. Good drinking water is a priceless possession to a person _____ in a desert.
(A) traveled (B) traveling
(C) travels (D) to have traveled

( ) 41. He was proud of his room; he liked to have it _____.
(A) admire (B) admiring
(C) admired (D) admirable

【精選模擬考題解答】

1. (**A**)　2. (**B**)　3. (**A**)　4. (**D**)　5. (**D**)　6. (**C**)
7. (**A**)　8. (**B**)　9. (**C**)　10. (**D**)　11. (**A**)　12. (**C**)
13. (**A**)　14. (**B**)　15. (**A**)　16. (**B**)　17. (**B**)　18. (**C**)
19. (**D**)　20. (**A**)　21. (**C**)　22. (**C**)　23. (**B**)　24. (**C**)
25. (**D**)　26. (**A**)　27. (**A**)　28. (**A**)　29. (**C**)　30. (**B**)
31. (**B**)　32. (**C**)　33. (**C**)　34. (**B**)　35. (**C**)　36. (**B**)
37. (**C**)　38. (**B**)　39. (**C**)　40. (**B**)　41. (**C**)

【解析】

1. 使役動詞＋物＋過去分詞，表「被動」。

2. 本題若 (A) 改為 kept shut，則亦可選。

3. excited (感到興奮的) 修飾人，exciting (令人興奮的) 修飾
   物。　　spectator〔'spɛktɛtɚ〕*n.* 觀眾

4. 「他雙臂交叉獨自坐在那裏。」　　fold〔fold〕*v.* 交 (臂)

5. 本句是由 His work *being* done，省略 being 而來。

6. 你有沒有聽過這首用義大利文唱的歌劇？
   opera〔'ɑpərə〕*n.* 歌劇　　Italian〔ɪ'tæljən〕*n.* 義大利文

7. 分詞構句的主詞應該一致，原句＝As *I* looked into the room,
   I found it empty.

8. 因為沒有連接詞，故本題是獨立分詞構句，將不同的主詞
   (there) 保留，並且將 be 動詞改成 being。

9. 抱歉讓你等這麼久。

11. porter〔'portɚ〕*n.* 挑夫；服務生
    get＋物＋過去分詞＋(by＋人)「使某物被 (某人) ～」

12. 你最好 (叫人) 把那顆蛀牙拔掉。
    decayed tooth 蛀牙　　***pull out*** 拔出

15. 我無法用英文使人了解我的意思。

    make* myself *understood 使自己被人了解

17. luggage (ˈlʌgɪdʒ) *n.* 行李

21. (A) 應改為 amusing (有趣的)，(B) 應改為 enjoyable
    (令人愉快的)。

    from beginning to end 從頭到尾

22. mend (mɛnd) *v.* 修理

23. translate (ˈtrænslet) *v.* 翻譯

24. 我看見她試圖除去地毯上的污點。

    remove (rɪˈmuv) *v.* 除去   stain (sten) *n.* 污點

27. 本題沒有連接詞，所以為獨立分詞構句，將不同的主詞保留。

    satisfactorily (ˌsætɪsˈfæktərɪlɪ) *adv.* 滿意地

29. province (ˈprɑvɪns) *n.* 省；領域

31. 「我的皮夾被偷了。」   wallet (ˈwɑlɪt) *n.* 皮夾

32. ***on one's way to***~ 某人到~的途中

35. tiring (令人疲倦的) 修飾物，tired (感到疲倦的) 修飾人。

36. ***an interested look*** 有興趣的表情

37. 溺者攀草求援；急不暇擇。

    (B) drowned (draʊnd) *adj.* 淹死的，與句意不合，故選
    (C) drowning (ˈdraʊnɪŋ) *adj.* 快淹死的。

40. ***drinking water*** 飲用水   priceless (ˈpraɪslɪs) *adj.* 無價的

    possession (pəˈzɛʃən) *n.* 所有物

41. ***be proud of***~ 以~為傲   admire (ədˈmaɪr) *v.* 欽佩；稱讚

3. 動名詞

具有名詞的性質，可做主詞、受詞、補語等，
又有動詞的性質，可以有受詞、補語，或由副詞修飾。

1. 動名詞的用法

1. 名詞性質的用法

(1) 做主詞

【例】 ***Studying*** all morning made him tired.
（讀了整個早上的書，使他感到疲倦。）

It was great fun ***playing*** with my dog.
（和我的狗玩很有趣。）

(2) 做受詞

【例】 I *enjoyed **lying*** in the sun after swimming in the sea.
（在海裡游泳之後，我喜歡躺在陽光下。）【動詞的受詞】

Illness prevented him *from **coming*** to school.
（生病使他無法來上學。）【介系詞的受詞】

(3) 做補語

【例】 My hobby is ***collecting*** stamps.
（集郵是我的嗜好。）

2. 動詞性質的用法

(1) 動名詞後面可接受詞

【例】 After ***reading*** *the novel* I went to bed.
（看完小說後，我就上床睡覺。）

(2) 動名詞後面可接補語

【例】 *Being idle* is the cause of his failure.

（懶惰是他失敗的原因。）

(3) 動名詞可由副詞修飾

【例】 Would you mind *speaking* more *slowly*?

（你能否說慢一點？）

(4) 動名詞可有完成式

【例】 I *regret* his *having neglected* his duty.

（他忽視職責，我感到很遺憾。）

(5) 動名詞可有被動語態

【例】 There is some hope of his *being saved*.

（他還有一點獲救的希望。）

2. 動名詞意義上的主詞

1. 不須再表明意義上的主詞

(1) 一些眾所週知的事

【例】 *Teaching* is more difficult than *learning*.

（教比學更難。）

Saying is one thing, *doing* another.

（說是一回事，做又是另一回事。）

(2) 動名詞意義上的主詞等於主要動詞的主詞時

【例】 I remember *reading* the detective story before.

（我記得以前讀過這個偵探故事。）

Would *you* mind *closing* the window?

（關起窗戶好嗎？）

2. 須表示出意義上的主詞

⑴ 生物名詞、代名詞，要用所有格的形式。

【例】 I am sure of *your brother's passing* the examination.
（我確信你弟弟會通過考試。）

Your being late has given us a lot of trouble.
（你遲到帶給我們很多麻煩。）

⑵ 無生物名詞或抽象名詞，用受格的形式。

【例】 Susan complains of *the kitchen being* so small.
（蘇珊抱怨廚房這麼小。）

I am glad of *the examination being* over.
（我很高興，考試結束了。）

3. 以動名詞為受詞的動詞

1. 只可接動名詞為受詞的動詞及片語

mind 介意	admit 承認	finish 完成
deny 否認	excuse 原諒	burst out 突然
envy 羨慕	can't help 忍不住	practice 練習
give up 放棄	avoid 避免	complete 完成
enjoy 喜愛	escape 逃避	put off 拖延

【例】 Would you *mind opening* the window?
（你介意開窗嗎？）

I could not *help laughing* at his joke.
（他的笑話使我忍不住發笑。）

I haven't *finished reading* the newspaper yet.
（我尚未看完報紙。）

She *denied having written* the letter.
（她否認寫過那封信。）

---

2. 可接動名詞或不定詞為受詞，但意義不同的動詞

(1) **remember, forget, regret** + $\begin{cases} \text{動名詞 ── 動作已經發生} \\ \text{不定詞 ── 動作尚未發生} \end{cases}$

【例】 (a) I *remember mailing* the letter.

（我記得已經把信寄出去了。）

(b) I must *remember to mail* the letter.

（我必須記得去寄信。）

(a) I will never *forget finding* the rare old coin.

（我永遠忘不了找到那枚稀有古幣的情形。）

(b) Don't *forget to close* the window before leaving.

（離開以前，別忘了關窗戶。）

(a) I *regret spending* so much money.

（我很後悔花了這麼多錢。）

(b) I *regret to say* that your letter didn't arrive in time.

（很抱歉，你的信並未及時送達。）

(2) **try** + 動名詞「嘗試；試驗」；**try** + 不定詞「努力；儘量」

【例】 (a) She *tried skating* for the first time.

（她第一次嘗試溜冰。）

(b) She *tried to solve* the puzzle.

（她努力去解開這難題。）

(3) **stop** + 動名詞「停止做～」；**stop** + 不定詞「停下來，開始做～」

【例】 (a) He *stopped reading* the notice when she came.

（她來的時候，他停止讀告示。）

(b) He *stopped to read* the notice.

（他停下來，並開始讀告示。）

☞　下列動詞接動名詞或不定詞，意義相同：

begin 開始	fear 害怕	plan 計劃
love 愛	can't endure〔bear〕不能忍受	
hate 憎恨	dislike 不喜歡	prefer 較喜歡
like 喜歡	attempt 企圖	continue 繼續

【例】 The baby began *crying*. = The baby began *to cry*.
（小寶寶開始哭了。）

☞　一般場合用動名詞，特定的場合用不定詞。

【例】 I like *swimming*, but I don't like *to swim* in the river.
（我喜歡游泳，但不喜歡在河裡游泳。）

4. 動名詞的慣用語

⑴ **cannot help V-ing**「不得不～；忍不住～」

【例】 He looked so funny that I *could not help laughing*.
（他看起來很滑稽，我忍不住笑了。）

⑵ **on V-ing**「一～就」

【例】 On *arriving* at the airport, he sent a telegram home.
（ = *As soon as* he arrived at the airport, he… ）
（一到達機場，他就發電報回家。）

⑶ **in V-ing**「當～時」

【例】 You cannot be too careful *in deciding* on your college.
（ = You…careful *when* you decide on your college. ）
（當你要選定讀哪一所大學時，再怎麼小心也不為過。）

⑷ **of *one's* own V-ing** 「自己～的」

【例】 I saw in his studio several pictures *of his own painting*. （我在他的畫室裡看到幾幅他自己畫的畫。）

⑸ **feel like V-ing**「想要～」

【例】 I *felt like jumping* up and down at the good news.
（聽到這個好消息，我真是雀躍不已。）

⑹ **be〔get〕used〔accustomed〕to V-ing**「習慣於～」

【例】 I *am* not *used*〔*accustomed*〕*to being* treated like a
lady.（我不習慣被當成淑女對待。）

He *got used*〔*accustomed*〕*to living* alone.
（他習慣獨居。）

<比較> He *used to treat* me like a child.
（他以前總把我當小孩看待。）

⑺ **cannot〔never〕…without V-ing** 「沒有…而不～；每…必～」

【例】 I *cannot* read such a story *without being* moved.
（每次讀到這種故事，我都會很感動。）

They *never* meet *without quarreling*.
（他們每次見面，就一定吵架。）

⑻ **look forward to V-ing**「期待～；盼望～」

【例】 I am *looking forward to seeing* you soon.
（我期待能很快見到你。）

⑼ **worth V-ing**「值得～」

【例】 This book is *worth reading*.
（= It is *worthwhile* reading this book.）
（這本書值得一讀。）

⑽ **want〔need〕V-ing**「需要～」

【例】 Your watch *wants repairing*（= needs *to be repaired*）.
（你的錶需要修理。）

My car *needs washing*.（我的車需要洗一洗。）

⑾ **There is no V-ing**「～是不可能的」

　　【例】　*There is no telling* what will happen in the future.
　　　　　(= *It is impossible to* tell what will happen in the future.)
　　　　　（要知道將來會發生什麼事，是不可能的。）

⑿ **It is no use V-ing**「～是沒有用的」

　　【例】　*It is no use crying* over split milk.
　　　　　（爲灑在地上的牛奶哭泣是沒有用的；覆水難收。）

⒀ **What do you say to V-ing…?, How about V-ing…?**
　「～如何？」

　　【例】　*What do you say to going* hiking next Sunday?
　　　　　（下個星期天去健行如何？）

　　　　　How about singing a few songs for us?
　　　　　（爲我們唱幾首歌如何？）

⒁ **go + V-ing**：go fishing（去釣魚），go skating（去溜冰），
　go skiing（去滑雪），go hunting（去打獵），go picnicking
　（去野餐），go mountain climbing（去爬山）。

　　【例】　I *went fishing* in the lake with my father.
　　　　　（我和爸爸去湖邊釣魚。）

⒂ **be busy + V-ing**「忙著做～」

　　【例】　He *has been busy preparing* for the examination.
　　　　　（他一直忙著準備考試。）

⒃ **spend + O + V-ing**

　　【例】　She *spent the whole afternoon* (in) *washing* her
　　　　　clothes.（她花了一整個下午的時間洗衣服。）

5. 動名詞與現在分詞的區別

動名詞和現在分詞型態上相同，但帶有名詞性質的是動名詞，帶有形容詞性質的是現在分詞。

【例】
{ a sleeping car (= a car for sleeping) 臥車【動名詞】
  a sleeping lion (= a lion which is sleeping)
    睡著的獅子【現在分詞】

{ a smoking room 吸煙室【動名詞】
  a smoking chimney 冒煙的煙囪【現在分詞】

{ a walking stick 柺杖【動名詞】
  a walking dictionary 活字典【現在分詞】

歷屆聯考試題

一、動名詞的用法

(　) 1. I would appreciate _____ back this afternoon.
  (A) you to call   (B) your call
  (C) your calling   (D) you're calling
  (E) to call you

(　) 2. I am very happy for your _____ our invitation.
  (A) accept   (B) accepted
  (C) accepting   (D) acception

(　) 3. Today men and women of all ages enjoy _____ music.
  (A) to listen   (B) listen
  (C) listening   (D) to listen to
  (E) listening to

(　) 4. She dislikes _____ by crowds of people.
  (A) to surround
  (B) surrounded
  (C) being surrounded
  (D) surrounding

(　) 5. The curious student kept on _____ questions.
  (A) asks   (B) asking
  (C) to ask   (D) asked

(　) 6. You must never cross the street without _____ for the light to turn green.

    (A) wait   (B) to wait

    (C) a wait   (D) waiting

(　) 7. After years of study, he succeeded _____ the English language.

    (A) master   (B) mastering

    (C) in master   (D) in mastering

    (E) by mastering

(　) 8. 我習慣於在這種燈光下看書。

    I _____ under these lights.

    (A) am used to reading

    (B) am use to read

    (C) am used to read

    (D) am using to read

    (E) was used to read

(　) 9. Peter soon became accustomed to _____ up early.

    (A) getting   (B) get

    (C) gets   (D) geting

(　) 10. I enjoy eating in good restaurants and _____ to the movies afterwards.

    (A) go   (B) to go   (C) going   (D) gone

(　) 11. It's not worth _____ there now; it's too late.

    (A) go   (B) to go   (C) gone   (D) going

(　　) 12. We should avoid ＿＿＿＿ mistakes again and again.

      (A) to make　　　　(B) make

      (C) made　　　　　(D) making

(　　) 13. Driving cars <u>is</u> full of excitement <u>but</u> driving lessons

          (A)　　　　　　　　　　　　(B)

      <u>is</u> rather <u>boring</u>. (改錯)

      (C)　　　　　(D)

(　　) 14. With a view to <u>prepare</u> for the <u>entrance examination</u>

              (A)　　　　　　　　　　(B)

      next year, he <u>has decided</u> to study hard <u>during</u> the

               (C)　　　　　　　　　　　(D)

      summer vacation. (改錯)

(　　) 15. ＿＿＿＿ something to eat is better than nothing.

      (A) Have　　　　(B) Having　　　　(C) Has

      (D) Had　　　　　(E) Has had

(　　) 16. I couldn't imagine ＿＿＿＿ all my life in my present job.

      (A) work　　　　(B) to work

      (C) working　　　(D) for working

      (E) to working

二、以動名詞為受詞的動詞

(　　) 1. 他記得過去曾寫信給她。

      (A) He remember to write to her.

      (B) He remembers writing to her.

      (C) He remembers has written to her.

      (D) He remembers already to write to her.

(　　) 2. Mary: Can I speak to Sue, please?

Anne: Sorry, she's gone _____.

    (A) to shop　　　　(B) shopping

    (C) for shopping　　(D) to shops

(　　) 3. After they finished _____ the dishes, the new couple went out for a drive.

    (A) wash　　　　　(B) washed

    (C) to wash　　　　(D) washing

(　　) 4. I'm tired. I must stop _____ a rest.

    (A) take　　　　　(B) to take

    (C) taken　　　　　(D) taking

    (E) took

(　　) 5. All the clerks in the bank stopped _____ to look at him.

    (A) to write　　　　(B) write

    (C) written　　　　(D) writing

(　　) 6. <u>Since</u> he is very <u>exhausted</u>, he does not <u>feel like</u> <u>to go</u>
    (A)　　　　　　(B)　　　　　　　　　(C)　　　(D)
anywhere now. (改錯)

三、動名詞重要句型

(　　) 1. He's such a strange person; there's no _____ what he'll do next.

    (A) know　　　　　(B) to know

    (C) known　　　　　(D) to be knowing

    (E) knowing

(　) 2. ＿＿＿＿ going to the movies tonight?
    (A) Would you like to
    (B) What do you think
    (C) I don't mind
    (D) How about

(　) 3. What ＿＿＿＿ going to the movies tonight?
    (A) on　(B) for　(C) about　(D) of

(　) 4. I can't help ＿＿＿＿ he is still alive.
    (A) thinking　(B) think　(C) to think

(　) 5. He couldn't ＿＿＿＿ being late. There was a traffic jam.
    (A) manage　(B) help　(C) escape
    (D) assist　(E) stop

(　) 6. She went out without ＿＿＿＿ good-bye to us.
    (A) say　(B) to say　(C) says
    (D) said　(E) saying

(　) 7. Our English teacher was busy ＿＿＿＿ the new lesson.
    (A) prepare　(B) preparing
    (C) prepared　(D) to prepare
    (E) to be prepared

8. 這絕不是說這本書值得一讀再讀。
    This is f＿＿＿＿ f＿＿＿＿ claiming that the book is
    w＿＿＿＿ r＿＿＿＿ over again.

_____ 9. There is _____ knowing when we shall meet again.

(　) 10. Your idea, although quite good, needs _____ out.
    (A) to try
    (B) trying
    (C) being tried
    (D) try

【歷屆聯考試題解答】

一、　1. (**C**)　2. (**C**)　3. (**E**)　4. (**C**)　5. (**B**)　6. (**D**)
　　　7. (**D**)　8. (**A**)　9. (**A**)　10. (**C**)　11. (**D**)　12. (**D**)
　　　13. (**C**) → are　　14. (**A**) → preparing
　　　15. (**B**)　16. (**C**)

二、　1. (**B**)　2. (**B**)　3. (**D**)　4. (**B**)　5. (**D**)
　　　6. (**D**) → going

三、　1. (**E**)　2. (**D**)　3. (**C**)　4. (**A**)　5. (**B**)　6. (**E**)
　　　7. (**B**)　　8. far, from, worth, reading
　　　9. no　　10. (**B**)

【解析】

一、　1. 今天下午你若能回電，我會很感激。
　　　　因意義上之主詞為人，故須用所有格形式。
　　　　call sb. back 回某人電話

　　　2. invitation〔ˌɪnvəˈteʃən〕*n.* 邀請

　　　4. 她不喜歡被人群包圍。

　　　5. curious〔ˈkjʊrɪəs〕*adj.* 好奇的
　　　　keep on V-ing 繼續（做～）

　　　7. ***succeed in V-ing*** 在～（方面）成功

10. 我喜歡在好的餐廳用餐，然後去看場電影。

   enjoy + V-ing 喜歡做～。and 在此連接「在餐廳吃飯」

   及「看電影」兩件事，故本題選 (C)。

11. 現在不值得去那裡；太遲了。

   worth + V-ing 值得做～

12. 「我們應該避免一再犯錯。」　***avoid + V-ing*** 避免～

13. driving cars（開車）爲動名詞當主詞，用單數動詞；

   但 driving lessons（駕駛訓練的課程）的 driving 是現

   在分詞，修飾 lessons，眞正的主詞是 lessons，故用複

   數動詞。

14. ***with a view to + V-ing*** 「爲了～」，在此 to 爲介系詞，

   接動名詞做受詞。　***entrance examination*** 入學考試

15. 「有東西總比沒得吃好。」本題需要一個主詞，故選動

   名詞 (A)。

16. ***imagine + V-ing*** 想像～

二、 6. 因爲他已筋疲力盡，所以他不想去任何地方。

   exhausted〔ɪgˋzɔstɪd, ɛg-〕*adj.* 筋疲力盡的

三、 1. ***there is no + V-ing = it is impossible to + V.***

   ～是不可能的

 2. 3. ***How (What) about + V-ing? = Would you like to +***

   V.? 「～如何」

 4. ***can't help + V-ing = can't help but + V.*** 「不得不～；

   忍不住～」

 10. 你的構想雖好，但需實際試驗。

   need + V-ing = need to be + 過去分詞「需要～」

   try sth. out 實際試驗某事

精選模擬考題

( ) 1. There is no _____ rid of the mice in the house.
    (A) get   (B) getting
    (C) gotten   (D) to get

( ) 2. We were looking forward _____ our friends next week.
    (A) to see   (B) to seeing
    (C) to be seeing   (D) shall see

( ) 3. The house needs _____.
    (A) being painted
    (B) painted
    (C) painting
    (D) to be painting

( ) 4. Mr. Smith quit _____ in order to improve his health.
    (A) smoke   (B) to smoke
    (C) smoking   (D) smoked

( ) 5. Is he equal _____ the task?
    (A) to perform   (B) to performing
    (C) performing   (D) performed

( ) 6. He is, so to speak, a _____ dictionary.
    (A) walk   (B) walking
    (C) walked   (D) walker

(   ) 7. He did not _____ the problem.
- (A) succeed solve
- (B) succeed to solve
- (C) succeed to solving
- (D) succeed in solving

(   ) 8. You must make an effort to avoid _____ the same errors.
- (A) to repeat
- (B) repeating
- (C) repeated
- (D) to be repeated

(   ) 9. When it comes _____ decisions, he is very cautious.
- (A) to make
- (B) to making
- (C) make
- (D) making

(   ) 10. This idea, though good, needs _____ out.
- (A) try   (B) trying   (C) tried   (D) trial

(   ) 11. I don't feel like _____ tonight.
- (A) study
- (B) to study
- (C) studying
- (D) studied

(   ) 12. He cannot bear _____ laughed at.
- (A) be   (B) being   (C) been   (D) to being

(   ) 13. Let's stop _____ some groceries on our way home. Our food is running short.
- (A) to buy
- (B) buying
- (C) bought
- (D) and bought

( ) 14. What prevented you _____ the work?

    (A) to complete   (B) from finish

    (C) from completing   (D) to finish

( ) 15. I love _____ in bed.

    (A) laying   (B) lain   (C) lying   (D) laid

( ) 16. He spent a lot of money _____ books.

    (A) buy   (B) buying

    (C) to buying   (D) bought

( ) 17. Everyone enjoyed _____ with her.

    (A) talks   (B) to be talking

    (C) talking   (D) to talk

( ) 18. Would you mind _____ a song for us?

    (A) sing   (B) to sing

    (C) singing   (D) sang

( ) 19. It is not a problem of _____ making.

    (A) he   (B) his   (C) one   (D) himself

( ) 20. I felt tired from walking, so I stopped _____ a rest for an hour.

    (A) take   (B) to take

    (C) taking   (D) to taking

( ) 21. Have you finished _____?

    (A) to write   (B) writing

    (C) written   (D) write

(　) 22. Don't forget ＿＿＿＿ this letter on your way downtown.

    (A) post　　　　　　　　(B) to post

    (C) posting　　　　　　　(D) to have posted

(　) 23. As she is looking forward to ＿＿＿＿ from me, please remember ＿＿＿＿ this letter on your way to school.

    (A) hear, post

    (B) be heard, posting

    (C) be hearing, to posting

    (D) hearing, to post

(　) 24. Would you mind ＿＿＿＿ the house?

    (A) of me to enter　　　　(B) that I enter

    (C) my entering　　　　　(D) for my entering

(　) 25. Your house needs ＿＿＿＿.

    (A) to paint　　　　　　　(B) painted

    (C) painting　　　　　　　(D) paint on

(　) 26. It is no use ＿＿＿＿ to teach a fellow who has no desire to learn.

    (A) to try　(B) trying　(C) try　　　(D) tried

(　) 27. He could not help ＿＿＿＿ that work.

    (A) to do　(B) do　　(C) doing　(D) does

(　) 28. It goes without ＿＿＿＿ that he is wise and well-＿＿＿＿.

    (A) says, speaking　　　　(B) says, spoken

    (C) saying, speaking　　　(D) saying, spoken

( ) 29. I felt like _____ upon hearing that.
      (A) laugh   (B) laughed
      (C) laughing   (D) to laugh

( ) 30. The girl is looking forward to _____ her cousin.
      (A) meet   (B) met
      (C) has met   (D) meeting

( ) 31. Uncle Bill went _____ for foxes last weekend.
      (A) for hunting   (B) to hunting
      (C) hunting   (D) hunted

( ) 32. This book is not worth _____.
      (A) to read   (B) reading
      (C) for reading   (D) read

【精選模擬考題解答】

  1.(**B**)   2.(**B**)   3.(**C**)   4.(**C**)   5.(**B**)   6.(**B**)
  7.(**D**)   8.(**B**)   9.(**B**)   10.(**B**)   11.(**C**)   12.(**B**)
 13.(**A**)   14.(**C**)   15.(**C**)   16.(**B**)   17.(**C**)   18.(**C**)
 19.(**B**)   20.(**B**)   21.(**B**)   22.(**B**)   23.(**D**)   24.(**C**)
 25.(**C**)   26.(**B**)   27.(**C**)   28.(**D**)   29.(**C**)   30.(**D**)
 31.(**C**)   32.(**B**)

【解析】

  1. 原句 = It is impossible to get rid of the mice in the house.
     get rid of 除去

  3. 原句 = The house needs to be painted.

4. quit〔kwɪt〕*v.* 停止；放棄　　improve〔ɪm'pruv〕*v.* 改善

5. *be equal to + V-ing*　能勝任～

   perform〔pə'fɔrm〕*v.* 履行（諾言等）；執行（任務）

   task〔tæsk〕*n.* 任務；職務

6. 在此 walking 是現在分詞而非動名詞。

   so to speak　可說是；好比是

8. *make an effort*　努力　　repeat〔rɪ'pit〕*v.* 重覆

   error〔'ɛrə〕*n.* 錯誤；過失

9. *when it comes to + V-ing*　一提到～

   cautious〔'kɔʃəs〕*adj.* 小心的；謹慎的

10. 這個主意雖然好，但需要徹底試驗一下。

    try out　徹底試驗

12. 「他不能忍受被人嘲笑。」　　*bear + V-ing*　忍受～

13. *run short*　快用完了

14. *prevent + 人 + from + V-ing*　阻止某人做～

23. *hear from～*　收到～的來信　　post〔post〕*v.* 郵寄

28. *It goes without saying that～*　不用說～

    well-spoken〔'wɛl'spokən〕*adj.* 說話文雅的；善於辭令的

31. *go + V-ing～*　去～

    hunt for～　尋找～；狩獵～

PART-5

一致・強調與倒裝・附加問句

命題焦點

▶1. 要注意兩個以上的主詞，用連接詞連接時，動詞的單、複數，如either～or, not only～but (also)等。

▶2. 否定副詞放在句首的倒裝最常考。

▶3. 須注意句中有否定詞seldom, never, hardly 等字的附加問句。

1. 主詞與動詞・時式的一致

> 主詞與動詞的人稱及數必須一致，
> 主要子句與從屬子句的時式也要一致。

1. 主詞與動詞的一致

1. 名詞單、複數的區別

(1) **every, each, either, neither**：用單數動詞。

【例】 *Every* boy and girl *likes* to play tennis.
（每個男孩和女孩都喜歡打網球。）

Either of the books *is* available.
（這兩本書中的任何一本，都是可以獲得的。）

Neither of the books *is* interesting.
（兩本書中，沒有一本是有趣的。）

(2) 集合名詞：(a) 指**集合體**用單數動詞，(b)指**集合體的組成分子**，用複數動詞。這類集合名詞有 family, class, audience（觀衆），crowd（群衆），committee（委員會），crew（全體船員）等。

【例】 (a) This *class* **is** made up of forty-five students.
（這個班級由 45 個學生組成。）

The *audience* **was** very small that night.
（那天晚上觀衆很少。）

(b) This *class* **are** all diligent.
（這個班級的學生都很勤勉。）

The *audience* **were** moved to tears by his speech.
（聽衆都爲他的演講感動得落淚。）

☞ 通常用做複數的集合名詞：police, cattle 等。

【例】 The *police are* investigating the matter.
（警方正在調查這件事。）

Cattle are raised here in great numbers.
（這裡大量飼養牛。）

☞ 通常用做單數的集合名詞：furniture（傢俱），machinery
（機械），clothing（衣物），scenery（風景），poetry（詩），
jewelry（珠寶）。

【例】 Our *furniture is* old-fashioned.
（我們的傢俱是老式的。）

All her *jewelry was* stolen by the thieves.
（她所有的珠寶都被小偷偷走了。）

(3) 下列**複數形名詞，表示單數意義時**，用單數動詞。

【例】 *Mathematics is* my favorite subject.
（數學是我最喜歡的科目。）

Physics was one of the subjects he had to study hard.
（物理是他得用功的科目之一。）

Measles is a disease that people usually get in
childhood.（麻疹通常在幼年時罹患。）

There *is* no *news* about the missing boy.
（沒有那個失蹤男孩的消息。）

The *United States consists* of fifty states.
（美國有五十個州。）

Ten years is too long for me to wait.
（對我而言等十年太久了。）

Ten miles is a long distance for a child to walk.
（對小孩子而言，走十哩路是一段很長的距離。）

<比較> *Ten years have passed* since he went abroad.
（自從他出國以來，已經過了十年。）

☞ **means**（方法；手段）**單複數同形**，因此要看前面的形容詞來決定動詞的單、複數。

【例】 *Is* there *any means* of finding out the secret?
（有任何方法可以找出這秘密嗎？）

All means of communication *are* not necessary.
（並非所有的交通工具是有必要的。）

☞ 由兩部分組成的物品，要用複數動詞，這類名詞有：
trousers（褲子）, gloves（手套）, glasses（眼鏡）,
spectacles（眼鏡）, scissors（剪刀）, pincers（鑷子）。
如果接 a pair of 時，則用單數動詞。

【例】 His *trousers were* too long for him.
（他的褲子對他而言太長了。）

Your *glasses are* too weak.（你的眼鏡度數太淺了。）

A new *pair of* glasses *is* needed.
（一副新的眼鏡是必要的。）

(4) **the ＋ 形容詞**：代表「全體」，視為複數的普通名詞。

【例】 *The rich are* not always happier than *the poor*.
（富人未必比窮人快樂。）

The learned are apt to despise *the ignorant*.
（有學問的人往往會輕視無知的人。）

(5) 複合主詞表示兩個不可分的東西，或表示同一個人、物或觀念時，用單數動詞。

【例】 *Curry and rice is* my favorite dish.
（咖哩飯是我最喜歡吃的。）

The *leader and teacher* of the people *was* shot to death.
（民眾的導師被槍殺了。）

2. 主詞的結構影響動詞的單複數

(1) $\left\{\begin{array}{l} \textbf{A or B} \\ \textbf{not only A but also B} \\ \textbf{either A or B} \\ \textbf{neither A nor B} \end{array}\right\}$ 動詞與靠近的主詞之人稱、數一致

【即在敘述句中，與 B 一致，在疑問句中，與 A 一致】

【例】 *Are you or* he to blame?（是你或是他該受責備？）

Not only he *but also* ***I am*** invited to dinner.

（不只是他，我也受邀參加晚宴。）

Neither you *nor* ***he knows*** the truth.

（你和他都不知道真相。）

(2) A + $\left\{\begin{array}{l} \textbf{as well as} \\ \textbf{(together) with} \end{array}\right\}$ + B，動詞與 A 一致

【例】 The ***books*** *as well as* the furniture ***are*** for sale.

（這些書和傢俱一樣，都要出售。）

My ***uncle with*** his children ***is*** staying with us.

（我舅舅和他的孩子，目前暫住在我們家。）

(3) $\left\{\begin{array}{ll} \textbf{a number of} \sim + \text{複數動詞} & \text{「一些} \sim \text{；許多} \sim \text{」} \\ \textbf{the number of} \sim + \text{單數動詞} & \text{「} \sim \text{的數目」} \end{array}\right.$

【例】 *A number of* ***books are*** missing from the library.

（圖書館丟了一些書。）

The number of ***cars has*** been increasing for many

years.（許多年來，車子的數目一直在增加。）

(4) 代名詞 half, all, part, most, some 以及分數當主詞時，視其後
名詞的內容，以決定動詞的單、複數。

> *All* of the ***children want*** presents on their birthdays.
> （所有的小孩生日時都想要禮物。）
>
> *All* of her ***money was*** spent on clothes.
> （她所有的錢都花在衣服上。）【money 為不可數名詞】

> *Half* of the ***students were*** successful.
> （有一半的學生成功了。）
>
> *Half* of her ***time is*** spent in practicing the piano.
> （她把一半的時間花在練琴上。）【time 為不可數名詞】

【例】 *Two-thirds* of the ***city was*** destroyed and *one-third* of
the ***people were*** killed.
（城市的三分之二地區被毀，三分之一的人死亡。）

---

3. 主詞與動詞一致的注意事項

(1) 先行詞為
> one of＋複數名詞，其後子句用複數動詞。
> the only one of＋複數名詞，其後子句用單數動詞。

【例】 Dick is *one of the **runners** who **are*** going to take part
in the long-distance race.
（狄克是要參加長途賽跑的選手之一。）

Mr. William was ***the only one*** of the members *that **was***
against the plan.（威廉先生是會員中唯一反對這計劃的人。）

(2) 強調句型：It is～that 中，若強調的部分是主詞，則 that 後動詞
的人稱和數要與 that 之前的（代）名詞一致，與 it 無關。

【例】 *It is **my brother** that **has broken*** the window.
（打破窗戶的是我弟弟。）
*It is **my brother and I** that **are*** to blame.
（該受責備的是我弟弟和我。）

2. 時式的一致

1. 時式一致的原則

主要子句的動詞是現在式，從屬子句的動詞可以用未來式、現在式、現在完成式及過去式。主要子句的動詞爲過去式，從屬子句動詞的變化爲未來式 → 過去式，現在式 → 過去式，現在完成式 → 過去完成式，過去式 → 過去完成式。

【例】 They *say* that he *will* be busy *tomorrow*.

　　　 (→ They *said* that he *would* be busy *the next day*.)

　　　 They *say* that he *is* busy *now*.

　　　 (→ They *said* that he *was* busy *then*.)

　　　 They *say* that he *has been* busy for a week.

　　　 (→ They *said* that he *had been* busy for a week.)

　　　 They *say* that he *was* busy *yesterday*.

　　　 (→ They *said* that he *had been* busy *the day before*.)

2. 時式一致原則的例外情形

⑴ 不變的眞理或格言，一律用現在式。

【例】 The ancient people *didn't know* that the earth *is* round.

　　　 (古人不知道地球是圓的。)

　　　 My grandfather *used to tell* me that a rolling stone *gathers* no moss.

　　　 (我祖父以前常告訴我，滾石不生苔。)

⑵ 至今仍未改變的習慣或事實，用現在式。

【例】 Nancy *told* me that her class *begins* at half past eight.

　　　 (南西告訴我她八點半開始上課。)

　　　 He *said* that he *takes* a cold bath every morning.

　　　 (他說他每天早上洗冷水澡。)

(3) 指歷史的事實,用過去式。

【例】 The teacher *told* us that Columbus *discovered* America in 1492.(老師告訴我們哥倫布於 1492 年發現美洲。)

(4) 含有「比較」的句子。

【例】 The lake *was* much deeper than it *is now*.
（這個湖以前比現在深多了。）

He *could* not sing so well as he *has done today*.
（他以前沒辦法唱得像今天這麼好。）

(5) 假設法的時式不受主要子句時式的影響。

【例】 He *says* that he *would help* me if he *were* not busy.
(→ He *said* that he *would help* me if he were not busy.)
（他說假如他不忙,他要幫我。）

I *wish* she *were* here with me.（但願她和我一起在這裡。）
(→ I *wished* she *were* here with me.)

She *speaks* English as if she *had been* brought up in America.（她說起英文來,好像她是在美國長大的一樣。）
(→ She *spoke* English as if she *had been* brought up in America.)

(6) 不論主要子句是何種時態,從屬子句的助動詞 must, ought to, should, need, had better 不改變。(指過去的 must 也可用 had to 代替。)

【例】 He *said* that she *ought to* be ashamed of herself.
（他說她應該自覺慚愧。）

He *said* that the woman *must* be over sixty.
（他說這女人一定超過六十歲了。）

Father *said* that he *must* [*had to*] have his hair trimmed.（父親說他必須給人修剪頭髮了。）

歷屆聯考試題

一、名詞的數

(　　) 1. Refusing invitations _____ not always easy.
    (A) are   (B) have been
    (C) can   (D) is

(　　) 2. Each boy and each girl _____ to look nice.
    (A) wants   (B) want
    (C) are wanting   (D) have

(　　) 3. Ten thousand dollars _____ a large sum of money.
    (A) is   (B) are   (C) have been   (D) were

(　　) 4. Chatting with them _____ my mind.
    (A) improves   (B) have improved
    (C) improve   (D) improving
    (E) is improved

(　　) 5. Whether I go or I stay _____ upon the news we get
about Mother's health.
    (A) depends   (B) depending
    (C) dependent   (D) depend

(　　) 6. Although there _____ many different sizes and types
of vending machines, they all work basically in the
same way.
    (A) is   (B) being   (C) are   (D) to be

( ) 7. The goods you ordered _____ arrived.

    (A) has   (B) have   (C) are   (D) is

( ) 8. There _____ sixty minutes in an hour.

    (A) are   (B) is

    (C) were   (D) shall be

( ) 9. The majority of the damage _____ easy to repair.

    (A) is   (B) are   (C) am

    (D) been   (E) be

( ) 10. 改錯：Playing <u>the piano</u> and <u>singing</u> <u>simultaneously</u>
                      (A)   (B)   (C)

    <u>are</u> difficult
    (D)

( ) 11. 改錯：The <u>number</u> <u>of</u> cars in Taipei <u>are</u> increasing year
               (A)   (B)   (C)

    <u>by</u> year.
    (D)

二、主詞與動詞的一致

( ) 1. One of his ambitions _____ to become an engineer.

    (A) be   (B) are   (C) were   (D) being   (E) is

( ) 2. The teacher with all his students _____ looking

    forward to _____ on a picnic.

    (A) are, going   (B) is, going

    (C) is, gone   (D) are, gone

    (E) are, go

(　) 3. Neither you nor I _____ happy.
　　(A) are　(B) am　(C) is　(D) be　(E) were

(　) 4. _____ are right in this matter.
　　(A) Both you and he　　　　(B) You as well as he
　　(C) Not only you but also he　(D) Both of you

(　) 5. Neither he nor I _____ willing to live there.
　　(A) are　(B) were　(C) be　(D) am

(　) 6. 改錯：At the bottom of the stairs <u>is</u> a door that <u>opens into</u>
　　　　　　　　　　　　　　　　　　　　(A)　　　　　　　(B)
　　the bedroom and <u>another</u> that <u>leads to</u> the garden.
　　　　　　　　　　　(C)　　　　　　(D)

(　) 7. <u>Only</u> one of all the young <u>people</u> who <u>graduated</u> from
　　　　(A)　　　　　　　　　　(B)　　　(C)
　　our high school <u>were</u> able to enter the college. (改錯)
　　　　　　　　　(D)

三、主詞與動詞的一致應注意事項

(　) 1. Smith was the only one of the members that failed to
　　keep his promises.
　　(A) 史密斯失敗了，因為他對所有的會員背信。
　　(B) 所有的會員都不守信，只有史密斯一人守信。
　　(C) 所有的會員中，只有史密斯一個人不能守諾言。
　　(D) 只有史密斯一個人要所有的會員守諾言。
　　(E) 所有的會員除史密斯外，都許下諾言。

( ) 2. In the <u>assembly</u> line, the product <u>that</u> is being
             (A)   (B)

     manufactured <u>move</u>, but the worker <u>stays</u> in the same
                  (C)   (D)

     place. (改錯)

四、時態的一致

( ) 1. Children _____ comic strips, don't they?

    (A) liked   (B) like

    (C) will like   (D) has liked

( ) 2. If Mary _____ here, she would help us.

    (A) has   (B) was   (C) had

    (D) were   (E) is

_____ 3. Had he known of your trouble, he would help you.

                                           (改錯)

( ) 4. We must be patient until _____ a satisfactory result.

    (A) we have to get (B) we are getting

    (C) we get   (D) we got

【歷屆聯考試題解答】

  一、 1.(**D**)   2.(**A**)   3.(**A**)   4.(**A**)   5.(**A**)   6.(**C**)

       7.(**B**)   8.(**A**)   9.(**A**)   10.(**D**) → is

      11.(**C**) → is

二、　1. (**E**)　2. (**B**)　3. (**B**)　4. (**A、B、D**)　5. (**D**)

　　6. (**A**) → are　　7. (**D**) → was

三、　1. (**C**)　2. (**C**) → moves

四、　1. (**B**)　2. (**D**)

　　3. would help → would have helped

　　4. (**C**)

【解析】

一、　1. 動名詞、不定詞，或子句當主詞時，用單數動詞。

　　　refuse (rɪ'fjuz) *v.* 拒絕

　　3. 此處 ten thousand dollars 指一筆錢，用單數動詞。

　　4. chat (tʃæt) *v.* 聊天

　　6. ***vending machine***　自動販賣機

　　7. 「你訂的貨已經到了。」本句的主詞是 goods，故

　　　選 (B)。

　　9. majority (mə'dʒɔrətɪ) *n.* 大部份

　　10. 同時又彈又唱是很困難的。

　　　simultaneously (,sɪml̩'tenɪəslɪ) *adv.*　同時地

　　　同時彈、唱在此視為一件事，故用單數動詞 is。

　　11. 「台北的車輛數目逐年增加。」本句的主詞是 number，

　　　故用單數動詞。

二、　7. 從我們高中畢業的所有年輕人，只有一個能上大學。

　　　先行詞為「Only one of + 複數名詞」，故用單數動詞 is。

三、　2. 本句的主詞是 product，故用單數動詞 moves。

四、　3. 本題是省略 if 的假設語氣，與過去事實相反，要用過去完

　　　成式。

精選模擬考題

( ) 1. A watch and chain _____ found on the floor.
   (A) has   (B) was   (C) are   (D) be

( ) 2. A poet and a musician _____ invited to dinner last night.
   (A) is   (B) are   (C) was   (D) were

( ) 3. All work and no play _____ Jack a dull boy.
   (A) make   (B) makes
   (C) be   (D) to

( ) 4. Fire and water _____ not agree.
   (A) does   (B) do   (C) is   (D) are

( ) 5. Early to bed and early to rise _____ a man healthy, wealthy and wise.
   (A) make   (B) makes
   (C) made   (D) have made

( ) 6. A number of students _____ absent today.
   (A) is   (B) are
   (C) was   (D) have

( ) 7. Not only she but also I _____ wrong.
   (A) is   (B) am
   (C) are   (D) must

(　) 8. This is one of the few novels that _____ been published this week.

    (A) has   (B) have

    (C) having   (D) will

(　) 9. Three-fourths of the earth's surface _____ water.

    (A) is   (B) are

    (C) has been   (D) had

(　) 10. Some of the furniture _____ bought last night.

    (A) was   (B) were

    (C) has   (D) will

(　) 11. The police _____ on the track of the murderer.

    (A) is   (B) are

    (C) has to   (D) must

(　) 12. Seven days _____ a long time to wait for him to come.

    (A) be   (B) am   (C) is   (D) are

(　) 13. He is the only one of those present who _____ with me.

    (A) disagrees   (B) disagreed

    (C) is disagree   (D) are disagree

(　) 14. These sheep _____ killed in the flood.

    (A) was   (B) were

    (C) all   (D) will

(　) 15. Ham and eggs _____ the main dish here.

    (A) is   (B) are   (C) be   (D) am

( ) 16. Our teacher told us that the earth _____ round the sun.
     (A) moves   (B) moved
     (C) move   (D) moving

( ) 17. The committee _____ been unable to agree on the plan.
     (A) has   (B) does
     (C) will   (D) do

( ) 18. The Chinese _____ said to be an industrious people.
     (A) is   (B) are   (C) has   (D) have

( ) 19. The rich _____ not always happy.
     (A) is   (B) are
     (C) was   (D) be

( ) 20. Five years _____ passed since he went to America.
     (A) has   (B) have   (C) is   (D) was

( ) 21. There _____ something to be said for both sides.
     (A) is   (B) are   (C) has   (D) have

( ) 22. Studying rules _____ helpful, but until such rules are applied, they can be of no value to you.
     (A) are   (B) were
     (C) is   (D) have been

( ) 23. The number of students in the class _____ limited to fifteen.
     (A) have   (B) are   (C) is   (D) has

(　) 24. _____ the rest of the audience refuse to go out?
　　　 (A) Do　(B) Has　(C) Is　(D) Are

(　) 25. One out of three motorcar accidents _____ caused by a teenage driver.
　　　 (A) are　　　　(B) is
　　　 (C) were　　　(D) has

(　) 26. Neither houses nor a church _____ enough to make a community.
　　　 (A) are　(B) is　(C) were　(D) have

(　) 27. There are only two rewards which _____ life worth living.
　　　 (A) make　　　(B) makes
　　　 (C) to make　　(D) have made

(　) 28. The United States _____ a republic.
　　　 (A) is　　　　　(B) are
　　　 (C) has been　　(D) were

(　) 29. Neither he nor I _____ responsible for it.
　　　 (A) is　(B) are　(C) am　(D) will

(　) 30. All my family _____ early risers.
　　　 (A) is　(B) are　(C) was　(D) be

(　) 31. Each of the seven girls _____ a dog.
　　　 (A) there is　　(B) are
　　　 (C) has　　　　(D) have

( ) 32. None of the money _____ left.
    (A) is   (B) are   (C) has   (D) have

( ) 33. Every student who _____ this examination must write with a pen.
    (A) take   (B) takes
    (C) took   (D) takes into

( ) 34. It is you, not I, who _____ in the wrong.
    (A) are   (B) am   (C) is   (D) was

( ) 35. My brother as well as my cousin _____ killed.
    (A) be   (B) are
    (C) has   (D) was

( ) 36. Both he and I _____ used to getting up early.
    (A) is   (B) am   (C) are   (D) be

( ) 37. The mayor, as well as all the members of the city council, _____ opposed to the idea.
    (A) was   (B) were
    (C) have   (D) be

( ) 38. Every means _____ been tried.
    (A) has   (B) have
    (C) must   (D) will

( ) 39. A new pair of glasses _____ needed.
    (A) is   (B) are   (C) has   (D) have

( ) 40. A lot of money _____ been spent.
    (A) have   (B) has
    (C) would   (D) must

( ) 41. Half of my salary _____ spent on rent.
    (A) is   (B) are
    (C) have been   (D) be

( ) 42. I lost the watch which my uncle _____ me.
    (A) giving   (B) had given
    (C) gives   (D) have given

( ) 43. I never expected that he _____ to the party.
    (A) would come   (B) came
    (C) comes   (D) have come

( ) 44. Fortunately, it was generally believed that the earth
    _____ flat.
    (A) has been   (B) were
    (C) was   (D) is

( ) 45. Columbus believed that the earth _____ round.
    (A) is (B) be (C) were (D) are

( ) 46. He says that they _____ English.
    (A) study   (B) studying
    (C) have study (D) have been studied

( ) 47. The lake was much deeper than it _____ now.
    (A) was (B) is (C) does (D) did

(　) 48. My grandfather used to tell me that a rolling stone
　　　　 _____ no moss.
　　　　 (A) gathered　　　　(B) is gathered
　　　　 (C) gathers　　　　 (D) gathering

(　) 49. He said that he _____ a cold bath every morning.
　　　　 (A) has taken　　　　(B) takes
　　　　 (C) was taking　　　 (D) is taking

(　) 50. He said that he _____ then.
　　　　 (A) was busy　　　　(B) business
　　　　 (C) has been busy　(D) busies

(　) 51. He said that there had been something of the great
　　　　 actress about the queen.
　　　　 = He said, "There _____ something of the great
　　　　 actress about the queen."
　　　　 (A) had been　　　　(B) has been
　　　　 (C) was　　　　　　 (D) is

(　) 52. She did not run so fast as she usually _____.
　　　　 (A) was　(B) is　　(C) does　(D) done

【精選模擬考題解答】

1.(**B**)	2.(**D**)	3.(**B**)	4.(**B**)	5.(**B**)	6.(**B**)
7.(**B**)	8.(**B**)	9.(**A**)	10.(**A**)	11.(**B**)	12.(**C**)
13.(**A**)	14.(**B**)	15.(**A**)	16.(**A**)	17.(**A**)	18.(**B**)
19.(**B**)	20.(**B**)	21.(**A**)	22.(**C**)	23.(**C**)	24.(**A**)
25.(**B**)	26.(**B**)	27.(**A**)	28.(**A**)	29.(**C**)	30.(**B**)
31.(**C**)	32.(**A**)	33.(**B**)	34.(**A**)	35.(**D**)	36.(**C**)
37.(**A**)	38.(**A**)	39.(**A**)	40.(**B**)	41.(**A**)	42.(**B**)
43.(**A**)	44.(**C**)	45.(**A**)	46.(**A**)	47.(**B**)	48.(**C**)
49.(**B**)	50.(**A**)	51.(**C**)	52.(**C**)		

【解析】

1. 懷錶被發現在地上。

   a watch and chain（懷錶）須用單數動詞。

2. 昨晚，一位詩人及一名音樂家受邀參加晚宴。

   本句的主詞是「一位詩人及一名音樂家」，故用複數動詞。

3. 只用功而不玩樂，會變成呆子。

   all work and no play 表示單一概念，故用單數動詞。

4. 水火不相容。

   fire 和 water 指不同的東西，故用複數動詞。

11. 警方正在追緝這名兇手。

    on the track of 追蹤　　murderer〔'mɝdərɚ〕*n.* 兇手

13. 他是在場的人員中，唯一不同意我的人。

    present〔'prɛznt〕*adj.* 在場的

    disagree with *sb.* 不同意某人

15. ham and eggs（火腿蛋）視爲一道菜，故用單數動詞。

17. 委員會至今仍不同意這項計劃。
committee 在此表集合體，指「委員會」，為單數名詞，故用
單數動詞。

18. 據說中國人是勤勉的民族。
the Chinese 為表「全國國民」的複數名詞，故用複數動詞。
industrious〔ɪnˋdʌstrɪəs〕*adj.* 勤勉的

22. studying rules 為動名詞片語，指「學會一些規則」這件事，
故用單數動詞。

25. 三起車禍中，就有一起是十幾歲的駕駛人所引起的。
本句的主詞為 one，故用單數動詞。

34. not I 為插入語，子句的真正主詞為 you，故選 (A)。

37. mayor〔ˋmeɚ〕*n.* 市長
council〔ˋkaʊnsl̩〕*n.*（市或鎮的）議會
be opposed to 反對

39. a pair of glass（一副眼鏡），視為單數名詞。

41. salary〔ˋsælərɪ〕*n.* 薪水　　rent〔rɛnt〕*n.* 租金

44. fortunately〔ˋfɔrtʃənɪtlɪ〕*adv.* 幸運地
flat〔flæt〕*adj.* 平坦的

2. 強調・倒裝

> do, oneself 等字詞、感嘆句或修辭疑問句等,可用以加強
> 語氣。爲了強調句中的某一部份,而變動語詞的位置,稱
> 爲倒裝。

1. 強 調

1. 加強語氣用法的字詞

(1) **do, does, did** → 務必;的確

【例】 *Do* come and see me as soon as you can.
(務必儘快來看我。)

I *do* believe he is innocent. (我確信他是無辜的。)

Why didn't you come to the meeting? — I *did* come.
You just didn't notice me.
(你爲何不來開會?— 我是來了,只是你沒注意到我。)

(2) **oneself** 的強調用法 → 自己;親自

【例】 The president *himself* came to meet the Prime
Minister. (總統親自來接見首相。)

His wife made tea *herself*. (他太太親自泡茶。)

I *myself* worked hard from morning till night.
(我自己從早到晚努力工作。)

(3) 利用重覆以加強語氣

【例】 If you fail, you should try *again and again*.
(你如果失敗了,就應該一再地嘗試。)

As she grew up, she became *more and more beautiful*.
(她長大後,變得越來越漂亮。)

⑷ 補述強調的字詞，用以加強語氣

【例】 (a) I am *awfully* sorry to have kept you waiting so long.

（讓你等這麼久，我極感抱歉。）

My dear, it's *simply* wonderful to see you again.

（親愛的，再見到你簡直太棒了。）

We are *terribly* lucky to find you here.

（我們幸運極了，能在這裡找到你。）

(b) What *on earth* is the matter with you?

（你到底怎麼了？）

How *in the world* did you solve the mystery?

（你到底怎麼解開這個謎的？）

If I had any money *at all*, I could go anywhere. But in fact, I have no money *whatever* (= *at all*).

（如果我有錢，我到處都可以去，但事實上，我一點錢也沒有。）

---

2. 加強語氣用法的句型

⑴ **感嘆句**可用以加強語氣。

【例】 *How good of you* to take me all the way to the station!

(= *It's very good of you* to take me…)

（你真好，老遠地把我載到車站！）

⑵ **修辭疑問句**可用以加強語氣。

【例】 *Didn't I tell you* to be quiet?

（我沒告訴你要安靜嗎？）

(= *I told you* to be quiet, didn't I?)

Who knows what will happen in the future?

(= *Nobody knows* what will happen in the future.)

（誰知道未來會發生什麼事？）

What would I not give to see my son again?

(= *I would give anything* to see my son again.)

（只要能再看到我兒子，我有什麼不願給的呢？）

(3) **強調句型：It is～that** 的用法。

【例】 *It was the actor that* went to Hawaii last month.

（上個月去夏威夷的就是這個演員。）

It was to Hawaii that the actor went last month.

（這演員上個月去的地方就是夏威夷。）

It was last month that the actor went to Hawaii.

（這演員是在上個月去夏威夷的。）

It is not what a man has but what he is that is most important in life.

（人一生中最重要的，不是他的財產，而是他的人格。）

What is it that you have been looking for?

（你一直在找的究竟是什麼呢？）

2. 倒　裝

1. 副詞（片語）放在句首的倒裝

(1) **地方副詞 + be + S**

【例】 Just *in front of the museum was* a beautiful garden.

(= There was a beautiful garden just in front of the museum.)

（有座美麗的花園就在博物館前面。）

High up in the sky were thousands of twinkling stars.
(= There were thousands of twinkling stars high
up in the sky.)
（有數千顆閃耀的星星高掛在天上。）

⑵ 副詞（片語）＋V＋S（名詞），副詞＋S（代名詞）＋V→ 多
用於不及物動詞

【例】 *Down fell* the big rock.（大岩石掉下來了。）
＜比較＞ *Down* it *fell*.
The door opened, and *in came* a tall young man.
（門開了，走進來一位高個子的青年。）

⑶ 副詞（片語）＋ 助動詞＋S＋V→ 多用於及物動詞

【例】 *Well do* I *remember* the good old days.
（以前那些美好的日子，我記得很清楚。）
In vain did he *try* to persuade her.
（他試圖說服她，但卻徒勞無功。）

⑷ 否定副詞（片語）＋助動詞＋S＋V

【例】 *Never have* I *heard* such beautiful music.
(= I have *never* heard such beautiful music.)
（我從未聽過這麼美妙的音樂。）
Little did I *dream* that I should ever see him again.
(= I *little* dreamed that I should ever see him again.)
（我沒想到會再見到他。）
Hardly had he *reached* the top before the fog cleared
up.（他一到達山頂，濃霧就消散了。）
(= He had *hardly* reached the top before the fog
cleared up.)

No sooner *had* he *left* than we burst out laughing.

(= He had *no sooner* left than we burst out laughing.)

（他一離開，我們就大聲笑起來。）

Not until then did I *realize* the danger of the situation.

(= I did *not* realize the danger of the situation *until then*.)（直到那時，我才了解情況有多危險。）

Not only did he *go* away but he never came back.

(= He *not only* went away but never came back.)

（他不只是離開，而且從沒回來過。）

---

2. 受詞放在句首的倒裝

⑴ 特別強調受詞時 → **O＋S＋V**

【例】 ***The door*** he *locked*, but ***the windows*** he *left* open.

（門他鎖上了，但窗戶卻讓它開著。）

That you *should put* into practice first of all.

（那是你首先應該實行的。）

What has become of the boy nobody *knows*.

（沒有人知道那男孩怎麼了。）

⑵ **O**（含否定意義）＋ **助動詞＋S＋V**

【例】 ***Not a single man*** did we *see* in the street.

（我們在街上一個人也沒看到。）

No help did he *offer* me after all.

（畢竟他沒提供我任何幫助。）

Only a little sleep did I *get* that night.

（那天晚上我只睡了一會兒。）

3. 補語放在句首的倒裝

⑴ **C + be** 動詞 **+ S**

【例】 *Great was* her delight when she discovered a new element. (當她發現一種新元素時，她高興極了。)

Quite satisfied was he with the result.
(他對結果相當滿意。)

Fortunate is the man who meets the right friends at the right moment.
(在適當時機，遇見適當的朋友，是很幸運的。)

⑵ **C + S + V，C + S + V + O**

【例】 *Very strange* his story *sounded* to me.
(對我而言，他的故事聽起來非常奇怪。)

Poor he *may be*, but *unhappy* you *should* not *think* him. (他或許很窮，但你不應該認為他不快樂。)

4. 倒裝的慣用法

⑴ **There + V + S；Here + V + S**

【例】 *There* once *lived* a poor farmer and his wife.
(從前，有一個貧窮的農夫和他太太住在那裡。)

There appeared a beautiful sight before us.
(在我們面前出現一個美麗的景色。)

Here comes the gentleman I have just spoken of.
(我剛剛提到的那位紳士來了。)

⑵ **so, neither, nor** 之後

【例】 I have made some mistakes. — *So have* I.
(我犯了幾個錯誤。—— 我也是。)

I don't like asking for money. — *Neither do* I.

（我不喜歡跟人要錢。—— 我也是。）

He was not rich then, *nor did* he wish to be.

（他當時並不富有，而且他也不渴望富有。）

(3) 假設法省略 if 的倒裝

【例】 *Were I* in your place, I would refuse the offer.

（假如我是你，我會拒絕這項提議。）

Had it not been for your advice, I could not have succeeded.（如果沒有你的忠告，我就不會成功了。）

(4) **the** ＋ 比較級～，**the** ＋ 比較級…「越～，就越…」

【例】 *The more* we get, *the more* we want.

（我們得到的越多，想要的也就越多。）

The higher we went up, *the colder* it became.

（我們爬得越高，天氣就變得越冷。）

(5) **as** 用在表讓步的副詞子句中，指「雖然」。

【例】 *Young as* he is, he is wise and reliable.

(= *Though he is young*, he…)

（他雖然年輕，卻聰明可靠。）

Child as she was, she was not in the least afraid.

(= *Though she was a child*, she…)【倒裝時，要省略冠詞 a】

（她雖然只是個小孩，但她一點也不害怕。）

歷屆聯考試題

一、強調

(   ) 1. _____ interesting it is!

     (A) What   (B) Where   (C) When   (D) How

(   ) 2. _____ he is!

     (A) What a clever man

     (B) How a clever man

     (C) What clever a man

     (D) What clever

(   ) 3. Never _____ ashamed to ask about what you do not understand.

     (A) is   (B) are

     (C) have been   (D) be

(   ) 4. It was between 1830 and 1835 _____ the modern newspaper was born.

     (A) then   (B) that   (C) which   (D) because

二、倒裝句

(   ) 1. Only when you are away from home _____.

     (A) will you realize how sweet home is

     (B) you will miss your parents

     (C) you know your parents do love you

     (D) then you want to write letters home

(　　) 2. Only after I had reached the supermarket ＿＿＿＿ that
I had forgotten to take my purse with me.
　　(A) I had realized
　　(B) I realized
　　(C) I have realized
　　(D) did I realize

(　　) 3. Not only ＿＿＿＿, but he saw her.
　　(A) did he come
　　(B) he came
　　(C) came he
　　(D) he comes
　　(E) he did come

(　　) 4. Hardly ＿＿＿＿ started when I heard a man call my
name.
　　(A) did the car
　　(B) had the car
　　(C) the car had
　　(D) the car did
　　(E) was the car

(　　) 5. I have never been to the U.S., ＿＿＿＿.
　　(A) nor he has
　　(B) so has he
　　(C) nor does he
　　(D) nor has he

( ) 6. Hardly _____ arrived when she started complaining.
     (A) did he   (B) was he
     (C) had he   (D) he had

( ) 7. He is going home _____ is she.
     (A) and neither   (B) but neither
     (C) and so   (D) so neither

( ) 8. She does not know how to operate the computer,

     _____.

     (A) nor am I   (B) I do, too
     (C) nor do I   (D) nor can I

  9. 他從來不曾這樣生氣過。
     _____ was he so angry.

( ) 10. Not only he is a famous pianist, but he is also a
              (A)   (B)   (C)
     great composer. (改錯)
          (D)

( ) 11. No sooner had the thief saw the policeman than he
       (A)   (B)
     took to his heels. (改錯)
     (C)   (D)

( ) 12. Never in my life I have heard such nonsense! (改錯)
          (A)   (B)   (C)   (D)

【歷屆聯考試題解答】

一、　1. (**D**)　2. (**A**)　3. (**D**)　4. (**B**)

二、　1. (**A**)　2. (**D**)　3. (**A**)　4. (**B**)　5. (**D**)

　　　6. (**C**)　7. (**C**)　8. (**C**)　9. Never

　　10. (**A**) → is he　11. (**B**) → seen　12. (**B**) → have I

【解析】

一、　1.2. 感嘆句中，How 後面直接接形容詞，What 只能接名詞。

　　　　*What **a clever man** he is!*

　　　　= *How **clever** he is!*

二、　1. only 置於句首，主詞和動詞要倒裝。

　　　4. *Hardly had* + S. + 過去分詞 + *when*～　　一～就…

　　　5. 我從沒去過美國，他也沒去過。

　　10. *not only～but also…*　不僅～而且…

　　　　composer〔kəm'pozɚ〕*n.* 作曲家

　　11. *take to one's heels*　逃走

　　12. 我這輩子從沒聽過這種歪理！

　　　　nonsense〔'nɑnsɛns〕*n.* 胡說八道

精選模擬考題

( ) 1. _____ was yesterday _____ I went downtown.
(A) It, then (B) It, that
(C) There, that (D) There, when

( ) 2. It is you _____.
(A) to blame
(B) to be blamed
(C) who are to blame
(D) who are to be blame

( ) 3. _____ this would come true.
(A) Little I dreamed
(B) Little did I dreamed
(C) Little did I dream
(D) Little do I dream

( ) 4. A: I went to the shopping center.
B: _____.
(A) So I did (B) So did I
(C) I did so (D) So I went

( ) 5. A: He didn't come to the party.
B: _____.
(A) Nor did she (B) Nor she did
(C) She did nor (D) She nor did

(   ) 6. A: I liked the actor.

           B: _____.

         (A) So I did   (B) So did I

         (C) I did so   (D) I so did

(   ) 7. How _____ say such a thing to me?

         (A) dare he   (B) dare he to

         (C) dares he   (D) he dares

(   ) 8. _____ come and see me as soon as you can.

         (A) Be   (B) Do

         (C) To   (D) Being

(   ) 9. She _____ sing beautifully.

         (A) do   (B) does

         (C) is   (D) was

(   ) 10. The President _____ came to meet the Prime Minister.

         (A) he   (B) him

         (C) himself   (D) she

(   ) 11. His wife made the tea _____.

         (A) her   (B) she

         (C) sheself   (D) herself

(   ) 12. Please help _____ to the fruit.

         (A) you   (B) they

         (C) yourself   (D) themselves

( ) 13. _____ to take me all the way to the station!
    (A) How you good   (B) How good of you
    (C) How good you   (D) How of you good

( ) 14. _____ the actor _____ went to Hawaii last month.
    (A) It is, whom   (B) It was, whom
    (C) That is, that   (D) It was, that

( ) 15. It was the window _____ I broke yesterday.
    (A) when   (B) how
    (C) which   (D) it

( ) 16. Not only _____ he _____ away but he never came back.
    (A) was, went   (B) did, go
    (C) did, went   (D) was, go

( ) 17. Not until then _____ I _____ the danger of the situation.
    (A) did, realize   (B) when, realize
    (C) was, realized   (D) but, realized

( ) 18. No sooner _____ he left _____ we burst out laughing.
    (A) had, but   (B) had, than
    (C) had, then   (D) had, so

( ) 19. _____ a poor farmer and his wife.
    (A) Lived there once   (B) Once lived there
    (C) There once lived   (D) Lived once

(　) 20. The more we get, _____ we want.

    (A) morer　　　　　(B) much more

    (C) the more　　　　(D) more

(　) 21. _____, he is wise and reliable.

    (A) Young as he is

    (B) Young he is

    (C) As he is young

    (D) Young is he

(　) 22. (A) Seldom she is so angry.

    (B) Seldom so angry she is.

    (C) Seldom angry so she is.

    (D) Seldom is she so angry.

(　) 23. Not for a moment _____ the truth of your story.

    (A) he has doubted　(B) he doubts

    (C) he did doubt　　(D) did he doubt

(　) 24. Not only _____ difficult, it is impractical also.

    (A) does it　　　　(B) has it

    (C) is it　　　　　(D) it is

(　) 25. Not until I lay in bed _____ of the people.

    (A) did I think　　(B) I did think

    (C) do I think　　(D) so I think

【精選模擬考題解答】

1.(**B**)	2.(**C**)	3.(**C**)	4.(**B**)	5.(**A**)
6.(**B**)	7.(**A**)	8.(**B**)	9.(**B**)	10.(**C**)
11.(**D**)	12.(**C**)	13.(**B**)	14.(**D**)	15.(**C**)
16.(**B**)	17.(**A**)	18.(**B**)	19.(**C**)	20.(**C**)
21.(**A**)	22.(**D**)	23.(**D**)	24.(**B**)	25.(**A**)

【解析】

2. 在 It is～that 的強調句型中，如果強調的是人時，that 可以用 who 取代。

7. dare（敢）可以做本動詞，也可以做助動詞。

12. **help** *oneself* **to**　自行取用
   祈使句省略主詞 you，故反身代名詞用 yourself。

21. reliable〔rɪˊlaɪəbḷ〕*adj.* 可信賴的

24. impractical〔ɪmˊpræktɪkḷ〕*adj.* 不切實際的

3. 附加問句

> 附加問句就是一個省略的疑問句。
>
> 前面如果是肯定，附加問句就用否定；
>
> 前面如果是否定，附加問句則用肯定。

1. 敘述句後面的附加問句

1. 附加問句的構成原則

⑴ 敘述句的動詞若是肯定，附加問句的動詞要用否定；敘述句的動詞若是否定，附加問句則用肯定。

【例】 He *is* a student, *isn't* he?（他是個學生，不是嗎？）

　　　 Mary *can't* play the piano, *can* she?

　　　（瑪麗不會彈鋼琴，不是嗎？）

⑵ 敘述句中，如果沒有 be 動詞、have 動詞，或其他助動詞時，附加問句的主詞前要用 do, does 或 did。

【例】 You learn German, *don't* you?（你學德文，不是嗎？）

　　　 He studied hard to pass the exam, *didn't* he?

　　　（他用功讀書，想通過考試，不是嗎？）

2. 應注意的事項

⑴ 敘述句的動詞 have, has, had，不作「有」解時，附加問句的主詞前要用 do, does 或 did。

【例】 You *have* a cold bath every morning, *don't* you?

　　　（你每天早上都洗冷水澡，不是嗎？）

　　　 He usually *has* ice cream for dessert, *doesn't* he?

　　　（他通常吃冰淇淋當甜點，不是嗎？）

⑵ 敘述句與附加問句裡動詞的時態要相同，而且附加問句的主詞一
定要用代名詞。

【例】 Tom *isn't* a teacher, *is he*?

（湯姆不是老師，不是嗎？）

Helen *was* a secretary, *wasn't she*?

（海倫是個秘書，不是嗎？）

We *will* go on a trip, *won't we*?

（我們會去旅行，不是嗎？）

2. 肯定祈使句後面的附加問句

⑴ 肯定祈使句之後，表示「請求」用 will you；表示「邀請；勸誘」
用 won't you。

【例】 Come here, *will you*?（過來這裡，好嗎？）

Have a drink, *won't you*?（喝杯飲料，好嗎？）

⑵ 否定疑問句之後，表示「請求」，則只用 will you。

【例】 Don't close the window, *will you*?

（別關窗，好嗎？）

⑶ 表示不耐煩，用 can't you。

【例】 Keep quiet, *can't you*?（保持安靜，可以嗎？）

⑷ 由 Let's 引導的祈使句，肯定的用 shall we
否定的用 all right 或 O.K.做附加問句。

【例】 Let's go, *shall we*?（我們走吧，好嗎？）

Let's *not* go, *O.K.*?（我們不要去，好嗎？）

Let's *not* go shopping, *all right*?

（我們不要去逛街，好嗎？）

3. 附加問句應注意的事項

(1) Let's 與 Let us 不同：

【例】 *Let's* go to the movies, ***shall we***?

（我們去看電影，好嗎？）

【shall we 是 shall we go 的省略，表「提議」】

Let us go to the movies, ***will you***?

（讓我們去看電影，好嗎？）

【will you 是 will you let us go 的省略，表「請求」】

(2) 附加問句以主要思想的子句爲準。

【例】 I think *the meeting is ending*, ***isn't it***?

（我想會議就快結束了，不是嗎？）

☞ isn't it 就是 isn't it ending 的省略，不能說成 *don't I*，因爲沒有 don't I think…這類沒有意義的疑問句。

(3) 含有 seldom, never, little, hardly 等否定副詞的句子，也視爲否定句，附加問句須用肯定。

【例】 He *seldom* went there, ***did he***?

（他很少去那裡，不是嗎？）

(4) 句中如有 had better，附加問句用 hadn't~；句中如有 had better not，則附加問句須用 had~。

【例】 I *had better* go home earlier, ***hadn't I***?

（我最好早點回去，不是嗎？）

He *had better not* stay here, ***had he***?

（他最好不要留在這裡，不是嗎？）

歷屆聯考試題

( ) 1. Mary has beautiful eyes, _____?
    (A) didn't she   (B) don't she
    (C) doesn't she   (D) don't they

( ) 2. Let's have a party tonight, _____?
    (A) shall you   (B) shall we
    (C) don't we   (D) do we

( ) 3. There were hardly any books in the classroom,
    _____?
    (A) weren't they   (B) weren't there
    (C) were there   (D) were they
    (E) would they

( ) 4. There is not much fun in being ill, _____?
    (A) is there   (B) isn't there
    (C) is it   (D) isn't it

( ) 5. There is nothing wrong with your car, _____?
    (A) are you   (B) isn't it
    (C) aren't you   (D) is there

( ) 6. We had better wait for your girlfriend Molly, _____?
    (A) hadn't we   (B) don't we
    (C) didn't we   (D) shan't we

(　) 7. You had better not go there again, _____?

      (A) hadn't you   (B) had you

      (C) do you   (D) don't you

(　) 8. Peter went to school by taxi yesterday, _____ he?

      (A) does   (B) don't

      (C) doesn't   (D) didn't

【歷屆聯考試題解答】

1. (**C**)　2. (**B**)　3. (**C**)　4. (**A**)　5. (**D**)

6. (**A**)　7. (**B**)　8. (**D**)

【解析】

1. have 當「有」解釋時，其附加問句可用 hasn't she? 或 doesn't she?

2. 祈使句 Let's～的附加問句須用 shall we?

3. hardly (ˊhɑrdlɪ) *adv.* 幾乎不

   句中如有具否定意義的字，如 hardly, never, seldom 時，則附加問句須用肯定。

5. There is nothing 爲否定句，故用肯定的附加問句 is there?

6. 7. 句中有 had better，附加問句用 hadn't～?

   句中有 had better not，附加問句用 had～?

8. 前爲肯定句，附加問句須用否定，且依句意爲過去式，故選 (D)。

精選模擬考題

( ) 1. It is very cold today, _____?
    (A) wasn't it   (B) will it
    (C) isn't it   (D) was it

( ) 2. She isn't studying English, _____ she?
    (A) does   (B) doesn't
    (C) is   (D) isn't

( ) 3. You did the work yesterday, _____?
    (A) didn't you   (B) do you
    (C) weren't you   (D) were you

( ) 4. Tom will come here next Tuesday, _____?
    (A) was he   (B) won't he
    (C) is he   (D) isn't he

( ) 5. You have never heard such a beautiful song, _____?
    (A) do you   (B) have you
    (C) don't you   (D) haven't you

( ) 6. They had a wonderful day, _____?
    (A) do they   (B) had they
    (C) didn't they   (D) hadn't they

(　) 7. Your father has few friends, _____?
    (A) does he   (B) has he
    (C) hasn't he   (D) doesn't your father

(　) 8. There is a car over there, _____?
    (A) is it   (B) is there
    (C) isn't it   (D) isn't there

(　) 9. It is a pity that nobody was saved in the accident,
    _____ it?
    (A) does   (B) doesn't
    (C) was   (D) isn't

(　) 10. Tom almost never studied while he was at college,
    _____?
    (A) didn't he   (B) did he
    (C) wasn't he   (D) was he

(　) 11. Let's go for a walk, _____?
    (A) do you   (B) don't you
    (C) will you   (D) shall we

(　) 12. Let us take a look at that photo, _____?
    (A) don't you   (B) will you
    (C) don't we   (D) shall we

【精選模擬考題解答】

1.(**C**)   2.(**C**)   3.(**A**)   4.(**B**)   5.(**B**)   6.(**C**)

7.(**A**)   8.(**D**)   9.(**D**)   10.(**B**)   11.(**D**)   12.(**B**)

【解析】

5. 句中如有具否定意義的字，如 hardly, never, seldom, few, little 時，則附加問句須用肯定；又 have 在本句中為助動詞，故附加問句用 have you?

6. had 是本動詞，且不作「有」解釋時，其附加問句不能用hadn't，應用助動詞 didn't。

7. has 作「有」解釋時，前為肯定，則附加問句用 hasn't he? 或 doesn't he? 前為否定，則附加問句用 has he?或 does he? 而 few「很少」，是具有否定意義的形容詞，故附加問句須用肯定，選 (A) does he?

9. 在那場意外中，沒有人獲救，真的是很可惜，不是嗎？
   主要思想為 It is a pity，故附加問句用 isn't it?
   pity〔ˈpɪtɪ〕*n.* 可惜的事

10. 湯姆唸大學時，幾乎沒在讀書，不是嗎？

11. Let's 開頭的祈使句，附加問句須用 shall we?

12. Let us 開頭的祈使句，附加問句須用 will you?